Beyond Telepathy

Andrija Puharich is a neurologist. After completing his studies at the medical school of Northwestern University, he set up his own laboratory in Maine for the study of extrasensory perception. A period with the United States Army at its Chemical Center aroused his interest in hallucination-producing mushrooms and brought about his first book, *The Sacred Mushroom*.

Ira Einhorn is a contributor to *Psychedelics* and is the author of *78–187880*.

Beyond Telepathy

By ANDRIJA PUHARICH

With an Introduction by Ira Einhorn

Anchor Books
ANCHOR PRESS/DOUBLEDAY
Garden City, New York   1973

Beyond Telepathy was originally published in hardcover by Doubleday & Company, Inc. in 1962.
Anchor Press edition: 1973
ISBN: 0-385-08376-9
Library of Congress Catalog Card Number 72–84967

Contents

Introduction

Andrija Puharich has written a book that is devoted to the material manifestations of the power of psychic energy. A unique book, for he has gone beyond the mere cataloguing of these manifestations, in order to produce a theory that attempts to understand both the source and the generation of these energies.

A THEORY
            at
                last,
allowing us to place psi phenomena on a level with other events within the matrix of scientific thought,

a theory that is very speculative,
a theory that often transcends the possibilities that the wealth of detailed information would normally allow.

N.B.—We really don't understand gravity, nor can we adequately quantize it.

Yet Puharich
            has created

A THEORY,

a beginning,
            a small favor
in a blithering confusion of data

which inundates anyone who wishes
                         to pursue
paranormal occurrences
with a scientific attitude.

   America woke up one morning 15 years ago to discover
                  S P U T N I K
That awakening
               produced
the first walk
              on the moon

   Beyond Telepathy discusses an aspect of human knowledge that official America
refuses to acknowledge.
For years
this book
         has been
                 out of print,
                        in America!
   It is a book that has no contemporary counterpart, and
will eventually rank as a classic.

A C O S M O S —
                  mechanistic to the core—is dying.
We are surrounded by the chaos of its passing.
Those who possess adequate presence of mind
                   are sifting the ashes
in order to utilize the information that
can be included
in the new formulations
that are
         destined to occur.
   The Aquarian Age is upon us, in ways that the clichés
of *Hair* and the popular press can't even begin to convey.
   Whole new octaves
of human awareness,
of cosmic energies,

previously expressed in terms
that only a few
could understand and accept,
are
  about to be unveiled
to
  mankind-as-a-whole.

We are poised on the edge of discoveries that will
totally transform man's conception of himself: Discoveries
that will dwarf the foolishness of

HIROSHIMA.

$E = MC^2$, the great poem of the twentieth century, is
a small adumbration of what awaits us as we plunge beyond the visible into realms that have been hinted at in the
past, without having been proven to the satisfaction of
that consensus that makes up the unique form of Western
scientific progress.

We are surrounded by pools of energy that we are just
beginning to tap.

The supposed
        "astral-etheric body"
is
  proving to be a biological reality.

Puharich shows a sure sense of the ground upon which
he walks, as well as an ability to theorize about the data
he has collected. His book is a welcome tonic to both the
wild claims of many, overwhelmed by the wonders of these
new realms, on the one hand; and the endless repetition
of experimental data, that is the meat of 99 per cent of the
books dealing with the psychic, on the other.

Einstein bounded the world of mass with his theories,
creating a limiting velocity
            of
            C,

allowing
        us
                to distinguish
between
        mass
                and
                        massless
entities,
as
   George Cantor's research
into

led to a distinction
                        between
ordinal
        and
                cardinal
                        numbers.

Much of what this book
                        deals with
are energies,
            physic,
                    which have no mass.
Thought;
        no mass;
                faster than C;
A world of difference
                        from what we have
been taught
            to expect.
  This book is
                an excellent gateway to
the experience,

the exploration,
and eventually the explanation
                              of that difference.

  We have become
                              so divided
in our ways
             that we have forgotten
the underlying unity
                      of the quest
that unites
           science and religion.
  Unified field theory—the quest of
Albert Einstein's
later years—
              has returned us
to the awareness
                  that science too
has its god term.
  Hence, once again we have the possibility
of a synergistic convergence
between
        science and religion—reinforcing
rather than demeaning
                       each other's goals.

The
     Pythagoreans
                  are loose
again   and the spirit of unity is
once again
           upon us—as this quote
from a recent letter,
written by Puharich,
so aptly demonstrates:
                        "That goal toward which I have
always moved all of my life—the understanding of some

aspect of ultimate reality in humanistic terms—appears
to be realizable here." (4/13/72—Tel Aviv, Israel)

IRA EINHORN
Philadelphia
April 1972
Paris—Senlis
June 1972

Ted Bastion provided me with information that was
germane to this introduction. I am entirely responsible
for the use to which it was put.

Foreword

This work provides a journey that every man can follow. It is an exploration of the personal world of your own mind. If you believe that this is not very interesting because your life has not been exciting, I want to show you that this is just not so. The nature of the individual mind is such that potentially every nook and cranny of the world can be reflected in it, and there are ways and means to experience this. Let me give you an example. You might say that you have never studied the circulation of the red blood cells under a microscope in a laboratory. Yet you have only to look at the blue sky, relax your mind, and you will directly observe the flow of myriads of blood cells in the fine vessels of your eye. You could lie down at absolute rest in a quiet room in your basement where there is no light or other disturbance, and within an hour or so you would begin to see, feel, and hear things whose existence up till now had never been suspected.

Man has been exploring his mind since time began, and out of it has come all that we know. When the mind becomes uncertain of what it finds, or thinks it knows, then it turns to the outer world and utilizes observation and experiment as a check upon itself. And this is a necessary precaution because a mind unchecked by facts can get out of control and create fantasies that can become injurious to one's existence, or to others. In this work I give you the stories of normal men and women who have explored the far reaches of their minds, and who were sure enough of their findings to check them against the facts, and be checked by outside observers. What they experienced are examples of telepathy, clairvoyance, the action of mind at a distance, and most remarkable of all—the personality freeing itself of the body and traveling where it will across the reaches of time and space.

These cases have all been carefully checked and each one reveals some new realm of exploration wherein others can follow. I have followed the cases principally as an observer, but have often had to devise ways of getting into this new world in order to better understand where others have been so that I could become a better reporter. For example, I wanted to have the inner feeling of what goes on during the act of telepathy, and found that by drinking the proper amount of the juice of a certain mushroom (*Amanita muscaria*) I could get the true feeling of telepathy, and prove it to others by objective laboratory tests. I feel that I can bring you this book with more authority by having viewed the subject both from the inside and the outside.

I have gone beyond this inside experience and outside observation and summoned all my scientific acumen to rationalize the anatomy and dynamics of the mind. I have tried to relate the facts of mind to the facts of biology and physics. I am the first to admit that this is a pioneering venture and that my interpretation may not entirely reflect the laws of mind. But I have taken this bold step in order to stimulate others to examine the same problems, and thereby draw more interest toward a seriously neglected area of knowledge. If I can serve as a catalyst, even though many of my ideas fall in the fray, I shall have accomplished one of my major purposes. My other purpose is to bring the latest thinking in this field to the attention of many intelligent seekers who in turn can utilize some of the techniques herein described in the private laboratory of their own mind. The more such private laboratories are placed in operation the quicker will the truth about ourselves be revealed. This is one of the last great frontiers of exploration, and fortunately it appears to be an infinite one, so we need not fear, as did Alexander, that there will be no more worlds to conquer.

I have written as simply of these explorations as I could in order to reach as many minds as are ready. However, in our present state of knowledge of the mind there are many complexities that resist simplification. This has led to the inclusion of two difficult chapters (Chapters 10 and 11). The reader who finds these hard to follow can get their general idea from Chapter 12.

ANDRIJA PUHARICH

Carmel, California, April 1, 1960

Beyond Telepathy

1

The Telepathic
Receiver and the
State of Cholinergia

Dr. Lawrence entered his office promptly at eight-thirty.
He nodded good morning to his dental assistant and quickly
walked to his desk. He sat down and began thumbing
through his morning mail. Suddenly a thought hit him. He
had an idea which he wanted to share immediately with
his research associate, Bill Harmon. He reached over to
the telephone and began dialing Bill's number.

Bill Harmon at this very instant was still asleep in bed.
He awoke abruptly with one thought in his mind, "Call
Joe Lawrence." Acting immediately on the impulse he
reached for the phone by his bedside. As he put the receiver to his ear, Joe was already saying, "Hello!" The
telephone bell had not rung.

This is an example of simple telepathy occurring within a
short time interval. From the moment Joe got the idea to
call Bill, and finished dialing the last digit of the telephone
number, perhaps fifteen to twenty seconds had elapsed.
Somewhere during the course of this fifteen to twenty second time span, Bill had got the sharp impression during
sleep that he should call Joe Lawrence. Between the dialing of the last digit of any telephone number and the en-
suing ring on the other phone, there is a time interval of
less than two seconds. It was within this time interval that

Bill picked up the telephone and found Joe already on the line.

It is important to note that Joe had a very urgent notion of calling Bill. However, he had no intention of using telepathy to reach Bill. He was going to use the much more efficient telephone. Bill on the other hand was peacefully asleep and experienced what might be called an abrupt arousal reaction. Such telepathic interaction between two individuals is not uncommon and in this case had no particular significance. In fact, we might say that the entire conversation which ensued was rather trivial.

While the interaction between Joe and Bill in this instance took place at an unconscious level, there are striking instances where the sender of a telepathic idea is fully conscious of his role as an agent. This phenomenon can be studied in the laboratory, where two people, that is a sender and a receiver, try to send messages to each other across the distance of several rooms. A simple instance of this occurs when one person, the sender, turns over one at a time an ordinary deck of playing cards while the receiver, who is in the other room, tries to tell whether the cards are red or black. Since there are 52 cards in a deck one would expect 26 correct calls by chance expectation alone. If the number of correct calls exceeds 26 by a certain margin the results are considered significant for telepathic interaction. In this type of scientific demonstration one can observe a telepathic sender consciously trying to send his message to a telepathic receiver, and conversely the telepathic receiver consciously trying to get the impression from the sender.

Such experiments have been repeated thousands of times in scientific laboratories, yielding overwhelming evidence of the reality of telepathic exchange of intelligence between two people.[1] We can accept the existence of telepathy with confidence, and go on to inquire as to how it works. Of prime importance in understanding telepathy is the biological state of the receiver. The following case is a good introduction to this problem.

On January 22, 1952, at 10:27 A.M., a routine telepathy experiment was begun with Mrs. Eileen Garrett as the receiver. Mrs. Garrett sat in a copper-screen (Faraday cage) room.[2] The sender in this experiment, Mr. Loren Wedlock, was sitting outside of the copper-screen room and observing Mrs. Garrett through the transparent mesh. Mrs. Garrett went into a self-induced trance, and thereafter the conversation was carried on between her alleged control personality, Abdul Latif, and Mr. Wedlock. The purpose of the experiment was to have Mrs. Garrett, via her control, guess the moment when an electrical charge of ten seconds' duration was placed upon the walls of the copper-screen room. Mr. Wedlock, through an indicator in front of him, was able to tell when the electrical charge occurred. This experiment is comparable to the Lawrence-Harmon story just described, where the purpose is to get one person to pick up the telephone at the instant when the other party finishes his dialing.

Mr. Wedlock led the conversation with Abdul Latif around to an inquiry on the use of vocal sounds in increasing telepathy. Abdul Latif obliged by giving certain vowels, demonstrating the sound production, and describing the effect this sound was to have. Mrs. Garrett, through her control, produced the sound *E,* and emitted a head-splitting version of this particular vowel. It was stated that this vowel, produced in this manner, was supposed to activate the "solar-plexus" center. The experiment continued in a routine fashion for thirty minutes. During this period three electrical charges of ten seconds' duration each appeared in a random sequence on the walls of the copper-screen room. In relation to these targets Mrs. Garrett made two correct calls, or hits. This was an unusually good demonstration of telepathy.

After the experiment Mrs. Garrett retired to her room. She reappeared in about an hour and said that as soon as she had awakened from the trance she had experienced severe abdominal cramps. Following the cramps, for a period of a half hour, she had had three watery stools in rapid succession. After this she felt unusually exhilarated and relaxed, the abdominal cramps disappeared, and she had the feeling of unusual mental acuity, and what she described as "traveling" clairvoyance. By this she meant that she had the distinct impression of literally looking in upon friends in New York City, Washington, D.C., London, and Southern France.

I was most intrigued by this description of her experience. Since in the trance state her control, Abdul Latif, had said that the production of the vowel sound *E* would activate the solar-plexus center, I casually assumed that she had been unconsciously influenced by this statement of her alter ego. However, to me this was not the important point. The important point was that she had had a massive activation of her parasympathetic nervous system. I took her blood pressure and found it to be twenty-five points lower than normal. Her pulse, which normally runs about ninety, was down to sixty-six. Her skin was flushed, her pupils pinpoint narrow, and her eyes were shining bright. These are the general symptoms of parasympathetic activation. In addition she had had a profound activation of the gastrointestinal tract.

The first order of business was to check her apparent "traveling clairvoyance," or what I would call highly active telepathy. I proposed that we do a telepathy test immediately, to which she promptly agreed. Mrs. Garrett entered the cage as usual with the expectancy of having to call out the moment when an electrical charge was present on the wall of the cage. However, since she had been so sensitized to looking for electrical targets, I thought it would be a better test of her sensitivity of the moment to eliminate the electrical charges, and see whether she would be deluded into making calls of targets that were not there. The experiment ran for thirty minutes, the usual time, and Mrs. Garrett did not make a single call during this period. During the course of the sitting she commented upon the fact that she had no sensation of any electrical charges being present at all. Upon the termination of this experiment she was given a twenty minute break and another experiment was run.

In this experiment the random switch was turned on so that the electrical charges would appear on the cage. During the course of the thirty minutes, six such charges appeared. Mrs. Garrett made six calls within fifteen seconds after the charge had appeared on the wall. This was a phenomenally good score and confirmed, for me, her statement that she was experiencing an unusually high degree of sensitivity for telepathy.

Two things struck me about Mrs. Garrett's experience. The first was the fact that parasympathetic activation was associated with an increased degree of sensitivity for telepathy. When the parasympathetic nervous system is activated there is an increased amount of acctylcholine released into the nervous system. For our convenience we will describe, henceforth, parasympathetic activation as being a state of cholinergia.[3] The second point of interest to me was the centrifugal reach of her mind in the state she described as traveling chairvoyance. It appeared as though her mind was a collecting vortex for people who had a deep personal meaning to her.

It was not until 1955 that my interest in these two points was again awakened by an experience I had with one of my telepathic subjects, Harry Stone. I have already described this experience elsewhere.[4] In summary, I had given Harry Stone some of the mushroom *Amanita muscaria*. The over-all effect of the *Amanita muscaria* ingestion was that Harry behaved like a person who had become inebriated with alcohol. He himself described a feeling akin to Mrs. Garrett's traveling clairvoyance. That is, he seemed to be able, in his mind, to see through walls, and to distant scenes and places. The *Amanita muscaria* induces cholinergia in an individual due to the presence of the drug muscarine, which is one of the very potent cholinergic drugs. I immediately gave Harry a laboratory test for clairvoyance in which he was supposed to correctly match two sets of ten different pictures. He completed this test, in spite of his inebriated condition, in three seconds. His score was perfect, he got ten correct matches out of ten trials. The statistical odds against getting this score were such that he would have had to do this test a million times before such a result would occur by chance.

This case set me to thinking again about my earlier observation on Mrs. Garrett. In Harry Stone we had artificially induced cholinergia by giving him a cholinergic drug, and he experienced both the usual symptoms of parasympathetic activation and the sense of traveling clairvoyance, verified by a laboratory test for clairvoyance.

A mild state of cholinergia is usually associated with a sense of relaxation, well-being, and even pleasure. For example, a viscerotonic individual according to Sheldon's[5] classification of temperament is in a state of mild cholinergia. Other states of relaxation which have been found to be associated with an increased ability for extrasensory perception are sleep and hypnosis.

In reviewing the literature I could find no mention of experiments that associated cholinergia with increased scoring in a telepathic receiver. Therefore, I devised two experiments to check this hypothesis.

Modern primitives[6] believe that their intuitive capacity is increased by eating certain species of mushrooms.[7] The muscarinic mushrooms were used in these experiments because of their availability in the United States. These produce a well-known cholinergic effect, and can lead to hallucinations.[8] (See Appendix H for a description of mushroom hallucinations.)

Intuitive capacity for telepathy was tested with a manual matching game made up of a fundamental probability set of ten consisting of two sets of ten cards each. The blindfolded subjects were asked to try to correctly match the two sets of randomized cards with their hands, while an observer watched their attempts, and scored the results. Twenty-six normal human subjects were used. A control test was given before the mushroom was eaten, and testing was continued after the mushroom was eaten.

There were 1140 trials of matching skill in the control series, resulting in 106 correct matches. This gave a critical ratio of −0.71, and this is a chance-expected score. Chance expectation in this series is 114 correct matches. None of the subjects showed intuitive capacity for telepathic reception.

Upon the completion of the control test each subject drank a water extract prepared from *Amanita muscaria.*[9] The matching test was then repeated. There were 1140 trials of matching skill in the test series, resulting in 141 correct matches. The critical ratio is +2.39, and is considered statistically significant at the 1% level. The subjects almost uniformly reported for the two hours or so following the ingestion of the mushroom extract that they experienced a sense of increased intuitive awareness. Once the hallucinations set in they still felt an increased sense of intuitive awareness, but the results of the matching test scores did not support this opinion.

On the basis of these indications that intuitive capacity is increased in the presence of a mild degree of cholinergia, it was decided to put the question to a critical test. In order to neutralize psychological bias in favor of the thesis, subjects were obtained who were either skeptical or hostile to the idea that drugs could influence intuitive capacity either positively or negatively. These subjects were four newspaper reporters from the Los Angeles area.[10] In order to minimize bias and error in the test procedure, the matching game was replaced by a computer[11] programmed to generate numbers from 1 to 9 (inclusive) in random order. The number generated by the computer was displayed on a typewritten sheet, and the subject had to guess this number by punching a keyboard in front of him. The subject's guess was then printed alongside the target number already displayed. At the end of each such nine trials of guessing skill the computer automatically calculated the statistics cumulatively up to this point. Various observers continuously witnessed the typewriter sheet containing the record of the random target number, and its accompany-

ing call by the subject. These observers also served the
function of telepathic senders. The computer was programmed by A. L. Kitselman, aided by technicians of the
Clary Corporation. The subjects were tested before taking
the mushroom and in two test series after taking the mushroom.

Of the four subjects, one did not participate in the control series due to the pressure of time. The three subjects
made a total of 35 correct guesses in 297 trials for the
control series. The chance-expected score is 33 hits in 297
trials. The critical ratio was +0.36, and odds against
chance, 2.7 to 1. It was concluded that the subjects in
the normal state could not out-guess chance expectation
and showed no evidence for telepathy.

All four subjects were then given two mushrooms of
the species *Amanita muscaria*. The subjects ate their
mushrooms at fifteen-minute intervals from each other.
This allowed the subjects to be tested on the computer in
staggered order. In the test series the subject had his turn at
the computer at an average interval of 41 minutes after
eating his mushrooms. The combined score of the four
subjects in test I was 65 correct guesses out of 432 trials.
The chance-expected score is 48 hits in 432 trials. The
actual deviation is 17 hits, the standard deviation is 6.52,
yielding a critical ratio of +2.60, probability, $P = 0.00467$,
and odds against chance occurrence, 214 to 1. This score
exceeds the 1% level of significance, and it was concluded
that the subjects' intuitive capacity (interpreted as telepathy) had increased as a result of the mushroom-induced
cholinergia.

Test II was repeated 2 hours and 26 minutes (average)
after the mushroom had been eaten. By this time all of the
subjects had achieved mild inebriation, had mild hallucinations, but still subjectively felt that their intuitive capacity was heightened. The four subjects made a total of
41 correct guesses in 351 trials in test II. The chance-
expected score is 39 hits in 351 trials. The actual deviation
was 2 hits, and this is a chance-expected score. It was ap-

parent that the period of cholinergia-induced intuitive capacity had passed.

When we compare the control-test results and the test I results, we find that the critical ratio of difference between the means, respectively 35/297 and 65/432, exceeds the 1% level, and hence is considered statistically significant. This conclusion is fortified by the total series of 3360 trials of guessing skill. From this series of experiments we can conclude that most normal humans will show extrasensory perception as telepathic receivers when they are under the domination of cholinergia.

The second group of experiments were based on the fact that an excess of negatively charged ions in the respiratory atmosphere produces mild cholinergia.[12] In these experiments only two subjects were tested, both of whom could normally score significantly above chance in telepathy tests. In both it was found that an excess of negative ions significantly increased their telepathy scores over the control-level scores.

While such experiments need confirmation by other workers, I am convinced of the basic finding that mild cholinergia[13] favors the receptive function in telepathy.

NOTES   Chapter 1

1. For a general introduction to laboratory research in ESP see: Pratt, J. G., Rhine, J. B., Smith, B. M., Stuart, C. E., and Greenwood, J. A., *Extrasensory Perception After Sixty Years*, Henry Holt, New York, 1940. This work contains an excellent bibliography of 360 references up to this year.

For a broad discussion of researches which cover the important later work see: *CIBA Foundation Symposium on Extrasensory Perception*, A. S. Parkes, Chairman; Little, Brown and Company, Boston, 1956.

For a broad survey of the entire field by a physicist see: Raynor C. Johnson, *The Imprisoned Splendour*, Harper & Brothers, New York, 1953.

For a definitive work on Telepathy researches see: Soal, S. G., and Bateman, F., *Modern Experiments in Telepathy,* Yale University Press, New Haven, 1954.

2. Puharich, *Tomorrow* magazine, Winter issue, 1957, Vol. 5, No. 2, "Can Telepathy Penetrate the Iron Curtain?" See Appendix A.

3. The biochemistry of cholinergia is described in Sir Henry Hallett Dale's *Adventures in Physiology,* Pergamon Press, London, 1953, Chaps. 11 and 30. The physiology of cholinergia is described in *Physiological Basis of Medical Practice,* Best and Taylor, 5th Ed., Williams & Wilkins Co., Baltimore, 1950, pp. 275 and 1083 ff. Some of the psychological aspects of cholinergia are described in *Forms and Techniques of Altruistic Growth,* Ed. by Pitrim A. Sorokin, Chap. 17, p. 283 ff; *Social Behaviour and Autonomic Physiology in Long-standing Mental Illness,* by J. Sanbourne Bockoven and Milton Greenblatt, The Beacon Press, Boston, 1954.

4. Puharich, *The Sacred Mushroom,* Doubleday & Co., New York, 1959, p. 118.

5. W. H. Sheldon, *The Varieties of Temperament,* Harper & Brothers, New York, 1944, p. 31.

6. These include tribes of Southern Mexico such as the Mixes, the Zapotecs, and the Chatinos; and tribes of Northeastern Siberia such as the Korjaks, the Chuckchees, and the Tungus. The author became interested in this problem while studying the Chatino Indians in the summer of 1960. This expedition included the following members: Andrija Puharich, M.D., Pacific Institute for Psychological Research, Stanford, Calif.; Barbara Brown, Ph.D., Riker Laboratories, Northridge, Calif.; Jeffrey Smith, Ph.D., Special Programs in Humanities, Stanford University, Palo Alto, Calif.

7. These are species of *Psilocybe, Stropharia, Paneolus,* and *Amanita.* Heim, R. and Wasson, R. G., *Les Champignons Hallucinogènes du Méxique,* Edition du Muséum National d'Histoire Naturelle, Paris, 1958.

8. V. P. and R. G. Wasson, *Mushrooms, Russia, and History,* Pantheon, New York, 1957.

9. The extract was prepared by using one gram of dried mushroom to 20 c.c. of distilled water. Extraction was carried out by soaking the mushrooms for thirty minutes in water at 180° F. The dosage was 2 c.c. of such extract per kilogram of body weight. The potency of the mushrooms varied depending on

where they were picked, and during which part of the season. The specimens came from the states of Maine, Vermont, Washington, and California.

10. The four subjects were chosen by the staff of Advance Public Relations Corporation of Los Angeles, acting in behalf of One Step Beyond Productions, Inc., for their sponsor the Aluminum Company of America. The subjects were unknown to the investigating team before the day of the experiment, December 2, 1960.

11. The computer was the Clary DE-60 made by the Clary Corporation. The author wishes to thank the officers and staff of this corporation for their generosity and co-operation in this experiment. The experiment was carried out at the Riker Laboratories, Northridge, Calif., and I wish to thank Dr. Edwin Hays, the Director of Research, for his co-operation in this experiment. I wish to thank Dr. Kurt Fantl, and Dr. Margaret Paul for assisting in the psychiatric supervision of the subjects.

12. This research was reported in an address to the Psychic Research Society, Massachusetts Institute of Technology, Cambridge, Mass., October 30, 1956. See Appendix A for details of this experiment.

An idea of the gain in telepathic test scores is given by considering the results from one telepathic team. Harry Stone was the sender, and Peter Hurkos was the receiver.

The control test (room) was done under normal room conditions without an ion generator. The control test (cage) was done inside an electrically floating cage without an ion generator. The test experiment was done in a cage whose outside walls were at 10 Kv DC negative charge (or higher) with respect to ground: and the cage contained a generator of negative ions.

	Trials	Hits
Control in room	140	30
Control in cage	100	24
Control totals	240	54

Control (Room plus Cage)		
Average Hits per run of ten trials		2.25
Test Series	570	246
Average Hits per run of ten trials		4.31

Statistical Analysis

Trials	570
Hits	246
Standard Deviation	7.16
Chance-expected	57
Critical Ratio	26.39
Probability $= -\log Q(X)$	148.606 (or better)

(Where $-\log Q(X) = -\log \{1 - P(X)\}$)

The order of increase in telepathic test scores is quite remarkable with the addition of an excess of negative ions in the atmosphere.

13. The *Amanita muscaria* is used for making an intoxicating beverage in Eastern Siberia. The Samoyeds, Ostyaks, and Tungus prepare watery extracts, cold or warm, also milky extracts from the dried red toadstool. Many of them chew it directly, taking care not to swallow it. The natives know that the active substances are expelled from the human body in the urine. The user, or his friends, collect his urine when he is intoxicated and drink it, to get the same effect.

Reko gives the following description of a *nanacatl* (the Mexican species) intoxication:

"The effect of the amanita toxin consists of a peculiar hypersensibility. The inebriated person will perceive a mere touch on his skin as highly unpleasant and disturbing. When you blow in their faces they will react with violent gestures of self-defense. The eyes are extremely sensitive to light. Hearing is overstimulated. The sense of smell is changed and they complain of every smell as being unpleasant—in an outright pathologic manner. A remarkable symptom is the strong outbreak of perspiration during the first few hours (the muscarine effect). They also complain of a strong need for urination while they are mostly unable to urinate at all. Psychological behavior is similar to a person heavily drunk on alcohol.

"Besides the muscarinic effects of amanita there are other effects: 1) Disturbances of the equilibrium. 2) Drunkenness. 3) Hallucinations. A fungus toxin has been isolated (from the amanita) which produces symptoms of the central nervous system in the cat, but has no effect on the gastrointestinal canal, the pulse or the pupils. The existence of an atropine-like substance has been established, as well as a camphor-like substance (volatile) called aminatol." Hess, *op. cit.*, Chap. 9. Quoted from V. Reko.

I am informed by the Wassons that the species of mushroom thus far discovered in Mexico are not those of the *Amanita*, but are of the genus *Psilocybe*, and two species of *Stropharia*, and *Conocybe*, hitherto unknown to science. It is the opinion of these authors that Victor Reko, in his *Magische Gifte*, F. Enke, Stuttgart, 1949, mistakenly identifies the Mexican inebriating mushrooms as a "Mexican" variety of the *Amanita*. See: Wasson, R. Gordon, "Hallucinogenic Mushrooms of Mexico," *Trans. of the New York Academy of Sciences*, Vol. 21, No. 4, pp. 325–36. V. P. and R. G. Wasson, *Mushrooms, Russia, and History*, Pantheon Books, New York, 1957.

When the author visited Mitla, Oaxaca, Mexico, in the summer of 1960, he was informed by Walter Miller that *Amanita muscaria* was found in the environs of Mitla by Roger Heim, the well-known French mycologist. The author was also informed by certain Brujos among the Chatino Indians (living in Southern Oaxaca) that they used the *Amanita muscaria* for hallucinogenic purposes. The proper dose is one half of a mushroom.

Muscarine stimulates the postganglionic parasympathetic receptors, and so reproduces all the effects of stimulating parasympathetic nerves, but this is not its only action. All its muscarine-actions are as follows:

A. PARASYMPATHETIC

1. Heart—Rate slowed; contraction weak and brief and followed by a brief refractory period. Heart block in the Bundle of His.

2. Arterioles in salivary glands and penis dilated.

3. Eye—Pupil constricted; circular fibers of the ciliary muscle contracted, causing spasm of accommodation which focuses the lens for near objects; fall of intraocular pressure, if this is raised from occlusion of the canal of Schlemm, by dilation of the pupil.

4. Stomach and Intestine—Increased tone and movements; increased peristalsis.

5. Bronchi—Constriction.

6. Coronary Vessels—Constriction.

7. Retractor Penis—Inhibition.

8. Glands—Secretion of tears, saliva, pancreatic juice, gastric

juice, intestinal juice, and bronchial secretion, but not milk, urine, or bile.

B. SYMPATHETIC

1. Secretion of sweat, contraction of the uterus and spleen; vasodilatation in muscles.

C. OTHER EFFECTS

1. Vasodilatation in the skin. Gaddum, *Pharmacology,* p. 187.

In the state of exhaustion and sleep the available evidence indicates that there is a predominance of the cholinergic or parasympathetic effect. It is the author's opinion from the observation of humans in light trance that they present a form of the psychological state described for mild *Amanita* inebriation.

2

The Telepathic
Sender and the
State of Adrenergia

When we come to analyze the physiology and psychology of the sender in telepathic interaction we have much less data to work with. Most of the attention in telepathic research has been centered upon the receiver. The role of the sender is usually taken for granted. However, in observing senders over many years I have formed some opinions as to his role in telepathic interaction. A striking case of telepathic sending has been reported by the highly competent investigator team of Betty and Fraser Nicol in *Tomorrow*, Vol. 5, No. 3, Spring issue, 1957. The following is a condensation of their case in their own words:

"In the late afternoon of June 14, 1955, Jack Sullivan was alone in a fourteen foot trench welding new thirty-six inch water pipes alongside busy Washington Street in the southwest section of Boston. By four-thirty P.M., the last pipe for the day had been laid in place by the power-shovel crew, who then stopped work, leaving Sullivan to finish welding the seam between the last two pipes in the trench.

"Sullivan pulled the welding shield back down over his face and was about to resume welding when the calamity happened. There was no noise, no rumble—no warning—

as tons of earth, clay and stone fell upon him from behind. The trench had caved in.

"He was knocked down against the pipe in a more or less kneeling position. His legs were doubled up under him, his head was knocked against the pipe, his nose was smashed against the inside of the welding mask. At first he was conscious only of the searing pain in his right shoulder, which was jammed against the red hot weld he had been making on the pipes. He tried to edge away from the hot pipe, but the burden of earth on top of him held him tight against it. He managed to work his left hand up along his body to the shoulder and, wiggling his fingers, tried to get some of the dirt to fall down between the pipe and his burning shoulder. This maneuver was futile, he only burned his hand badly.

"Though buried under the earth, he shouted for help, hoping the children might still be around and hear. But after a few shouts he became short of breath. He thought it best to take things easily and not use up the air around the mask too quickly. With the generator running on the truck, probably no one could hear him anyhow, he realized.

"Then a vivid picture of Tommy Whittaker came into his mind. Whittaker was his best friend—a welder too, who had been working for Sullivan's welding company this spring. Whittaker, he knew, was working that day on another part of the water-main project some four or five miles away, near Route 128 in Westwood. Somehow Sullivan got the idea that Tommy Whittaker might help him.

"Whittaker didn't even know that Sullivan was at the Washington Street job. Sullivan had planned to spend the day working in Chelsea, north of Boston. Nobody had worked on the Washington Street job for several weeks. The project there had been held up when the trench-cutting crews had run into rock ledges. Sullivan himself had not been informed of resumption of the pipe-laying there until noon that day. So he knew Whittaker would think he was up north still in Chelsea. But still, Sullivan had a very clear mental picture of his friend working near the golf course in Westwood a few miles away."

Here we must make a brief digression. A physiologist, the late Walter B. Cannon,[1] has made us aware that the emotional condition of extreme danger, or a tendency to flight or fight, is associated with a massive action of the sympathetic nervous system. The sympathetic nervous system in general acts as an antagonist in the body to the parasympathetic nervous system. What one does, the other counteracts. For example, the parasympathetic inhibits or slows down the heartbeat. The sympathetic, on the other hand, accelerates the heartbeat. Sympathetic action prepares the body for great exertion. In general the parasympathetic causes blood vessels to dilate and relax, whereas the sympathetic causes them to constrict. One exception to this rule is in the case of the coronary vessels, where the parasympathetic causes constriction and the sympathetic causes dilatation. The parasympathetic causes the muscles of the pupil of the eye to constrict, and the sympathetic causes the pupil to dilate. In general the parasympathetic causes most of the sweat and salivary and gastric glands to secrete juices, whereas the sympathetic in general causes inhibition of such secretions. In general the parasympathetic, as we have noted earlier, causes marked contraction or increased tone and motility of the gastrointestinal tract. The sympathetic on the other hand causes an inhibition of such motion.

The sympathetic nervous system is activated by adrenalin and related adrenalin-like compounds. Therefore, dominance of the sympathetic nervous system is called adrenergia. The parasympathetic system on the other hand acts on the effector cells, that is, muscle and gland cells, by liberating acetylcholine, and its dominance is called the cholinergic system. When Sullivan was buried under the earth, he obviously suffered all the sense of great danger, at the same time suffered great pain because of the severe burn to his right shoulder. These two conditions plus his determination to fight his way out of this could only result in a massive activation of the sympathetic nervous system. In short, he was chemically under the domination of adrenergia. Let's see what happened to him.

"Farther south in Boston, in Westwood, Whittaker was welding more water pipes. Working with him was Danny, a welder from another company. They were welding overtime in order to finish up a seam before stopping for the night.

"Welding becomes an automatic job" (Whittaker later told us), "so that all sorts of irrelevant things run through your mind and you hardly know you are working." Into Whittaker's mind, as he worked that afternoon, came the idea that he ought to go up to Washington Street and check. It was so vague that he can hardly explain it. He felt that something was wrong. No particular person came to mind, only the persistent idea that he should go and check.

We here note that Whittaker is in an ideal condition for what we have earlier described for the receiver in telepathy. In the first place, he was working physically on a hot day. This activation of the skeletal muscle system alone is sufficient to induce a mild state of cholinergia. Secondly, because of the routine and monotony of his work, he was able to drift into a daydreaming, relaxed state of mind. This again is a good condition for telepathic reception.

"Whittaker got up and started to pack up his equipment.

" 'Where are you going?' asked Danny.

" 'I'm going up to the Washington Street job,' answered Whittaker.

" 'There's nobody working up there now, is there?' said Danny.

" 'No, but I think I'd better go.'

" 'But we'll finish up here in half an hour,' Danny pointed out.

" 'Well, I think I'd better go now. There might be something wrong.'

"So he drove off, leaving Danny alone to finish up. It was about 5:30 P.M.

"Usually when he quit work there, he went straight on to Route 128, the super-highway around Boston, and on home to Stoneham in the north. This night, he turned back into the heavy traffic and drove to Washington Street. He still doesn't know exactly why he did it—something seemed to be drawing him on.

"Nearing the trenches on Washington Street (near De Soto Road), he saw one of his company's trucks standing there with the generator running. He drew up behind it. No one was around. He got out and walked over to the trench. At first all he saw was dirt. Then he realized there had been a cave-in. Finally he saw the hand sticking out.

"Sullivan says, 'When Tommy jumped into that hole, I felt the earth shake and knew that help had come. Thank God.'

"It was 6:30 P.M. when he was lifted out. Whittaker had made the discovery about 6, so his friend must have been buried over an hour."

This case clearly shows that the sender in this telepathic interaction was Sullivan. Sullivan was under great stress and as described earlier, had a massive adrenergia. Whittaker, as the receiver in the telepathic interaction, was probably in a mild state of cholinergia, very relaxed, and therefore most receptive for receiving a telepathic impression. The fact that Whittaker went back into the city during the heavy traffic hour against his usual routine, is proof enough that he was guided by some telepathic urge, unformed though it was.

There is another case which brings out certain aspects of the role of the sender in a different way. John Hayes was a second-year student at San Jose State College in California. He was engaged in a fraternity hazing party. This occurred on a Saturday. It was John's mission to take a group of freshmen up into the High Sierras where spring snow conditions still prevailed. The distance to the Sierras was about 150 miles and John left sometime after midnight on this wild journey. He was in the mountains driv-

ing fast and rather recklessly when suddenly in the car
lights there appeared a gaping hole in the road ahead.
The car plunged down a seventy-five-foot embankment.
John was terror-stricken as the car plunged off into the
dark unknown. Miraculously the car landed right side up
and after plunging ahead about two hundred yards
through the brush and undergrowth came to a safe stop.
No one was injured in this accident.

In the meantime John's mother and father were asleep
in Salinas, California, about 180 miles away from the
scene of the accident. John's mother awakened abruptly
from a deep sleep and across her mind there flashed a
vision of her son being in an automobile accident. She
looked at the clock, it was exactly 5:30 A.M. She had no
idea where her son was or why he should be in an auto
accident at this hour. She awakened her husband, who
simply grunted something about "women and their prem-
onitions" and went back to sleep. Mrs. Hayes, however,
was so sure of her vision that she arose and placed a telephone call to the college. No one at the college could tell
her where her son was. As a matter of fact, it was about
twelve hours before her son was able to reach a phone
and telephone her. One of the first things that Mrs. Hayes
said to her son when she heard his voice was, "Did you
have an accident? Are you well?" Her son replied that he
was well, but how did she know that he had had an accident? Then she related to him her experience. He confirmed then and there that it was about 5:30 in the morning when his car had plunged down into the washout.

The son obviously experienced a sudden adrenergia as
his car plunged over the washout. His mother on the other
hand was asleep and relaxed. John had no thought, as
near as he can recollect, as he plunged down the washout,
of thinking at all of his mother or family. The mother's
mind on the other hand reached out and projected to the
scene and it seems that she saw only the relevant portion
of the scene: she knew her son was involved in an auto
accident. She had no idea where it was or the fact that he

was plunging down a washout. Here we have an ideal illustration of the adrenergic state of the sender, and the relaxed cholinergic condition of the receiver, the mother.

Crisis cases like this impressed me forcibly as I observed telepathic senders in the laboratory. I was well aware that in general a telepathic sender made a determined effort to concentrate during tests. The receiver on the other hand generally tried to remain relaxed and stated the first thing that entered his blank mind. I tried in a number of ways to induce an artificial state of adrenergia and pinpoint concentration in senders. I must say that most of these attempts were unsuccessful. It is very difficult to artificially bring on a true crisis adrenergia[2] based on a feeling of flight, fright, or fight.

However, the opportunity eventually arose to test this notion. While working with Peter Hurkos I observed that he seemed to have an abnormal fear of electricity. I knew that Hurkos, as a telepathic sender working with Harry Stone under normal room conditions, could achieve an average score of about twelve hits out of fifty ESP-test trials. This is barely significant for telepathy in one run. I therefore planned an experiment in which he, as the sender, was supposed to sit on a foot plate which had a ten-thousand-volt direct current charge on it. Actually the nature of the charge was such that even though he was sitting on the foot plate and the electricity was turned on, he would not experience any shock. I explained this carefully to Peter and assured him that he would not in any way be hurt. He was enterprising enough to go ahead with the experiment, but I could see grave doubts and fears written all over his face as the experiment began. The experiment was extraordinarily successful. The average score jumped from the twelve correct hits out of fifty to thirty-one correct hits out of fifty trials.[3] This is overwhelming evidence of telepathic interaction. There was no doubt that Hurkos' fear was profound as he sat on the electrically charged foot plate. I repeated these experiments seven times with the same results.

In repeating the same test with other sender subjects I found that the results were variable.[4] Some subjects got higher scores when they were thrown into an artificial state of fear by being on an electrically charged plate, and others got lower scores. In general this seemed to correspond with the individual's psychological reaction to electricity. For example, I know of some people who love to see lightning. It gives them great elation and joy to watch this awesome display of nature. Others are terrified by a flash of lightning and by the rumble of thunder. In general I was never able to create under laboratory conditions a consistent situation which would maintain sustained adrenergia in different senders during a telepathic test.

The basic act of sending in telepathy appears to be psychologically a centripetal one, concentration. In fact, the word *sender* in telepathy is a misnomer in that the sender does not send anything out, but rather serves as a center of attraction drawing to him the attention of the receiver. It is as though the sender creates a mental vacuum toward which the receiver's mind is drawn. The sender by his need and desire prepares a mental stage; the receiver in turn populates the stage with his own symbols and images.

NOTES   Chapter 2

1. Cannon, W. B., *Bodily Changes in Pain, Hunger, Fear, and Rage,* Appleton, New York, 1920.

Cannon, W. B., *The Wisdom of The Body,* Norton, New York, 1932.

2. The difficulty in reproducing adrenergic effects on one sender, or getting uniform responses from different senders to the same stimulus situation, may be due to the several actions of adrenalin itself. We have stated that adrenergia is a condition of fright or flight due to hyperactivity of the sympatho-adrenal system with the assumption that the net effect is an excitatory one. It is true that the classical response to adrenalin is excitatory, but the work of Marrazzi and others (see references a and b) has shown that adrenalin, noradrenalin, amphetamine, and ephedrine exercise an inhibitory effect on ganglionic and synaptic transmission. Certain hallucinogens such as amphetamine, and

mescaline show structural similarities to adrenaline (c), and it has been argued that they exert their effect through an adrenergic inhibitory effect on cerebral synapses. This may be accomplished by a direct action, or, as has been argued, by an effect in altering the metabolism of adrenaline (d). It has been demonstrated that some of the indole compounds exert an adrenergic type of inhibitory effect on cerebral synapses (e). If hallucinatory activation is dependent to some extent on an inhibitory effect on cerebral synapses (and this matter has not been entirely settled yet), we can argue that the excitatory phase of the ritual of the irrational sets the stage for an inhibitory process.

The possible proof of the thesis that adrenergic inhibitory blockade of the cerebral synapses of the temporal cortex is an essential step in producing self-sustained repetitive synchronous discharge in the cells of the temporal cortex (after excitation by the effects of camphor and interrupted sonic stimulation) would lie in finding an adrenergic blocking agent that has such an effect. (See Chap. 8.) There is the possibility that such a compound exists, as shown by the work of Nickerson and Goodman (f) with Dibenamine (N,N-dibenzyl-beta chloroethylamine) and congeners. They make the following statement in regard to Dibenamine:

A peculiar psychic feature of the central effect of Dibenamine deserves comment. In some patients, there occurs a type of transient repetitive temporal hallucination—or re-duplicative paramnesia in which an event seems to have been already experienced at the very moment when it is being experienced. With regard to the visual component this is the well known phenomenon of déjà-vu (g).

Such evidence would suggest adrenergic blockade of the synapses of the temporal cortex. Since there are a number of congeners of Dibenamine it appears that work with this group of drugs holds high promise. This drug is the more interesting in that while it blocks excitatory adrenergic functions, inhibitory adrenergic functions are not blocked and in fact are brought into sharp relief. Although the effects of Dibenamine persist for 36–96 hours (and this would be desirable) it is promptly destroyed by sodium thiosulfate, thus giving the possibility of counteracting an overdosage in the subject.

a   Amadeo S. Marrazzi, "Electrical studies on the pharmacology of autonomic synapses. II. The action of a sympathomimetic drug (epinephrine) on sympathetic ganglia," *J. Pharm. & Exp. Therap.,* 65: 395, 1939.

—— "Electrical studies on the pharmacology of autonomic synapses. III. The action of ephedrine analysed by a study of its sympathetic central and ganglionic effects," *J. Pharm. & Exp. Therap.,* 67: 321, 1939.

—— "Inhibition at sympathetic synapses," *Am. J. Physiol.,* 126: 579, 1939. "Adrenergic inhibition at sympathetic synapses," *ibid.,* 127: 738, 1939. "Relation between structures of epinephrine and ephedrine homologs and analogs and ability to inhibit sympathetic ganglia," *J. Pharm. & Exp. Therap.,* 69: 294, 1940.

—— "Distribution and nature of ganglionic inhibition in the sympathetic system," *Fed. Proc.,* 1: 57, 1942.

—— "Cholinergic excitation and adrenergic inhibition common to peripheral and central synapses," *The Biology of Mental Health and Disease,* Hoeber, Harper & Brothers, New York, 1952.

Krivoy, Hart, and Marrazzi, "Inhibition of phrenic respiratory potentials by adrenaline and other sympathomimetic amines," *Fed. Proc.,* 12: 338, 1953.

Marrazzi, "Some indications of cerebral humoral mechanisms," *Science,* 118: 367, 1953.

"Ganglionic and central transmission," *Pharm. Rev.,* 6: 105, 1954.

b   For a comprehensive review of the work of others in this field see: *Progress in Neurology and Psychiatry,* Grune & Stratton, New York, Editions of 1949, 1950, 1951, 1952, 1953, and 1954. See particularly the chapters on Pharmacology of the Nervous System. I am particularly grateful to Dr. Marrazzi and Dr. Harry H. Pennes for invaluable discussions on this subject.

c   I am particularly indebted to Dr. Humphrey Osmond for his ideas on this subject. Abram Hoffer, Humphrey Osmond, and John Smythies, "Schizophrenia, a new approach: II. Result of a Year's Research," *J. Mental Science,* 100: 29, 1954.

D. W. Woolley and E. Shaw, "A biochemical and pharmacological suggestion about certain mental disorders," *Science,* 119: 587, 1954. Amadeo S. Marrazzi and E. Ross Hart, "The Relation of Hallucinogens to Adrenergic Cerebral Neurohumors," Prepublication copy, 1955.

d   Rinkel, Max, *Psych. Quart.,* 26: 33–53, 1952.

e   See Marrazzi, Note (a), *The Biology of Mental Health and Disease.*

f   Mark Nickerson and Louis S. Goodman, "Pharmacologic and Physiologic aspects of Adrenergic Blockade, with special reference to Dibenamine," *Fed. Proc.*, 7: 397–409, 1948.

g   Nickerson and Goodman, *ibid.*, p. 407.

3. Hurkos—sender
   Stone—receiver

Control 2.4/10	
or 12/50	
Test Trials	350
Hits	223
Average Hits for 10 Trials	6.37
Average Hits for 50 Trials	31.85
Mean	35
Standard Deviation	5.61
Critical Ratio	33.5
Probability $= -\log Q(X)$	238.39

4. When I reversed the role of this telepathic team, Stone being the sender and Hurkos the receiver, there was not the same dramatic jump in scoring.

Trials	200
Hits	60
Average Hits for 10 Trials	3/10
Average Hits for 50 Trials	15/50
Mean	20
Standard Deviation	4.24
Critical Ratio	9.43
Probability $= -\log Q(X)$	18.94

When Stone was the receiver and four other persons, who were electrically charged, acted as senders, the following results appeared.

Trials	200
Hits	42
Average Hits for 10 Trials	2.10/10
Average Hits for 50 Trials	10.5/50

The scores fell below control levels.

3

Telepathic Networks
with Individuals
Serving as
Unconscious Relays

Telepathy is never as simple a process as dialing a telephone to get your party. I was conducting an experiment with Mrs. Eileen Garrett in which she was to guess when a switch was turned on in another building. This experiment is very much like waiting for a telephone to ring and guessing when the phone would ring, as in the instance cited earlier between Joe Lawrence and Bill Harmon. As I sat with Mrs. Garrett, and she was waiting for an impression of when the switch would be turned on in the other building, she suddenly said to me, "You have a friend, Dr. Henry Wilson?" I looked at her quizzically and said, "How did you know that I know Dr. Wilson?" She replied that she didn't know this before but had just gotten the impression mentally that I knew a Dr. Henry Wilson.

The entire conversation with Mrs. Garrett, as well as the entire experiment, was recorded on tape and provisions were made so that the exact times when these conversations occurred were recorded too. The experiment ended about three minutes after this exchange between Mrs. Garrett and myself.

As I left the laboratory I was called by my secretary to answer the telephone. The telephone was about twenty feet from where Mrs. Garrett and I had been sitting. I was surprised to find Dr. Wilson on the phone, the same Dr. Henry Wilson referred to by Mrs. Garrett some moments earlier. Dr. Wilson told me that he was traveling through Maine and had stopped at a university about fifty miles from where I lived. He had had an impulse to call me a few minutes earlier just to see how I was getting along. I must make it clear that I had not been in touch with Dr. Wilson for about six months and was not at all familiar with his movements. Likewise he was not familiar with what I was doing at the moment and therefore would have had no normal way of knowing that I was engaged in a telepathic experiment with Mrs. Garrett. I invited him over for dinner that evening and he promptly accepted.

I turned back to the experiment just completed with Mrs. Garrett, which had run thirty-six minutes, and played the tape recording of our session. When I reached the point where Mrs. Garrett had unexpectedly brought up the name of Dr. Wilson, I noted that twenty seconds following her utterance of the words "Dr. Henry Wilson," there were three faint phone rings on the tape. The question arose as to whether this was Dr. Wilson ringing me. I checked back with my secretary and found that the phone had rung about three minutes before I had reached it. She had not wanted to disturb me until the experiment was completed and had asked the operator to hold the call for a few minutes.

When Dr. Wilson arrived at my home I told him of this curious coincidence, and he, wanting to make sure that it was his phone call that was heard on the tape, called the long distance operator to get the time at which he had placed his call earlier that afternoon. His call had been placed within a minute of the time that the phone ring was recorded on the tape. Therefore, allowing for small variations in the recording of time at both ends, we felt sure that the phone ring on the tape was due to Dr. Wilson's call. Furthermore it was found that no other telephone

calls had come into the laboratory during the half-hour
period of this particular experiment.

I was curious about this event. Mrs. Garrett was in a
state of consciousness which can best be described as a
light trance in which she was scanning her mind for a
telepathic impression. I myself was unaware that Dr. Wilson was trying to call me. Mrs. Garrett, however, being
sensitive to telepathic impressions and being in my presence, must have intercepted the unconsciously sent telepathic message intended for me.

In this situation we have the following elements: Dr.
Wilson had an abrupt impulse (adrenergia?) to call me
on the telephone. He carried out this act as soon as he
could get near a telephone. Concurrently with his desire
to phone and going through the process of phoning he
must have released a telepathic message unconsciously.
This of course was intended for me. However, I was completely unconscious of it since my mind was taut and
concentrated on the experiment. But in my presence was
a person highly sensitized (cholinergia?) at the moment
to receiving telepathic impressions. This penetrated her
consciousness and she without knowing why merely passed
the name of Dr. Wilson on to me.

In the Lawrence-Harmon story we had a simple two-termed situation where there was a sender and a receiver
for a telepathic message, and an immediate confirmation
of the interaction because of the use of a telephone. In
the Garrett-Wilson story we have Wilson as the sender and
Garrett as the receiver, but we have a third party interposed between the sending and the receiving function. Our
attention is drawn to this third party because he appears
to act as a relay station between Dr. Wilson and Mrs.
Garrett. If Puharich had not been present it is almost certain that Mrs. Garrett would not have received the telepathic message. If Mrs. Garrett had not been present it
is certain that Puharich would never have been aware of
a telepathic message. We ask whether Puharich in this
instance actually reflected the message of Dr. Wilson in

his unconscious? Did Mrs. Garrett read the message of Dr. Wilson in his unconscious? Or did Mrs. Garrett, in a way unknown to herself, use Puharich as a tuning device which allowed her to get the message directly from Dr. Wilson? This is a critical question in this early stage of our examination of telepathy. We shall have to discuss another instance of three-termed telepathy in order to begin to understand the question that has been posed.

Peter Hurkos and I were relaxing in the kitchen having our after-dinner coffee. We were both looking at the mock afterglow in the western sky caused by northern lights. As we watched this dramatic scene, Peter suddenly turned to me and in great excitement said, "I see it. I see it, just like a film. I see a hand in front of my eyes. It's hanging, the wrist is cut and there is blood coming from it." I was startled by this abrupt interruption of my reveries about the northern lights.

I had studied Peter Hurkos for a year in the laboratory in Maine. I had become used to his spontaneous outbursts of ideas, visions, and telepathic messages. Therefore I assumed that in this instance his vision had some special significance for him. "Peter," I said, "what are you talking about?" "It's a hand! I saw a hand in front of my eyes and the wrist is cut, and it's nothing in this room; it's in my mind that I see it." I knew now that his vision could either be a literal telepathic impression, or one that could have a symbolic meaning. When I pressed Peter further, he told me that this really had a symbolic meaning to him, and that it had to do with suicide. "Whose suicide?" I asked. He pondered a moment over this question and announced that it might be connected with Jim Middleton.[1]

Now I must explain a situation that had existed for several weeks between Peter Hurkos and Jim Middleton. Peter had a pilot film for a TV series in his possession that he was trying to sell to some television producer. Today was December 1, 1957, and several weeks earlier he had been in New York visiting Jim Middleton. He had persuaded Jim Middleton to show this pilot film to some of his friends in the television industry. Jim had obliged by taking the film and was trying to arrange showings for it. Peter returned to Maine shortly after giving Jim the film and began to worry over the fact that the film was not in his own hands. He would call Jim up every day or two and ask him if anybody was interested in the film. The next time he would call to ask him to send back the film, only to countermand the request by a subsequent phone call. Jim was very disturbed by this pressure, and would have been glad to be rid of the whole problem. Peter on the one hand was very anxious to sell the film, and on the other hand he kept worrying that it would get lost. In this way quite a tense situation had arisen between Peter and Jim in the past few weeks.

Peter's wife, Maria, now turned to Peter and said, "Peter, I think you are all worked up about Jim having your pilot film, and this is why you are thinking of him now." Peter was irritated by this remark and stated that the pilot film was not on his mind at all, but that he had a very strong impression of a possible suicide in Jim's family. As a peacemaker I took up the questioning and finally asked Peter to identify the member of Jim's family involved with this vision. Peter now began to feel strongly that the threat of suicide had nothing to do with Jim but with Jim's brother, Art. Now as far as I have been able to determine, Peter had never met Art. Peter and I lived at Glen Cove, Maine; Jim lived in New York City; and Art was living in Albuquerque, New Mexico. However, Jim had at times talked about his brother and therefore both Peter and I knew of his existence, although we had never met him physically.

Peter got more and more worked up about his feeling that there was some danger of suicide in the case of Art Middleton. He insisted that we place a call to Jim in New York City, a distance of some 440 miles. Maria resisted this idea because she felt he would merely irritate Jim, who would think it was another phone call about the pilot film. However, I saw that Peter was so worked up that there was nothing to do but place the call to New York

City, so I went ahead and did this. I turned the phone over to Peter, who said, "Hello Jim, this is Peter. I am sorry to bother you again but I am not calling about the movie film this time. I have a very unpleasant feeling that your brother might try to commit suicide."

"It's amazing that you should call me now," Jim replied. "About twenty minutes ago I got a phone call from Art's psychiatrist in Albuquerque, who told me that Art was feeling rather depressed, and that it would be a good idea if I came out to visit him and cheer him up. I told the psychiatrist that it was very difficult for me to get away and I could not promise immediately that I would come. I told him I would call him back as soon as I could see my way clear to leave. However, now that you have called, I am impelled to go out there as soon as I can. Thanks for calling me, and I will let you know what happens. I am going to get a plane reservation as soon as I can for Albuquerque."

After this telephone conversation we were all quite impressed with the fact that Peter had sensed that something was wrong with Art, even though none of us could yet take seriously Peter's vision of a cut wrist and a suicide threat. I noticed during the telephone conversation that Peter had not mentioned his vision of a cut wrist.

Several weeks passed before I got another phone call from Jim Middleton. At this time he was in the state of Washington and was calling to say that his brother, while depressed, was not seriously ill. But in view of Peter's warning he had persuaded both Art and the psychiatrist that Art should be hospitalized until he was better. He was now safely hospitalized and Jim was going to take a trip to Mexico and get some rest after the tension of the past few weeks. Jim then asked me to repeat the entire story as it had happened on the evening of December 1, when Peter had called Jim. I repeated the story in great detail to Jim. He was surprised that Peter had originally seen a cut wrist with blood flowing from it. He recalled that Peter had not mentioned this to him while on the telephone. After this telephone call it was another week before I heard from Jim. This time his story was quite remarkable.

After hearing about the cut-wrist vision from me, he went back to the hospital and begged the attending physician to place Art under maximum security as far as a possible suicide attempt was concerned. The physician complied with Jim's request and put Art in a room by himself where there was no object or instrument available that could be used for suicidal purposes. Art was left with his hospital gown and a pair of paper slippers. The second day after Jim left for his trip to Mexico, Art requested the attendant to get him a newspaper, which the attendant did. Art then said that he could not read the newspaper without his glasses and requested the use of them. The attendant produced the reading glasses. As soon as the attendant had turned his back Art smashed the glasses on the floor, picked up one of the larger pieces of glass, and slashed both wrists. Fortunately he was given immediate medical attention and recovered completely. The date on which this suicide attempt occurred was December 23, 1957.

What particularly interests us in this story is the function of Jim as a relay between Art Middleton in the Southwest and Peter Hurkos in Maine. In checking out the time factor afterward it was established that Peter had probably had his vision sometime during or shortly after Jim had received a telephone call from Art's psychiatrist. It must be noted that Peter and Jim were very much on each other's minds as a result of the tension that had built up over the pilot film. Secondly, it must be noted that Peter got his vision, and correctly ascribed it to Art Middleton, some short time after Jim had become aware and was of course worried that his brother was ill. Now the key information had to do with a cut wrist. This information could not have been in Jim's mind at the time of the telephone call on December 1. It could have unconsciously been in Art's mind on this very day. But it was impossible to establish this probability after the event. On the other hand we could look upon this as a case of precognition on Peter's part, whereby he saw an event twenty-three days before it occurred. It must be noted that Art himself was not influenced toward this mode of suicide because neither Peter Hurkos nor his brother Jim ever conveyed this vision to him before the suicide attempt.

The Garrett-Wilson and the Hurkos-Middleton cases clearly show that telepathy can exist between more than two people at a time even though some of the members of this network may be totally unconscious of their participation in the phenomenon. In both cases the receivers were relaxed and in the state of cholinergia. In both cases the senders were under tension. In both cases the unconscious relay agent was tense, concentrated, and perhaps even worried, a state fitting adrenergia. We have thus far considered only a three-termed telepathic network, and the question naturally arises as to how large such a network can become?

Dr. Rudolf von Urban, Dr. Alexander Pilcz, and some colleagues made a study of the Indian Rope Trick.[2] They were interested in the problem of mass hallucination and it was their idea that the Indian Rope Trick would serve as a good experiment for their purposes. They collected several hundred people and a Fakir to put on the show. All of the observers, including the scientists, saw the Fakir throw a coil of rope in the air and saw a small boy climb up the rope and disappear. Subsequently dismembered parts of this small boy came tumbling down to the ground; the Fakir gathered them up in the basket, ascended the rope, and both the boy and the Fakir came down smiling. It is astonishing that several hundred people witnessed this demonstration and agreed in general on the details as described. There was not a single person present in the crowd who could deny these facts. However, when the motion pictures of this scene were developed subsequently, it was found that the Fakir had walked into the center of the group of people and thrown the rope into the air, but

that it had fallen to the ground. The Fakir and his boy
assistant had stood motionless by the rope throughout the
rest of the demonstration. The rope did not stay in the air,
the boy did not ascend the rope. In other words, everyone
present had witnessed the same hallucination. Presumably
the hallucination originated with the Fakir as the agent or
sender. At no time in the course of the demonstration did
the Fakir tell the audience what they were going to see. The
entire demonstration was carried out in silence. In view of
this fact we must assume that the hallucination was telepathically inspired and therefore extended to the several
hundred people present as receivers of this delusion.[3]

In this instance we have one powerful agent who acts
as the sender of a telepathic drama, and we have several
hundred people who expect a wonder and simultaneously
act as receivers for a very complex and orderly drama.
Other instances reported from earlier times[4] by many travelers show that the Indian Rope Trick hallucination can
extend to thousands of observers at one time. This gives
us an idea of the large network that telepathic interaction
can assume. We have no final idea as to how large a
number of people can be embraced by one telepathic
situation, that is, with a single sender.

We can look at telepathic networks from the opposite
point of view, namely, where there are multiple senders
and a single receiver. I was fortunate enough to study this
phenomenon in the laboratory through one subject, Harry
Stone. Harry had the uncanny ability to find a small
object hidden in a room. The demonstration would be run
with a dozen observers present in a room. Harry was asked
to leave the room and was always accompanied by someone who acted as a monitor. One of the persons in the
room would then take a small object such as a dime and
hide it out of sight at any place in the room. Before re-
entering the room Harry was blindfolded. He then entered the door and usually paused for a few moments,
apparently concentrating. His next move invariably was
in a straight line for the place where the object was hidden

and usually within two or three minutes he had found the object no matter how well it was concealed. Here he was under the mass influence of a dozen telepathic senders.

I observed this phenomenon several hundred times. Once I gave a dime to a visitor to hide in the room. I noticed that the visitor went to four different places thinking he might hide the object there, but finally decided on a fifth place. He then sat down with the rest of the observers. Harry entered the room blindfolded, as usual, and concentrated for a few minutes at the door. I then observed that Harry retraced the steps of the individual who had hidden the object by going to each of the four places the person had thought of as a possible hiding place, and Harry finally went to the fifth place and recovered the dime. This demonstration set me to thinking as to whether or not Harry was actually following the entire thought process[5] of the person who had hidden the object. I determined to test this in a number of different ways, and the first was to ascertain what it was that Harry was responding to. Was it the hidden object itself? Was it the mass influence of all the people present in the room? Was it specifically the thought processes of the person who had hidden the object? Was it a particular person in the room from whom Harry received the strongest telepathic impression?

First a series of tests was run to determine if Harry did indeed retrace either the steps or the thinking processes of the person who hid the object. It was soon found that as a rule he did retrace the steps of the person who had hidden the object. The next question was to find out if Harry was really influenced by the thinking of that person whom we shall call the Agent.

The Agent was asked to hide the object in the first place in the room that came to his mind. Then after hiding the object he was to sit down with the other observers. At the moment that Harry entered the room the Agent was to concentrate not on the right location, but on a completely different one. Now the question was, would Harry go to the place where the object was hidden? Or would he go to the place where the person was telepathically trying to divert him? It was found that Harry invariably first went to the place where the Agent was trying to divert him. After a few minutes of feeling around in this place Harry soon realized that the object was not there and then usually went to the correct hiding place as his next move.

This experiment was used many times to prove to observers that Harry could reach the mind of the Agent— since no one else in the room knew the wrong location which the Agent had selected. This sort of demonstration obviously ruled out the possibility that somebody in the room was directing Harry by unconscious cuing. It is also interesting to observe in this situation where there may have been at least a dozen observers in the room each concentrating on the problem, that Harry was able to selectively follow the thinking of the person who had hidden the object. It was further noticed that if Harry did not know who had hidden the object he invariably wasted a lot of time in random movements around the room before finding the object. This ruled out the possibility that he was following some physical scent or track. It was not necessary to have the Agent remain in the same room with Harry. On the contrary, the Agent could remain outside the room, and still Harry would follow his thought process either by repeating the sequence of possible hiding places, or being diverted to a spot chosen by the Agent where the object was not hidden, and going on to find the place where the object actually was hidden.

This observation brings out the unusual selective aspects of the telepathic process. On the basis of a mass reaction alone one would assume that Harry would be primarily guided in his choices by the largest number of individuals who either consciously or unconsciously were thinking about the place where the object was actually hidden. In my experience it turned out that Harry usually responded to the person who was most vitally interested in influencing him.

It is simple enough to see a one-to-one relationship be-

tween a telepathic sender and a telepathic receiver when
the intelligence transmission and reception is contemporaneous. It is perhaps puzzling to include a third person
into this simple telepathic relationship and look upon him
either as an unconscious relay, or an unconscious tuning
mechanism, or an amplifier of the telepathic signal. When
we look at a large broadcasting effect emanating from a
single telepathic sender as in the case of the Indian Rope
Trick, or look at the converse phenomenon of a large
number of telepathic senders focusing on a single receiver,
we indeed begin to get into the deeper complexities of
telepathy.

NOTES   Chapter 3

1. Jim Middleton is a pseudonym used to protect the privacy
of the family concerned.

2. I have had this story directly from Dr. Rudolf von Urban.
He has published a short account of this experiment in his book,
Beyond Human Knowledge, Pageant Press, New York, 1958,
p. 184.

3. The Indian Rope Trick has also been described as an
elaborate illusion. Here the Fakir is alleged to suspend a taut
cable between two high points in such a way as to be invisible
to the audience. The rope with a ball on the end is thrown over
the cable. John Keel, *Jadoo,* Gilbert Press, New York, 1957.

4. *Travels of Marco Polo,* Trans. and Ed. by Sir Henry Yule,
Cordier Edition, John Murray, London, 1921, Vol. 1, Chap. LXI,
p. 314 ff.

5. Experiments of a similar nature with positive results have
been reported by Prof. W. H. C. Tenhaeff in *Beschouwingen
Over Het Gebruik Van Paragnosten,* Erven J. Bijleveld, Utrecht,
1957.

4

General Extrasensory Perception Networks Containing an Object as a Relay

There is a curious form of general extrasensory perception called psychometry in which the sensitive person uses an object as the primary inductor of intelligence. How psychometry[1] fits into the network of telepathy which we have been sketching can best be brought out by a selected series of cases.

In 1958 Mr. W. H. Belk arranged with Professor C. J. Ducasse to find out how much information Peter Hurkos could get from an object sealed in a cardboard package. The object was furnished by Professor C. J. Ducasse of Brown University. Professor Ducasse sent the following letter after the reading by Hurkos was completed: "The object contained in a sealed package I gave Mr. Loring to submit to Hurkos for psychometrizing is a small pottery jar, that was broken but mended, which was given to me in 1922 by the late Dr. Stevenson Smith, Professor of Psychology at the University of Washington. He said that it came from the ruins of Pompeii, in Italy, buried in 79 A.D. in the ashes thrown up by the eruption of Vesuvius. I think, but am not positive, that Dr. Smith said he had bought the jar on a trip he made to Pompeii excavations. So far as I can remember, this is all the information I have ever had concerning that little jar." Dated May 10, 1958, signed C. J. Ducasse.

The sealed package was brought to New York City by Mr. Paul Loring from Providence, Rhode Island. There were several witnesses present at Mr. Belk's apartment when the package was handed to Peter Hurkos, and his statement concerning the package was tape-recorded. I give below the reading by Peter Hurkos. The order of the statements has been rearranged for easier reading since his sentences were repetitive.

This is what Hurkos said about the sealed package: "This object blew up—an explosion. There was an explosion—a long time ago. I hear a strange language. It is very old. It had to do also with water. I don't know what it is. I see a dark color. It is not straight, not regular. It is very jagged, sharp points. It belonged to three people. I am sure of this. Dr. Ducasse didn't buy this. It was given to him, and it was repaired. A souvenir. I am sure that the owner of the cylinder is dead. I do not mean Dr. Ducasse, he is well."

As the reader may judge for himself, Hurkos' statements are a fair approximation of the contents of the sealed package. He was not able to specifically state that it was a jar. He seemed to sense the object more as it existed when it was fragmented in connection with an explosion. However, he does state that it was repaired and therefore it would appear that he should have been able to guess that this was a container or jar. In general I would say that he did have knowledge about what was in that package, and more so of the people who had owned it. For example, he was quite certain that Dr. Ducasse had not bought this, but that it had been given to him; that the person who had given it to Dr. Ducasse was dead; that the object was very, very old. This indicates that he knew things about the object that could not be known from visual inspection of the object itself. However, we can say that he knew no more about the object than did Dr. Ducasse. It is my opinion that the object in this case acted as a tuning device which allowed Hurkos to tap, in an approximate way, the mind of Dr. Ducasse with specific reference to the object in hand. This in itself is a most interesting phenomenon in that we would have to ascribe some sort of relay function to the object, as we did earlier to the unconscious participants in a telepathic triad.

There are many instances of Hurkos' ability to gain intelligence through the mediation of an inanimate object. On November 6, 1959, Hurkos was giving a demonstration of his talent before a group of three hundred Naval Reserve Officers at Charleston, South Carolina.[2] About three dozen of the officers sent personal objects on a tray up to Hurkos, who was on stage. Hurkos picked out of this collection of personal objects a wallet which was devoid of contents. He fingered the wallet for a few moments and then said, "The man who owns this was in an auto accident very recently. I see three people injured in this accident. The man was not responsible when he was driving. I see big trouble with the police. Yes, this was an accident."

The story behind this reading is interesting. One of the men in the audience, a Commander, had been driving home from a meeting the previous night about 3:00 A.M. The Commander admits to having some drinks before starting out in the car. On the roadside ahead of him a police car had stopped another car for speeding. The police officer and the two occupants of the car which had been stopped were standing on the roadside in the headlights of the police car. The Commander was driving about fifty miles an hour and apparently did not realize that the tail lights in front of him were standing still, and he rammed into the rear end of the police car. All three people, the police officer and the two citizens, suffered injuries as a result of this rear-end collision. Because of the early hour, the story was not to be found in the newspapers on the following morning when Hurkos was giving his readings.

We have an instance where an inanimate object that has

been in close personal contact with an individual serves as a mediator between Hurkos' mind and the mind of the party to whom it belonged. Again we note that Hurkos in this instance was not able to recover any more intelligence about the situation than was present in that person's mind at the moment.[3]

Two businessmen, Mr. C. V. Wood and Mr. Tom Slick, wanted to test Hurkos' ability to get intelligence from an object sealed in a package. At this time, May 1959, Hurkos was staying in Miami and the two gentlemen visited him there. They had arranged to have Mr. Wood's secretary, in Los Angeles, California, mail them a sealed package whose contents were not to be revealed to them until after the experiment was completed. In this particular instance Hurkos was not allowed to touch the sealed package. Furthermore, it was held by another gentleman who went into the next room so that Hurkos could not even see the shape of it. Hurkos' statement about the contents of this package was as follows:

"I see in this package some brown hair from a dog. I see a leather collar from a dog with brass trimmings on it. This package is about a small dog, brown in color. The dog has a lame left hind leg. The owner of the dog does not know what is wrong with it. The doctor of the dog is not sure what is wrong with it. The doctor thinks that it is some sort of an arthritis. I think that this is not an arthritis but is due to neuritis. I believe this dog will be cured by some sort of a shock."

The facts in the case are that the sealed package contained some brown dog hairs, and it contained a metal chain from a dog. There was no leather brass-trimmed dog collar in the box; in this respect Hurkos was wrong. The other statements were remarkable in their knowledge of the situation. The dog in question was a brownish poodle called Cocoa. The dog had been sick for several weeks, limping and favoring his left hind leg. No definite diagnosis had been established by the veterinarian in charge. The most curious aspect of this case is that a week after the reading by Hurkos, the dog was hit by a car but merely rolled over, and after this accident the limp disappeared and the dog has been well since that time.

Apparently Hurkos received intelligence about a situation several thousand miles away which was not known by the owner of the dog. I'm referring of course to the actual diagnosis of the dog's malady and the suggestion of a cure by shock. I think it is fair to assume that the dog suffered some shock when hit by the car.

Here we have a case where Hurkos not only got knowledge that was in the mind of the owner of the dog, but knowledge that was privy to the dog in the sense that the dog had the affliction connected with the limping. But no one at the time of the reading had any knowledge of how the dog would be cured. Certainly not the two businessmen who were with Hurkos in Florida, nor the owner, nor the veterinarian. In this instance we have some evidence that Hurkos' mind was focused on the far-off dog through the mediation of the chain and the hairs sealed in the package. We have reason to believe that the intelligence that he gained from this object was outside of that of the human beings concerned in the case, therefore pure clairvoyance.

That Hurkos can get intelligence from an object when this intelligence is not present consciously or unconsciously in the mind of the person connected with the object can be illustrated from another case. A friend of mine gave Peter Hurkos a letter sealed in a manila envelope. Hurkos handled this letter and then made the following statements to my friend in my presence.

"This letter is from your wife. She seems to be in good health at the moment, but she will have trouble with her female organs." Hurkos then drew a diagram of the uterus and the Fallopian tubes of this woman, showing the left Fallopian tube with a large mass in the center portion. Hurkos then went on to say that in about six months the female organs would give rise to complications which would require surgical intervention.

Six months after this reading the woman in question began to develop severe cramps, irregular bleeding, and low back pain. She went to a number of specialists who eventually referred her to the Mayo Clinic. At the Mayo Clinic a hysterectomy was performed. In this case the husband was shown the removed surgical specimen. He was told by the attending physician, and confirmed it by his own observation, that the left Fallopian tube had a large sealed-off mass.

This particular case illustrates two important features of the mediation of an inanimate object in the process of extrasensory perception. In the first place it shows that Hurkos' mind could see anatomical arrangements within an individual that are not consciously known to that individual. Secondly, he seemed to be able to make a guess as to the course of the pathology connected with this particular anatomy, and this was subsequently confirmed following surgery.[4]

It was found over a two-year period of study of Peter Hurkos' psychometry that he was most successful at getting a reading from objects when he used photographs. For example, it was found in the case of photographs of the same person that his best intelligence was obtained from a negative film of that person, less intelligence from a positive print of that negative, and very little or no intelligence from a printed reproduction of the photograph.[5] This meant that there was a closer connection between the individual and the photograph when one dealt with the negative.

Peter Hurkos was giving a demonstration before a movie-studio audience in Amsterdam, Holland, in December of 1956. Members of the audience sent up various objects to be handled by Peter. One of the objects that Peter picked up was a photograph of a family group. The photograph had been placed in an envelope so that he could not directly see the image on the photograph. Peter immediately gave a description as follows:

"I see a small boy of age nine or ten. He goes to school

and follows such a route through the streets. At a certain
point he crosses an intersection." Peter went on to sketch
the details of that intersection. "I am sorry to tell you this
but I see this boy involved in some kind of an accident
with a yellow bus on a Wednesday at twelve noon."

The parents were quite disturbed by this reading. The
reason they were disturbed was that every detail that Peter
had given them could be verified on the basis of his description of their son and the route he walked to school. They
knew that Peter was definitely referring to their son. They
asked him after the meeting what they could do about this.
Peter said that the only thing he could think of was to keep
the boy home on Wednesdays. The parents then asked
him how long this should be done. Peter thought that the
next four weeks would be sufficient.

The parents did as instructed and for the next four
weeks kept the boy home on Wednesdays. After four weeks
they began to be relieved of their anxiety and decided to
send the boy back to school. On the sixth week after the
reading the boy was injured by a large tan American car
(not by a yellow bus) at the crossing that Peter had mentioned, at twelve noon on a Wednesday. He was not seriously injured and recovered satisfactorily.

Peter got this intelligence about a boy he had never
seen simply by handling a photograph (a positive print)
sealed in a manila envelope. It can also be said that Peter
foresaw an accident that occurred six weeks afterward.
Peter was inaccurate in some details of this accident but
his essential intelligence was correct. It must be remembered that the boy in question had been informed, and
was thereby probably alarmed by the possibility of an
accident at such a corner and therefore may have been
accident prone. This case is not very clear-cut for evidence
of precognition, because of this complicating factor.

These cases make it appear as though something is transferred from a human being to an inanimate object and
that thing is carried for long periods by the object. When
an object is placed in the hands, or in the vicinity, of a

sensitive person[6] like Peter Hurkos, he is able to use that something to sharply focus upon the problem and glean verifiable intelligence. This raises the enormous question as to whether what we call memory can exist outside of biological organisms. There is another case which illustrates another aspect of this puzzling question.

Julian Huxley and his wife visited the laboratory in Maine on the twenty-sixth of August 1956. In this test Mr. Huxley handed a sealed envelope to Harry Stone, who went to the opposite side of the room. Peter Hurkos was to concentrate on Harry Stone holding the sealed envelope and see if he could get any impression. These are his words:

"What a sweet character. Never caught in a lie. Open nature. Not proud. Has been in a hospital. A serious sickness. I now go to the hospital room and I see a bureau and a blonde woman. There are two persons at home. Death was around here. I see a woman who lives outside of town. A musical person. A ring has been lost. This woman had an accident on the legs. I see a picture in the house with children in it. I see airplanes and bombs. 'Don't forget me, Frank and Lillian would.' I see writing on a photograph. I feel a woman."

At this point Mr. Hurkos was allowed to actually touch the envelope and he now held it in his hands.

"I see dogs and cats. This picture is of a lady, blonde hair with a round face." At this point Julian Huxley emphatically stated that Peter was entirely wrong, and went on to say that the envelope contained a photograph of his son.

Peter was taken aback by this vigorous denial of the accuracy of his reading. But he recovered and said, "I now see that you are absolutely right. The impressions that I have been getting are from a photograph of a woman which was next to this photograph in your wallet. If you will look in your wallet you will see that you have a photograph of the woman whom I have been describing." Mr. Huxley then looked in his wallet and verified that there was a woman's photograph next to where his son's photograph had been and that the description Peter gave was in reference to it. Mr. Huxley affirmed that Hurkos' description of the photograph still in his wallet, sketchy though it was, was accurate.

This case is of interest for a number of reasons. It is obvious that Mr. Huxley had firmly in mind the knowledge that the photograph Peter was handling was of his son. It apparently had not even occurred to him that the photograph next to his son's, and which was still in his wallet, was at all under discussion. If we consider the possibility that there is something connected with a physical object which has been transferred to it from a person, then in this case we have further evidence that something can be transferred from one object to another. This something that is transferred, in this case from one photograph to the next by long proximity, was actually picked up as a piece of verifiable evidence by a sensitive. I have seen this type of case repeated many times.

We must squarely face the possibility that memory or intelligence is not strictly limited to the human mind. It can, as a sort of network extending from a living individual, reach not only into other minds and cause them to respond, but register on physical objects which serve as reservoirs of discrete intelligence that can be recovered in the future. This presents us with one of the greatest mysteries about the mind.

Let us look at this phenomenon a little more closely. A photograph is being taken of a person. Light from some source strikes the individual being photographed, is reflected from his surface, and enters a camera box. Here the reflected light falls upon a photo emulsion. The photo emulsion is made of tiny grains of silver halide. The photonic energy activates discrete specks on the silver-halide crystal, and the distribution of these specks of activated silver form what is called the latent image. The latent image is amplified by a subsequent chemical developing process which reveals an image that has a one-to-one correspondence with the person originally photographed.

What is there in this purely physical process of light reflection from an individual as registered on film emulsion that allows an individual like Peter Hurkos, and other sensitives, to gain intelligence about that person? Many experiments have shown that Hurkos is not only capable of describing images on the photograph, but also of getting intelligence other than that physically recorded on the film. Much of the intelligence that he gets comes from other segments of time and space than the one in which the picture was taken. This means that whatever it is that is transferred from the person to the film remains on the film as a permanent record ready to be read by a sensitive mind, and is of a nature quite beyond our comprehension. It almost seems as if the film captured a good deal of the life history of the subject and stored it away for many years. At the time that much of the subject's past history is transferred to the film, some bits of his future history are also added to this record. This process has absolutely no analogy in any of the known dynamics associated with matter or energy. These puzzling findings, and some of the conjectures and deductions drawn therefrom, led me to devise an experiment whose chief purpose was to try to capture or detect an emanation associated with the photographic process as outlined above.

NOTES   Chapter 4

1. Johnson, Raynor, *The Imprisoned Splendour,* Harper & Brothers, New York, 1953. On pages 185–89 Johnson presents a sketch of a telepathic theory of psychometry in which an "aetheric structure" couples brain to mind, as well as permeating objects. The aetheric structure provides the linking mechanism between the object, the owner of the object, and the psychometrist's mind.

2. Reported in the Sixth Naval District Naval Reserve publication, *Guidelines,* December 1959, p. 1.

3. Comparable experiments are reported by J. Hettinger, *Exploring the Ultra Perceptive Faculty,* Rider & Co., London, 1940. The Agent (owner of the object) is placed at a distance from the psychometrist. The psychometrist holds an object of the Agent. The Agent looks at pictures in an illustrated magazine. The psychometrist then tries to give impressions of the mental content of the Agent. The psychometrist was able to get a high percentage of correct impressions of the pictures viewed by the Agent.

4. Hettinger reports a study of psychometrists in which a total of 172 different objects was tested. This was a quantitative study in which the deviation from the chance score was 14.6. The correct statements about the owner of the object covered both the past history and some of his future history. Hettinger, J., *The Ultra Perceptive Faculty,* Rider & Co., London, 1940. A critical evaluation of Hettinger's researches is given by Christopher Scott in *Proc. Soc. Psych. Res.,* Vol. 49, 1949, pp. 16–50.

5. There is a report of a closely related phenomenon in which hypnotized, carefully blindfolded subjects were found to be able to see photographs, read newsprint, and read the time by psychometry. See Boirac, Emile, *Our Hidden Forces,* Tr. by W. de Kerlor, F. A. Stokes Co., 1917. In repeating these experiments with subjects who claimed to have such "Eyeless Sight" I have not been able to confirm the existence of such a faculty. If the phenomenon exists, it must be a form of telepathy and not eyeless sight as reported. In the case of photographs, and not newsprint, it would be psychometry.

6. For reports on the psychometric ability of other sensitives see: Osty, Eugene, *Supernormal Faculties in Man,* Trs. by Stanley de Brath, Methuen & Co., London, 1923. Maeterlinck, Maurice, *The Unknown Guest,* Methuen & Co., London, 1914. Bender, Hans, and Tenhaeff, W. H. C., "The Croiset Experiments," *Tomorrow,* Vol. 2, No. 1, 1953.

5

The Memory Capacity
of Objects, and the
Impregnation of Such Objects
by Mind Action

It appeared that if a photo carried a memory decipherable by psychometry, then the photographic emulsion might be a good starting point for this investigation.[1] I prepared a room which was light-tight, that is, where there was no external or internal source of stray light. Then I searched for a photographic system which offered the least possibility of artifact by chemicals, and found that the Polaroid-Land camera satisfied my requirements. I used Peter Hurkos as the subject. I briefly outlined to Peter the possibility that the human mind could influence a photographic emulsion. I asked him to use whatever means, conscious or unconscious, he was in command of, and concentrate upon a film with the idea of getting an image or density upon it. He cheerfully agreed to attempt this experiment, even though it was completely new to him.

In the first trial I went into a dark room and held a Polaroid camera in my hands. I sat there for about fifteen minutes until my eyes were thoroughly adapted to the dark. As far as the eye could see, there was no leakage of light into this room. Then I pointed the camera into the dark, and snapped the shutter. I carried out the processing of the film according to the standard method, but in the dark room. The film was developed in sixty seconds. Upon examination, both the negative and the positive films were found to be homogeneously dark, showing no image or activation by light.

In the next trial I asked Hurkos to sit in the same spot in the dark room that I had occupied. I asked him to concentrate until some image appeared in his mind. When this image appeared, he was to try to transfer it consciously to the film in the camera. In order to give him some sense of synchronization between mental image and camera image, I asked him to snap the shutter in the dark at the instant that he felt he could transfer this image to the camera. This he carried out as directed. Before I developed the film I asked him in the presence of six witnesses to describe what it was that he was trying to impress upon the film. He said that he had been concentrating on the bust portrayal of a human head. It was no particular head, just a human head.

I developed the Polaroid film in sixty-five seconds. The positive print showed a hexagonal light spot, 14 mm. by 16 mm. in size, in the upper left-hand corner of the film. The negative film showed an 8-mm. oval light in the lower left-hand corner. There was no comparable image present on the positive film for this latter spot. After I had looked at this spot on the negative film I passed it to each of the six observers present and asked them to independently form a judgment as to what they thought this oval light spot looked like. No one was to give their opinion until everybody had had a chance to look at the film. Each of the six observers wrote down that the light spot looked like the faint image of a human head, and some of them thought that it looked like a child's head. This was a most extraordinary result, and in order to make sure that some error had not occurred, a new roll of film was placed in the camera.

In trial number three Hurkos again held the camera in a dark room and was again asked to open the shutter at that moment when he thought he had an image clearly fixed in his mind. After completing his part of the experiment he stated that he had seen in his mind's eye the image of a pipe, which looked like an Indian pipe, with smoke rising from it. The film was then developed in sixty seconds. It could be clearly seen that both negative and positive films in this trial showed a long-stemmed pipe, 5 cm. long, with a 3-cm. column of smoke rising from it. This was clearly a direct hit for Peter. It began to look as though the human mind can consciously activate a photo emulsion even though no light is striking the film.

In the next trial Hurkos held the camera in a dark room, but this time was not allowed to snap the shutter at the moment when he had an image clearly in his mind. He silently handed the camera back to me when he had completed the period of concentration. He stated that the image in his mind contained "Chinese lines with figures, none of which makes any sense to me." The film was developed in sixty seconds. The lower right corner of the film showed a sharp image of a white light about 1 mm. wide and 1 cm. long, and in the same corner of the film there was a diffuse and faint light-pattern which had no determinate form. It looked like a cloud-like luminosity.

Experiment number five was carried out under the same conditions and again Hurkos held a camera in the dark room and again Hurkos was told not to snap the shutter. Upon returning the camera to me he stated that "I see an image that is symbolic of the head of the government of the United States, and there are many lines connected with it." The film was developed in sixty seconds. In the lower right-hand corner there was seen a spheroid of bright white, shaped like a bald-head profile, surrounded by a light halo effect. The spheroid was 24 mm. by 33 mm. in size, and this section of the film looked overexposed even though we knew that no light had reached it. Above it were a number of wavy lines which looked like a triple exposure of indeterminate shape. So far this was the strongest activation of the chemicals in the emulsion. There could be no question up to this point of any stray light emanating from outside the room or from Hurkos and somehow reaching the camera.

In trial number six Hurkos held a camera in his hands in the dark room and when he snapped the shutter he said that he saw "Lines, just lines." The film was developed in sixty seconds. The film showed an image all along the right-hand border that was made up of tubular lines resembling lattice work that was thought by some to look like a rib cage. The individual lines were quite distinct even though the over-all form was indeterminate and looked like "Lines, just lines."

In trial number seven I held a camera in my hands in exactly the same position occupied by Hurkos previously in the dark room. I snapped the shutter as before, aiming the camera in the general direction of the wall. The film was developed in sixty seconds. The positive and negative films were found to be homogeneously black and devoid of any images.

Another method of control was attempted in trial number eight. This time the camera was held by myself in a room illuminated by several sixty-watt light bulbs. I then took a picture of Hurkos holding his baby daughter. The film was developed in sixty seconds. It showed the expected image of Hurkos holding his daughter although the quality of the photograph was poor due to underexposure.

Still another control was attempted in trial number nine just to make sure that the images somehow were not due to some factor which hadn't occurred to us. I held a camera in the dark room pointing it toward my body and snapped the shutter. The film was developed in sixty seconds. Both the positive and negative prints were uniformly and homogeneously dark and blank.

In trial number ten one of the people present held the camera in the same position that Hurkos had, and tried to concentrate on an image. The film was developed in sixty seconds and found to be uniformly dark and blank.

The findings of these ten trials can be summarized. There were five control films and five test films in the series.

Of the five control films four were taken in the dark and turned out to be blank as expected. The fifth control was exposed in the light and showed an image as expected.

Under the conditions of this experiment and according to all the laws of optics and photochemistry the five test films should have shown no light exposure, and should have been blank for density or image formation. We found that each of the five test films showed an activation of the film as though it had been struck by light rays or photons with a resulting image. Yet no light had entered the camera or fallen upon the film. Of the five images thus developed three correspond more or less accurately to the predictions Hurkos had made. The other two images did not correspond to his predictions, but nevertheless showed an activation of the chemicals in the film emulsion. We can only conclude that Hurkos' mind was able to mimic the effects of light on a photosensitive surface. This experiment clearly reveals the mind's potential as an action center.

Experiments with the photographic process were repeated at a later date with Hurkos. This time instead of using the Polaroid camera and film, I used plate film, Ansco Orthochromatic contrast process film. With the film I used the developer and fixer recommended by Ansco, and followed their directions for processing implicitly. Hurkos held the film in his hand in a dark room. He was asked to concentrate upon some mental image. His father had died a few months previously and he decided to concentrate upon getting an image of his father on the film for every trial. He made eight different trials on eight different plates of film, each time concentrating on the image of his deceased father. Upon development only one of the eight films had any density, and this density fell into an image pattern. The image so developed on this film was shown to ten different people, as one would show a Rorschach Ink Blot, and they were asked what they thought the image represented.

Eight of the ten individuals thought they saw the head

of a man in this image. I must admit that although the head did appear to be there, it was quite fuzzy in outline, and one had to really imagine to see it as a head. But the important point is that density and some image did form where there should have been none, considering the care exercised during this experiment. While the frequency of activation in this experiment was lower than with the Polaroid film, the results nevertheless indicated that the human mind could activate Orthochromatic process film. This mental "something" which activates film must be that which also registers a personal memory pattern on an object which is later recoverable by the technique of psychometry as intelligence.

This action of the mind at a distance is called psychokinesis. Psychokinesis is studied in the laboratory with attempts to influence the fall of a group of rolling dice.[2] In other words the mind tries to interact with a moving mechanical system and tries to get certain die numbers to appear face up. Such experiments have been conducted at Duke University,[3] Columbia University,[4] and at Pittsburgh University,[5] and the results indicate that dice can be controlled far beyond the expectations of chance. This kind of evidence from dice experiments shows that the mind can influence the behavior of inanimate objects in motion.

There have been reports that the human mind can activate static mechanical systems, that is, inanimate objects that are at rest. Such, for example, are cases of table tipping, furniture being moved across the room by unknown agencies, and the acceleration of objects from a position of rest to a high velocity. The latter are normally referred to as poltergeist incidents.[6] I was curious about such developments but had never personally witnessed any. However, a friend, Si Slavin in Los Angeles, persuaded me to investigate some alleged table tapping that occurred in the presence of a housewife, Mrs. C. Ross. I observed this for the first time in the spring of 1959.

Mrs. C. Ross is a woman in her early fifties who is very

pleasant and speaks quite factually about her experience with table tapping. She said that she had done this sort of thing as a game when she was a girl of twelve or thirteen. At this time she and her playmates had been successful in getting a table both to tip and to emit sounds in the form of raps. She had discontinued these experiments for many years and had come back to them eleven years ago when some friends encouraged her to try to repeat the phenomenon. Since then she had been holding table-tapping sessions at irregular intervals for family friends. She had never used this ability in any professional or commercial sense.

A group of people sat down around a wooden table. They placed their hands on the surface of the table and chatted about matters of current interest. The room was fully lighted, and I was allowed to inspect everybody's feet and the relation of their feet to the table legs. I was satisfied upon examination that nobody had any object on his person that could account for an artificial table tap. After about a half hour of such sitting I distinctly heard taps emitting from the table. I carefully checked the position of everybody's hands and feet again and could not observe any irregularity that would account for the tapping. The tappings proceeded merrily for about an hour. One of the people at the table would ask a question and the table would respond by giving one tap for no, and three taps for yes. I decided to look into this phenomenon a little more seriously.

A group[7] of us arranged to have weekly sittings with Mrs. Ross. She readily submitted to personal examination and it was found that when she sat at the table she had no concealed noise-making instruments on her. It was observed that it usually took ten to thirty minutes for the rapping to begin. To make sure that the table taps were not hallucinations we recorded the low-frequency sounds of the table with a seismographic pickup connected to an oscilloscope and photographed the wave output of the table. The speech of the people and the sounds of the table were also tape-recorded on a separate system. The people sitting at the table were measured for muscle movements by means of an electromyograph and these were ruled out as the sound source. Many different tables were tried and found to work with equal success.

At several sessions all the people around the table were asked to keep their hands on the table but to move their feet and legs as far away from it as possible. After this had been done each individual slowly lifted his hands from the table while the table was actually tapping. It was found that all individuals present could raise their hands about four inches above the level of the table and the table still continued to tap. When the hands went beyond the distance of four inches the tapping ceased.

It was also found that the table tapping occurred only when Mrs. C. Ross was present. Hence one could look upon her as a source of suspicion, or one could consider her as the agent for this psychokinetic phenomenon. I, myself, didn't believe that Mrs. Ross was producing the table raps by any fraudulent method. The tests which were made ruled out the possibility of fraud.

During the course of four months Mr. Jochems, one of the people involved in these experiments, was able to develop the ability of getting table taps to the point where he and his wife could do it alone. It was also found that when Mr. Jochems was present at the table, Mrs. Ross could leave the table and the phenomenon would continue.

These experiments clearly convinced me that pulsed sounds can appear out of a wooden table when there seems to be no possibility of any of the people present at the table making these sounds by fraudulent means. It would appear that the mediumistic individual is an agent in the release of pulsations of either positive or negative energy which in turn energize the table in a manner that is audible to the human ear. One of the peculiar characteristics of the sound waves produced by the table is that in certain instances the waves did not slowly damp out at the end of the sound production, but instead the waves rose to a high amplitude at the beginning of the sound production, continued for some time at the same intensity, and then abruptly dropped off to zero oscillation. This is called critical damping and is very difficult to produce by artificial means.

It occurred to this group that if Mrs. C. Ross or Mr. Jochems were able to release enough energy to activate the table, it should be easy enough for them to produce the small amount of energy necessary to cause an image to appear on a film. Therefore I made a number of attempts to get them to activate Polaroid-Land film, in this case placed in individual packs which were light-tight and could be used under ordinary room conditions. I asked them to concentrate upon this film while the table tapping was going on. Upon developing these films I found them to be uniformly blank. Neither Mrs. C. Ross nor Mr. Jochems was able to produce a density or an image on the film as Mr. Hurkos had done in the experiments cited earlier. It became quite clear that whatever mechanism was involved in the table tapping it was not the same as that which Mr. Hurkos had released in activating the density and image on the film without light.

We have presented highly selected evidence thus far to show that the human mind can collect intelligence by extraordinary and uncommon means. We have further presented selected examples of the ability of the human mind to serve as an action center, in the absence of any of the other known energies, and create mechanical or other physical action on objects.

We see mind breaking through the barrier of space to reach another mind with an exchange of intelligence. We see mind going through a network of other minds and reaching its goal with a high degree of selectivity. We see mind extending outward with invisible threads to blanket hundreds of minds at one time to bring about a common or mass hallucination in the group. We have seen how mind can be relayed, stored, and even projected into the future, through the mediation of inanimate objects such as pieces of paper, pottery, and photographs.

It is difficult to escape the conclusion that mind at certain levels of operation is ubiquitous and can pass through the barriers of the physical world around us. In fact, there are times when it literally transcends time as it leaps ahead to cognize physical events not yet born, or leaps backward in time to reconstruct scenes long since perished from the physical realm.

NOTES   Chapter 5

1. Other investigators had already pursued this problem with positive results. One of the pioneers was a professor at the University of Tokyo who began his experiments in the early part of the twentieth century, T. Fukari, *Clairvoyance and Thoughtography*, Rider & Co., London, 1931. His subjects were able to concentrate on a Japanese character and reproduce it on film by thought alone, and with great fidelity compared to the original.

2. See chapters VI, VII, and VIII of *The Reach of the Mind* by J. B. Rhine, Faber & Faber, London, 1948. For a critical review of this book, consult West, D. J., *Proc. Soc. Psych. Res.*, Vol. 47, 1945, p. 281.

3. *Ibid*. For the work of others consult the *Journal of Parapsychology*, Duke University. Humphry, B. M., "Simultaneous High and Low Aim in PK," pp. 160–74, 1947. Nash, C. B., and Richards, A., "Comparison of Two Distances in PK Tests," pp. 269–82, 1947. Rhine, J. B., "The Psychokinetic Effect: I. The First Experiment," pp. 20–43, 1943; "The Psychokinetic Effect. A Review," pp. 5–20, 1946. Pratt, J. G., and Forwald, H., "Confirmation of the PK Placement Effect," pp. 1–20, 1958, and other articles in this journal.

4. Professor Gardner Murphy, then of Columbia University, repeated the Duke University PK experiments in 1946, and confirmed the findings of Rhine and his associates.

5. McConnell, R. A., Snowden, R. J., and Powell, K. F., "Wishing with Dice," *Journal of Experimental Psychology*, pp. 269–75, 1955.

6. For a general introduction see: Osborn, A. W., *The Super-*

physical, Ivor Nicholson & Watson, London, 1937. This work contains numerous references and quotations from the original researches carried out by such competent investigators as Dr. Schrenck-Notzing, Dr. Eugene Osty, Dr. Gustav Geley, Sir William Crookes, Mr. Harry Price, and others.

7. This research was carried out under the auspices of the Consciousness Research Foundation, Inc., San Pedro, Calif., under the guidance of Dr. Kurt Fantl, Dr. Margaret A. Paul, and Dr. Hal Dorin—all physicians. It was reported by Dr. Fantl at the annual meeting of the Pan American Medical Association held in Mexico City on May 2, 1960. The most important finding in this study was that the carrier wave induced in the table had a frequency range of 300–400 cycles per second, and this was pulse-modulated 2–18 times per second—the actual audible taps. This paper was published in *The Proceedings of the 35th Congress of the Pan American Medical Association.*

6

The Dynamics of the Mobile Center of Consciousness when Separated from the Physical Body

The best way to understand the dynamics of the mobile center of consciousness is to study the experiences of an individual who has had many different degrees of separating mind from the physical body. The subject is a forty-four-year-old highly successful New York radio producer, writer, and business executive. He is happily married and has a glowing and warm home life. I cannot use his real name because of his professional status, but shall call him Bob Rame. What follows are extracts taken from a diary which he has kept of his own experiences. I have carefully checked the entire series of episodes and spent much time interviewing him. He writes as follows:

"I wish to write it down in the event I, for some unknown reason, or unforeseen one, cannot repeat it in the future. It is not intended for any other purpose than to place it down in some kind of record, for someone, I know not whom, for what reason, I know not. I shall not tear it up or destroy it, in spite of future developments, as it is as honest and objective a record as I can make it. And as candid.

"I was constructing a set of built-in drawers and a cupboard in our children's room. In a desk cubbyhole, a piece of plywood had to be glued in place with a cement. As I brushed on the cement, I noticed a feeling of light-headedness and for a period I remembered nothing; when I was conscious again I was still brushing on the cement, but my arm and face were covered with it where I had evidently simply laid down on the newly spread surface. Fom the smell, I realized that I had probably been 'out' for a moment due to the ethyl ether content of the cement. The can had a big warning notice on the top to use with adequate ventilation.

"I thought about this experience for a while. I remembered as a child experimenting with a can of gasoline, smelling it until a dizziness came over me. I remembered the strange effect of ether and nitrous oxide in the few times I had had it, and my puzzlement over the strange *feeling,* not dreams, but *feeling.* I remembered having dental work years back, and while waiting for the dentist to finish another patient, I experimented with his 'auto feed' nitrous oxide machine.[1] It was a pleasant memory.

"My first attempt at inhalation from the can ended in my first surprise. One night, unable to sleep, at around two in the morning I went into the room where I had been working, obtained a can, and went downstairs and sat, occasionally taking a casual smell from the can. Nothing out of the ordinary happened for a while, not even dizziness. Then quite suddenly, as I looked at the can, I felt as if a ray or some kind of energy[2] had come down from a low angle and bathed the upper half of my body. I could not see this ray, everything in the room appeared the same, otherwise I felt and thought the same, it was as if I could *sense* the outline of it. It did not spread over the room, it was as if a flashlight had been turned on me, the outline of the beam being in that shape. The feeling was that of some slight warmth, a very low frequency vibration in the lower part of my body, a sense of relaxation,[3] and a knowledge that this was some form of communication. I had the feeling that I was participating in a communication, as though I were listening in on a telephone line where no one was speaking. After several minutes, the ray seemed to fade away, and did not return. Puzzled, I went to bed and slept.

"I repeated this inhalation experience a number of times thereafter. These are my impressions of what went on within me. Several times I seemed directly in contact with a place that appeared to be a night club, although it may not have been that, I was in both auditory and visual contact with the place. It looked to be a room some twenty by forty feet. It had a raised platform at one end, similar to a small bandstand. The center of the room was bare, such as a dance floor. Except for the bandstand, the room was dimly lighted, and cigarette smoke drifted across the lighted area on the bandstand. There seemed to be many people around the dance floor, and they seemed to be waiting for announcements. There was a microphone on the bandstand, but no orchestra. There was a slight buzz of conversation from the people around the floor, and the room felt quite warm.

"My vantage point was to the left as you face the stand, at the edge of the floor, as seen from a standing position. As I watched, a man in an ill-fitting suit, rather chubby, walked up to the stand with several pieces of paper in his hand, made some announcements to the assembled people, reading from the papers, then stepped two steps down from the stand and walked away. I waited for sometime more for something to happen, then left. On successive visits to the same place, the place was completely empty, or the same condition existed as on my first visit. I have never been able to understand this particular experience.

"Other times after inhaling from the can it was as if I tuned into various radio stations and people were talking, mostly along the line of jazz, foreign languages, odd music, and fast chatter. I made no attempt to do other than to listen, and no awareness of me was present, nor was any attempt to communicate with me present. Several times I was overwhelmed by what seemed to be a tightly jumbled series of voices, mostly in languages I did not understand. The 'messages' were coming so thick and fast that I couldn't seem to get through to anything.[4] The feeling that accompanied it was that these were unimportant, personal messages, and that it was too bad that the 'line' was tied up with these.

"At other times no matter how much inhalation, nothing seemed to happen. I would get the feeling that I was being wound up tighter and tighter, as if something were being speeded up faster and faster (my pulse stayed the same, and I had the definite knowledge that I overshot the 'point'), and I was doing nothing more than getting a jag.[5] This same incident occurred many times during my experimentation with exactly the same results. In the end I would get sluggish in speech and body movement, and decided to lie down and sleep. Upon awakening I seemed to suffer no more than a consuming thirst, and the entire sensation was gone, as a matter of fact, at no time have I ever felt serious after effects.

"My first experience that struck me as being more than a dreamlike state was one night when I lay down to go to sleep. Not being very successful at sleeping, I picked up my can of cement and began to breathe it deeply. I suddenly slipped into the condition I have described earlier, namely where there was some sort of ray either entering my body or leaving it.[6] I do not know which. I began to feel tired and forced myself out of this condition. I waited awhile and a heavy roaring started in my head, and some sense of low vibration appeared in my legs, and I decided to stay with it this time. A force seemed to be sweeping up and down my body regularly,[7] and I got a little used to it. I thought I would try a little of its power. I mentally tried to force the power to move me upward out of bed, it did! I floated upward to about four feet over the bed. Rolling in the air, I looked back down at the bed and there was my body, still in bed!

"My wife was sleeping alongside my body, and I could clearly see her. I floated over her, by willing it, and then moved down and patted her on the cheek. She didn't respond, then I floated back over my own body, and began to have concern about my getting 'back in.' Floating down I came in face to face contact with my body, but felt nothing. My physical body was lying face up, and I had floated down facing downward. I grew worried, and then I seemed to remember, and rotating on my body axis, I turned around and faced upward. There was a sudden blending, and I was in my physical body again, eyes open, looking out through the window into the half dark sky. I sat up in the dark, smoked a cigarette, and thought about it.

"Later I went into a similar condition when lying in bed. I curiously reached over the side of the bed and felt the floor. Using my sense of 'power' I pushed on the floor, and suddenly my hand slipped right through it to the sub-floor. I felt around on the sub-floor and there was a nail, a chip of wood, and some sawdust. I pushed deeper, and my hand went through the sub-floor and went into a small stream of running water. I moved my hand around in the water for some time, and didn't go deeper simply because my arm was extended as far as I could make it go. I then carefully withdrew my hand, looked at it, but it was dry, then my sense of power faded after which I felt my hand with the other to be sure it wasn't wet. I have often wondered what would have happened if I had let go of the power when my hand was stuck elbow deep in the floor?

"Around three in the afternoon I lay down to think, as is my habit. The weather was rainy and it was quite humid, the month being June. Without any feeling of the vibrations I've mentioned previously, I found myself floating against the ceiling of my office. A friendly thought came into my mind which said, 'If your soaring is that good, go to it,' and proceeded to open the door so I could go outside and higher. I felt that the door in this impression was merely a symbol. It seemed as if somebody who was quite friendly opened that door and was amused at the soaring on my part, as if a friendly understanding teacher was letting a child out to play for a while because he was too restless to concentrate. I went out through the door and picked my way upward through the trees, ducking branches until I came into sight of what seemed a mesh of wires and tree branches. I seemed to be able to go no further until I thought, and realized, that these were not branches and wires obstructing me, but were instead some sort of power or force field. Immediately upon this thought the wires and branches disappeared,[8] and I was soaring upwards strongly, faster and surer. It was an ecstatic exhilaration that I felt as I extended my arms out from my shoulders and soared in great joy. I sailed far above an enormous white cloud bank that extended in both directions as far as I could see. I was about to go higher, when I felt myself being pulled back, not a tug, but a gentle definite elastic type of motion.[9] I started backward and down, realizing I must, and not disappointed or depressed because I had to return. The clean joy and beauty I had experienced could not be dampened.

"Then I was back on my couch in my office, feeling very smooth vibrations in my body. I opened my eyes, fully awake and conscious, and looked around and everything seemed normal. I then moved my arms, which were folded across my chest, and held them to one side outstretched, as I lay on my side. They felt outstretched, and I was surprised when I looked, because there were my real arms still folded. I looked to where they felt they were, and I saw the shimmering outlines of my arms and hands in exactly the place they felt they were. I looked back at my folded arms, then at the 'bright shadow' of them outstretched. I could see through them to the bookshelves beyond. It was like a bright outline, which moved when I felt them move, or made them.[10] Then I started to feel a slight pain in my chest, and decided that I had had enough of this exercise, and moved the 'arms' back in place, shut off the sense of vibration, and thought about the experience.

"The chest pain continued for about an hour afterwards, right in the middle of the chest, not sharp or severe. I had

recently been checked by two insurance doctors who both
stated that my heart was in good condition. Another time,
about a week later, I had some diarrhea and abdominal
cramps. For reasons I cannot explain I took a thousand
milligrams of Vitamin C hoping this would relieve the
cramping. In the afternoon, I lay down in my office, and
after a few minutes of relaxation, there was what seemed
like an explosion—quick roaring sound, a feeling of deto-
nation.[11] There was no transition to sleep. The next
instant I was walking into a house, entering by the rear,
and went past what seemed to be many coats lying stacked
upon a table. I could hear the voices of a number of people talking in the next room. I then went into a bathroom,
looked into the mirror and saw myself. As I stood there
staring new vibrations came on and the next instant I
was back in my office with the vibrations still continuing.

"I now realized I was awake again but I quietly lay
where I found myself. I lay on the couch testing the vibrations and opened my eyes to see the room, which looked
normal. I felt the lower half of my body (legs and hips)
swing upward, float over the side of the couch and, like a
feather, float down and touch the floor. After testing this
several times, I 'brought' them back into place, and diminished the vibrations. Then, as I lay there still fully conscious, I knew I was not asleep, with my eyes closed I
saw in my mind's eye a book in front of my eyes. The
book was riffled, turned around so that I could be sure that
it was a book. The book was then opened and I started
to read. The gist of what I read was that in order to wil-
fully bring back a condition, it was necessary to re-create
the experience similar to the one desired that had occurred
in the past: I took this to mean that you should 'think'
of the feeling, more than remember the incident. I was
fully aware that the book was simply a convenient image
for my mind which was digesting my own understanding
of my experiences.

"A most astounding 'trip.' It started in the same manner
as the others except that instead of floating upward, I

seemed to be traveling rapidly through space. After what seemed a long time, I suddenly was standing in what seemed to be a theater, to one side of the audience, smoking quietly in the semi-darkness. Some kind of period piece was being performed on the stage—at least the costumes were not modern dress that I recognized. As nothing more happened, I decided to leave. Again a feeling of speeding rapidly through space and then I opened my eyes and I was in a strange bed.

"A strange woman smiled as I opened my eyes, and an older woman was with her. They expressed happiness that I had finally come to, I had been ill for a long time, but that now I would be all right. They helped me get out of bed and I was dressed in some form of robe (their dress seemed normal to me), and I knew that I was not the person they thought I was, I tried to tell them, but they seemed to think it was still some form of delirium. I asked what day it was, and they smiled. I asked for a calendar, and then decided it was better simply to try to find out the year. I asked the woman who seemed to be my wife, and she replied that it was 1924. I then was sure I shouldn't stay here any longer, and despite their objections went out a door into the open air. I stood there trying to move upward, I got the definite feeling I had to move up, very far up; with 'someone' holding on to me, I tried to 'take off.' At first nothing happened, and I became worried. I then remembered a breathing trick, and started to breathe in a gasping manner through the lips. I started to rise, slowly, above the building which was U-shaped, with 'someone' still holding on to me, trying to keep me from rising. I breathed harder and harder, faster, and I moved faster, until the now familiar blue blur was all around me. I opened my eyes, and far below, I saw what looked like a world as seen from a very high airplane.

"I thought hard of two friends with whom I had discussed my experiences, and who had asked that I try and 'visit' them the next time I was in this 'free state.' With this thought, I immediately felt myself in a body, in a large darkened room. A man, big and round shouldered, was supporting me on my left, much taller than I, his shoulders seeming to glisten, and holding me up on my right was a young girl. They were walking me in circles around the room, and I was having difficulty walking, thus they were half supporting me under each arm. I heard them comment on the strange type of hands that I had, most unusual. They were not unfriendly, but again I was sure this was not the place for me, I wanted to get back quickly to my own body, and again the feeling was that it was somewhere far far away. With this thought, I was again speeding through the blur, and I did this for what seemed a very long time. Then, I opened my eyes and I was lying in my own bed. I sat up, smoked, and thought over the whole thing. I'm sure there is more but I could not recall all of it at this moment of writing. Sitting up and smoking a cigarette, I decided that if this was a dream, it was totally unlike any I'd ever had before, and certainly didn't seem to have the characteristics of a dream; all places and people were unfamiliar to me, consciously at any rate. I speculated this might have been a trip to some other time and that I simply was going around and invading bodies whose conscious mind is weak at the moment, thus permitting me to 'get in and out' due to this weakness.[12] This was the most unusual 'non-inhalation' experience to date.

"Then came the most impressive and convincing non-inhalation experience to date. Propelled by some unconscious urge, I left my studio, and went up the side of the hill to my office retreat. Lying on the couch at about four in the afternoon, sun streaming in through the window from the west, I took pencil and paper and began to think out the problem that had confronted me in the studio—the exact relationship between fields of force and forces themselves—specifically electrostatics, electromagnetic waves, and magnetism. Proceeding from known areas, and trying to think out the relationship between the three, I suddenly—quite suddenly grew sleepy—so quickly that my eyes closed, and I had to open them again. I put down the paper and pencil (the paper was covered with symbols which were my mind's representation of these forces and their inter-locking generation), turned over and closed my eyes.

"I lay there for a moment, then raised my head. I looked unintentionally directly at the sun. Immediately the vibrations and a familiar deep pressure rumble came into my head and I closed my eyes. The force was very strong and I felt no fear. I opened my eyes again, feeling completely conscious, and everything seemed normal, except the vibration and roar-rumble still in my head.[13]

"I closed my eyes again, and they both grew in strength. I decided to try to 'lift up,' and I floated off the couch (mentally only, I assume, since I had no witnesses). 'I' then floated over to the center of the room, and floated downward very gently, I touched the floor, and my head and shoulders seemed against the rug, with my hips and feet angling up into the air. I then opened my eyes, and my view was from the floor at an angle looking up at the ceiling, and definitely not from the couch. I then floated upwards again, and mentally decided to 'go somewhere.'

"Seeming to know how, I rolled over, arched my back, and dove easily into the 'floor,' which felt like slipping into a tunnel that exactly fitted my body dimensions. The next moment, almost instantaneously, I was standing in a stall shower. I clearly saw the drain, and the water on the tiled floor. I went out of the shower, through two louvred doors, down a sand-colored tiled hall for about twenty feet, where the hall made a ninety-degree turn to the left. Some ten feet beyond the turn was a desk against the left side of the hall or corridor. A man was sitting at the desk, and I believe wearing a white uniform. He looked at me startled, and stood up. Another man came from the other end of the corridor, wearing a bathrobe, my impression was that of an attendant, and gave me a strange look and passed by heading in the direction I had come.

"Shortly thereafter, a second attendant came up, and I

asked him where I was. He stated rather uncomfortably, staring more at my body than my face (clothes or no clothes?) that I was at —— Baths, and gave the address. I am sure that I will know the name and address when I hear it again. At this moment I simply cannot remember it clearly. I then asked both if they would remember me if they saw me again. They nervously assured me that they would. I repeated the question, and more emphatically they stated, oh yes, they certainly would. My intent in asking this question was a hope that in some way I would be able to document this visit.

"After these assurances, I turned and walked back around the corridor through the louvred doors and into the shower. I floated into the air, turned on my back, and dove, and again in the tunnel, my thought was to return to my office, which I did, coming seemingly out of the tunnel and floating in the office. I floated over the top of my body, then down, rotated on my body axis and merged. That is the only way to put it. After merging, I opened my eyes, and I was lying on the couch, seemingly in the same position as when I started.

"Everything seemed normal, so I decided to try it again. Closing my eyes brought the sensation back, but this time with a tingling all over the body, similar to the one felt when a foot is asleep. Again, I floated upward deciding to visit my two friends Boris and Lomar. Realizing Boris was ill and in bed, I thought I would visit him in the bedroom, which was a room I had not seen and thus if I could describe it later, they could document my visit.

"Again came the turning in air, the dive into the tunnel, this time the sensation of going uphill. Boris and Lomar live on a hill some five miles distant from my office. Momentarily, I saw (in the sky?) a figure of a rounded human form, seemingly dressed in robes and a head piece on his head, sitting, arms in lap, perhaps cross legged, then it faded. After awhile the uphill traveling became difficult, and I had the feeling that the energy was leaving, and I felt I wouldn't make it.

"With this thought an amazing thing happened. It felt precisely as if someone had placed a hand under each arm and lifted me. I felt a surge of lifting power, and I rushed quickly up the hill. There I came upon Boris and Lomar. They were outside the house, and I was momentarily confused, as I had reached them before I had got to the house which I didn't understand. Boris was dressed in hat and light overcoat, Lomar in dark clothes and coat.

"They were coming toward me, so I stopped. They seemed in good spirits and walked past me unseeing in the direction of some building like a garage. I floated around in front of them, waving, trying to get their attention, without result. However I thought I heard Boris say to me, 'Well I can certainly see you won't have to use the cement can fumes anymore.' Thinking I had made contact, and feeling I should return, I dove back into the ground, and returned to the office, rotated into my body, opened my eyes. Everything was just as I left it.

"The vibration was still present, but I felt I had had enough for one day, so I decided to check up on the house. Immediately upon closing my eyes, I was in the main house, four hundred feet away, and I could hear my wife talking and the children running up the stairs. Satisfied, I returned to my office, again opened my eyes. The vibration faded. I got up, looked out the door, and my wife and children had returned. I did not feel tired, or anything unusual, and after awhile returned to the main house. My wife reported that they had returned only a few minutes previously. The children up the stairs coincided with my visit, as near as I could estimate.

"The aftermath came when I called Boris and Lomar that evening. I made no statement other than to ask where they were between four and five that afternoon. My wife, upon hearing of the 'visit' I made, had flatly stated that it could not be so, because Boris was in bed sick. With Lomar on the phone, I asked the simple question. Lomar stated that roughly at four twenty-five, they were walking out of the house toward the garage; she was going to the post office, and Boris had decided that perhaps some fresh air might help him, and had dressed and gone along. She knew the time by back checking from the time she arrived at the post office, twenty minutes to five. It takes roughly fifteen minutes to drive to the post office from their house. I had come back from my trip from them at approximately four twenty-seven P.M.

"I asked what they were wearing? Lomar stated she was wearing a black skirt, a red sweater which was covered with a black car coat. Boris was wearing a light hat and a light coat. It is an important point that I did not tell them first what I knew. I instead asked them for the information. The reason? I was not interested in proving to them or anyone else the validity of what had happened. I was much more interested in proving it to myself. The coincidences involved were too much, and this documentation of my 'mental' events by actual incident was deeply significant. It proved to me, at any rate, that there might well be more to it than the normal science of dreams and psychology allows—more than an aberration, trauma, hallucination, etc. and I needed some form of proof more than anyone else, I'm sure. It was unforgettable, and a step, a tentative step, in controlling this new factor in my life."

NOTES   Chapter 6

1. Sir Humphry Davy was probably the first person to report this type of experience when he inhaled pure nitrous oxide on April 9, 1799. However, we must remember that since time immemorial man had been inhaling one gas or another in order to experience revelation. It is believed that the oracles of ancient Greece were familiar with the use of carbon-dioxide inhalation for this purpose. Benjamin Paul Blood published two works on his personal experiences with nitrous-oxide inhalation: *The Anaesthetic Revelation and the Gist of Philosophy*, Amsterdam, New York, 1874; and *Pluriverse*, Marshall Jones Company, Boston, 1920. These works inspired William James to seek the same

experience, and the result was his monumental work, *The Varieties of Religious Experience*, Longmans, Green and Co., London, 1908. Anyone interested in the meaning of the mystical experience should read this book.

2. The statement, "A ray or some kind of energy had come down from a low angle and bathed the upper half of my body," catches our attention. I am convinced that this was not an hallucination, but an expansion of what I call in Chapter 8, the psi plasma. Psi plasma is that "something" which expands outward from the telepathic receiver, and that which imprints a personal memory pattern on an object. Later on in the same paragraph Bob notes that at the same time he felt this ray around the upper half of his body, he had the feeling of "a very low frequency vibration in the lower part of my body." This low-frequency vibration is what, in Chapter 9, we describe as the awakening of the Kundalini force at the base of the spine in the Yogin. It is interesting that we are shown here a polar relationship, in that the "ray" expands in the upper part of the body, and the low-frequency vibration is felt in the lower part of the body, i.e., at the base of the spine.

3. The sense of slight warmth and relaxation, etc., is the classical description of what we have called cholinergia, especially as it occurs in connection with an expansion of the psi plasma. This interpretation is fortified by the feeling of Bob that this was "some form of communication." This is the prelude to an uncontrolled form of telepathic reception in our theory.

4. This experience confirms our impression of an uncontrolled form of telepathic reception where the recipient has been opened up to too many channels of communication at once.

5. Bob was well aware of the fact that he could overshoot the state of optimum cholinergia, and this is similar to what is described in Chapter 8, page 97, where the Shaman gets drunk and cannot give a true Shamanistic performance.

6. Although I speak of the expansion of the psi plasma, and Bob speaks of a ray and does not know whether it is entering or leaving his body, the two are equivalent. I do not believe that the psi plasma has any direction to it, as we ordinarily know direction, and Bob shows his acuteness as an observer by being aware of this.

7. The force that Bob felt was an intensification of the low-frequency vibration that he had earlier noticed only in his legs.

Now as it increased in power, it swept from head to foot regularly and had the characteristics of a resonant standing wave. This is a good description of volume transmission through the nervous system, described later in Chapter 10.

8. The observation that the "mesh of wires and tree branches" was a construction of his own thought again impresses us with the accuracy of observation of our subject. It illustrates the fact that as soon as we know that our inhibitions are of our own making, we are in a position to remove them by a simple act of will.

9. The sense of being pulled back by a "gentle elastic type of motion" is an excellent description of a contraction of the psi plasma due to a decrease in the cholinergic condition. It is just the type of elasticity that we would expect in the psi plasma during contraction. For the opposite we would expect that the psi plasma has a mushroomic type of expansion.

10. This is a beautiful description of the way in which the will can manipulate the imaginary arms of psi plasma independently of the position of the physical arms. It illustrates an aspect of Sir Geddes' case in Chapter 7, where the percipient becomes aware that each of the organs of his body has a separate psi-plasma constitution.

11. Here we have an example of the cholinergia becoming massive (as evidenced by diarrhea and abdominal cramps), as in the case of Mrs. Garrett in Chapter 1. This was followed by an explosive or mushroomic separation of the nuclear psi plasma from the physical body. Later, Bob tried to repeat this experience, and believing that it may have been brought on in some way by the ingestion of 1000 mgm. of Vitamin C, he resorted to the use of Vitamin C, not knowing about the state of cholinergia. In order not to delude himself, he arranged with his wife to have her surreptitiously slip 1000 mgm. of Vitamin C into one of his frequent fruit drinks. He believed for a time that when he was given the Vitamin C he had an unusual experience of the separation of the nuclear self, but never in such an explosive fashion as on the first occasion. Eventually he realized that there was no causal relation between Vitamin C and his experiences.

12. One of the problems of proving that the state of a mobile center of consciousness exists concerns its confusion with clairvoyance. This experience offers an experimental test of the reality of the nuclear psi plasma in that we can attempt to get it

to carry out an action. We could attempt this by having the nuclear psi plasma enter a weakened person's body, and then getting the "invader," as per previous instructions, to carry out an act to prove that he was there.

I have coined the phrase "Mobile Center of Consciousness" because it seems to me to be descriptive of the state in question. The first point to be noted is that consciousness is no longer limited to the locus of the body. In this state one has a complete body image as a part of such consciousness, secondly, the MCC can at will go to any point in space that it desires, and be there in an instant as an observer. This sense of a complete body image and mobility of that body image with a sentient state of consciousness is, I believe, described by the term I have introduced.

13. We note here that Bob had been experimenting with the separation of the nuclear psi plasma for about nine months now, and had obtained considerable control over the process mentally. He no longer had to rely on the ethyl-ether inhalation. Now we notice that under voluntary control he has localized the low-frequency vibrations to his head, and that their power increase is evidenced by the sensation of a "roar-rumble." This is an important description of the psychological control of separation of the nuclear self.

7

The Mobile Center of Consciousness Completely Independent of a Living Physical Body

The foregoing account in Bob's own words scarcely needs comment. However, there are some points that are taken up in the notes to Chapter 6 which the reader should review in preparation for the difficult material of Chapter 8. We note that Bob's initial experiences with the inhalation of ethyl ether can be divided into a number of groups. His first experience was that of sleep, and this was a pleasant feeling, associated with warmth, relaxation, and a low-frequency vibration in the body. These early inhalation experiences resulted either in symbolic dreams, or in a confused jumble of ideas, associations, and perhaps telepathy. At other times none of these ideational experiences were present. He merely felt sluggish and sleepy. However, the inhalation experiences did culminate in the sense of leaving his body as a mobile center of consciousness, and re-entering his body as a nuclear mental entity with an existence separate from his physical body.

We see that Bob eventually attained a certain mental control over the process of leaving the body and therefore gave up the use of ethyl-ether inhalation. Among his most remarkable experiences are those in which during a light sleep state, at times oscillating between wakefulness and light sleep, he was able to control and manipulate imaginary counterparts of his limbs outside of his physical body. He also found that such imaginary parts, for example his hand, could pass through the solid matter of the floor. He was able at times to simultaneously observe his physical body, his folded arms, and at the same time independently separate from these their imaginary counterpart and manipulate the imaginary part. Among his experiences which have not recurred too often was the sense of a line force, or ray, making a certain angle with his body. The ray appeared to be nondirectional, in that he never could decide whether it was entering his body or leaving his body. Such a ray is what we will describe in Chapter 11 as the imaginary lines of psi plasma involved in telepathy.

It is interesting that Bob was able to realize that much of the imagery which he encountered in his mobile center of consciousness experiences was a product of his own imagination, and that he could set these up, or take them down if they appeared to block his way. When mind is in isolation from its physical roots, it is dealing with and manipulating other imaginary products of the mind, and it is most difficult for us to follow the dynamics. It may well be that the idea forms it encounters as a mobile center of consciousness can be manipulated as the mind wishes.

Bob has had quite a number of experiences, of which only a few are cited, of finding himself in a physical body which did not belong to him. It must be pointed out that he never was able to find proof that he was in another physical body. It could have been one of the imaginary bodies created by his own ideational process. His mode of travel as a mobile center of consciousness encompasses a wide range. We see him going through floors, ceilings, and walls, diving into the earth, and soaring high above the clouds. In general Bob's experience did not admit any obstruction in travel by any of the known physical structures. The greatest obstruction he encountered in his travels was that created by what he describes as "lines of force." And in many instances he seems to feel these are creations of his own mind.

In general his experience shows all gradations from simple imagination during conscious states in his own body, through symbolic dreams in sleep-like states, leading to confirmed telepathy as a nuclear mobile center of consciousness. Not only did he encounter people and scenes familiar to him from everyday waking experience, but he also encountered "entities" which are not known in the everyday world. Some of these were highly unpleasant and engaged him in mortal combat which was very trying and soul-shaking. At other times he encountered friendly and pleasant "entities," and one of these he became attached to, and looked upon him as a "father" and/or "mentor." It must be noted that Bob's real father is alive, and that his use of the term *father* does not refer specifically to his parent.

In Bob's experience of a nuclear mental entity behaving as a mobile center of consciousness outside of the body, we have used a case in which the physical body of the percipient was alive. Therefore, one would be inclined to look upon the nuclear mental entity as a product of the physical, and energy as the constitution of a living organism. This would be a fair assumption, and since apparitions are always seen by some living person, it is very difficult to dissociate in our thinking the existence of a nuclear mental entity from the living organism, either of the sender or the receiver. However, there are a number of cases of apparitions in the literature which deny this premise, and we must examine them closely before making a judgment.

Mrs. Sidgwick presented a paper to the British Society for Psychical Research in which she reported the case of the Honorable Miss K. Ward. Here is the abridged version of this case from Johnson's book.[1]

"Two years ago, on awakening one morning at 8 o'clock, I saw a distinct appearance of my sister Emily, seated at the foot of my bed in her nightgown. She was rocking herself backwards and forwards as if in pain. Putting out my hand to touch her, the phantasm vanished. Going into my sister's room half an hour later, I related to her my experience, and she (being still in much pain) informed me that at 8 o'clock she had actually been in the position above described, *on her own bed,* and had meditated coming into my room, but had not liked to disturb me. (She had been perfectly well the night before.) My sister's room is at some distance from mine, being divided therefrom by a corridor and cross-door."

Here we have a classical instance of the receiver-and-sender relationship in telepathy. Miss Ward is asleep and upon awakening sees the image of her sister at the foot of her bed. Her sister at the same moment is in great pain, acting as the sender, sitting at the foot of her own bed. The receiver is in a mild state of cholinergia due to relaxation and sleep, and the sender is in a state of adrenergia due to severe pain. We ask the question why did Miss Ward see so clearly the image of her sister, in severe pain, not where her sister was, but in Miss Ward's own room? It would appear that Miss Ward had a clairvoyant vision of her sister which was transferred to her immediate surroundings. However, this is by no means certain since there are many instances in the literature where an apparition has appeared sometimes thousands of miles distant from the body, without that person being aware of any separation of his nuclear mental self.[2] It could be well in this instance that there was an unconscious separation of the nuclear mental self which appeared to Miss Ward. However, in most instances of an authenticated apparition that I know about there is no residual consciousness associated with the body once the nuclear self has separated. And yet in this case Miss Ward's sister, while in great pain, was fully aware of herself remaining in her own room. My opinion in this case would be that there was a temporary separation of the sender's nuclear mental entity, and that there was a momentary marked degree of activation of Miss Ward's clairvoyant faculties which led her to briefly perceive the apparition of her sister in her presence.

Our second case is reported by Sir Auckland Geddes. Here is Tyrrell's[3] abridged version of Sir Auckland's address before The Royal Society of Medicine on February 26, 1927.

"On Saturday ninth, November, a few minutes after midnight, I began to feel very ill, and by two o'clock was definitely suffering from acute gastro-enteritis, which kept me vomiting and purging until about eight o'clock. By ten o'clock I had developed all the symptoms of acute poisoning; intense gastro-intestinal pain, diarrhea; pulse and respiration became quite impossible to count, I wanted to ring for assistance, but found I could not, and so quite placidly gave up the attempt."

The symptoms here portrayed are those of massive parasympathetic activation where the individual is going into shock. These symptoms are often seen in the profound cholinergia that occurs with poisoning by certain mushrooms.

"I realized I was very ill and very quickly reviewed my whole financial position. Thereafter at no time did my consciousness appear to me to be in any way dimmed, but I suddenly realized that *my* consciousness was separating from another consciousness which was also me. These, for purposes of description, we could call the A and B consciousness, and throughout what follows the ego attached itself to the A consciousness. The B personality I recognized as belonging to the body, and as my physical condition grew worse and the heart was fibrillating rather than beating, I realized that the B consciousness belonging to the body was beginning to show signs of being composite—that is, built up of 'consciousness' from the head, the heart, and the viscera. These components became more individual as the B consciousness began to disintegrate, while the A consciousness, which was now me, seemed to be altogether outside of my body, which it could see. Gradually I realized that I could see, not only my body, and the bed it was in, but everything in the whole house and garden, and then realized that I was seeing not only 'things' at home, but in London and in Scotland, in fact wherever my attention was directed, it seemed to me; and the explanation which I received, from what source I do not know, but which I found myself calling my mentor, was that I was free in a time-dimension of space, wherein 'now' was in some way equivalent to 'here' in the ordinary three-dimensional space of every day life.

"I saw someone enter my bedroom; I realized she got a terrible shock and I saw her hurry to the telephone. I saw my doctor leave his patients and come very quickly, and heard him say, or saw him think 'he is nearly gone.' I heard him quite clearly speaking to me on the bed, but I was not in touch with my body and could not answer him. I was really cross when he took his syringe and rapidly injected my body with something which I afterwards learned was camphor. As the heart began to beat more strongly, I was drawn back, and I was intensely annoyed, because I was so interested and just beginning to understand where I was and what I was 'seeing.' I came back into the body really angry at being pulled back, and once I was back, all the clarity of vision of anything and everything disappeared and I was just possessed of a glimmer of consciousness, which was suffused with pain."

The interesting aspect of this case of advanced cholinergia accompanied by shock is that the centrifugal mental tendency earlier described for Mrs. Garrett and Harry Stone now seemed to have an independent existence like that experienced by Bob Rame. Where Mrs. Garrett and Harry Stone felt they were being whirled outward mentally toward scenes that interested them, the patient in this case was fully aware of himself as a nuclear ego entirely detached from his body. The nuclear mental self operated as a mobile unit and was able to observe the body in which it had formerly been intimately locked.

This "A consciousness," it appears, is the true self that is involved in telepathy and other forms of ESP. It is this self or a ray of it which in a telepathic receiver appears to go toward the object of its interest. It is as though some mental plasma bridges toward the object of its attention. There are a number of cases of apparitions which Tyrrell has described as post-mortem cases. I give one of his cases, described as case number 5, in his book entitled *Apparitions*.[4]

"Mrs. P. and her husband had gone to bed, but she, wrapped in her dressing gown was laying on the outside of the bed, waiting to attend to her baby which lay in a cot beside her. The lamp was still alight and the door of the room was locked. She says, 'I was just pulling myself into a half sitting posture against the pillows, thinking of nothing but the arrangements for the following day, when to my great astonishment I saw a gentleman standing at the foot of the bed, dressed as a naval officer, and with a cap on his head, having a projecting peak. The light being in the position which I had indicated, the face was in shadow to me, and the more so that the visitor was leaning upon his arms which rested on the foot rail of the bedstead. I was too astonished to be afraid, but simply wondered who it could be; and instantly touching my husband's shoulder (whose face was turned from me), I said "Willie, who is this?"

"'My husband turned, and, for a second or two, lay looking in intense astonishment at the intruder; then, lifting himself a little he shouted, "What on earth are you doing here, Sir?"

"'Meanwhile the form slowly drawing himself to an upright position, now said, in a commanding yet reproachful voice, "Willie, Willie!"

"'I looked at my husband and saw that his face was white and agitated. As I turned towards him he sprang out of the bed as though to attack the man, but stood by the bedside as if afraid, or in great perplexity, while the figure calmly, and slowly moved towards the wall at right angles with the lamp. As it passed the lamp, a deep shadow fell upon the room as if a material person shutting out the light from us, by his intervening body, and he disappeared, as it were into the wall.

" 'My husband, in a very agitated manner, caught up the lamp and, turning to me said, "I mean to look all over the house and see where he has gone." By this time I was exceedingly agitated too, but remembering that the door was locked, and that the mysterious visitor had not gone towards it at all, remarked, "He has not gone out by the door!" But without pausing, my husband unlocked the door, hastened out of the room, and was soon searching the whole house.' Mrs. P. was wondering if the apparition could indicate that her brother, who was in the Navy, was in some trouble, when her husband came back and exclaimed, 'Oh no, it was my father!' She continues, 'My husband's father had been dead fourteen years: He had been a naval officer in his young life.' "

What strikes me as being unusual about this apparition is that it was not dependent for its existence upon a living organism for the form which it represented. If this were an hallucination it could only have proceeded from her husband's mind, because the wife did not know that her husband's father had been a naval officer. Not knowing this, it is difficult to see how she could have created an hallucination, and that her husband without any prompting or coaching immediately saw it. Another unusual feature of this apparition is the fact that both the husband and the wife clearly heard the words "Willie, Willie!" proceeding as if from the apparition. Here we have an instance of an auditory response, added to a visual response emanating from an apparition. Whether we regard this as an hallucination, or the independent existence of a nuclear mental entity, we certainly have an answer to our basic question as to whether or not the *appearance* of an apparition is necessarily dependent on a living physical organism which has the same form.

The distinguished British physicist Sir William Crookes spent much of his time studying the powers of individuals with psychic gifts. One of his long studies carried out in the 1870's was on the medium Florence Cook. While in deep trance she was able to produce the visible apparition of a girl who called herself Katie King. Crookes was not satisfied with his visual observations of this apparition, and demanded of Katie King that he be allowed to photograph her presence. This was arranged in due time, and Crookes worked out the technique that would be the least harmful to the medium. I had best allow Crookes to describe his results in his own words.[5]

"During the week before Katie took her departure she gave seances at my house almost nightly to enable me to photograph her by artificial light. Five complete sets of photographic apparatus were accordingly fitted up for the purpose, consisting of five cameras, one of the whole-plate size, one half-plate, one quarter-plate, and two binocular stereoscopic cameras, which were all brought to bear upon Katie at the same time on each occasion on which she stood for her portrait. My library was used as a dark cabinet. Those of our friends who were present were seated in the laboratory facing the curtains (wherein the medium lay in trance), and the cameras were placed a little behind them, all ready to photograph Katie when she came outside, and to photograph anything also inside the cabinet, whenever the curtain was withdrawn for the purpose.

"Each evening there were three or four exposures of plates in the five cameras, giving at least 15 separate exposures at each seance; some of these were spoilt in the developing, and some in regulating the amount of light. Altogether I have 44 negatives, some inferior, some indifferent, and some excellent. Katie instructed all the sitters but myself to keep their seats and to keep conditions, but for some time past she has given me permission to do what I like, to touch her and to enter and leave the cabinet almost whenever I please. I have frequently followed her into the cabinet and have sometimes seen her and her medium together, but most generally I have found nobody but the entranced medium lying on the floor, Katie and her white robes have instantaneously disappeared."

Cases like this could be multiplied many times,[6] but this one is sufficient to answer our questions as to whether the nuclear mental entity, or a psi plasma, can affect a photographic plate as in the telergy of a sensitive like Hurkos. If we can accept this evidence in the good faith in which it was obtained by many distinguished researchers, one wonders why something has not been done with it? The principal reason why little has been done with it is that the experiments themselves are not readily repeatable, and this has been the chief obstacle to an acceptance of the facts. This condition could be reversed if we had some control over the dynamics of the psi plasma, and in the next chapter we take up an analysis of the biological conditions which may lead to such control.

NOTES   Chapter 7

1. Johnson, Raynor, *The Imprisoned Splendour,* Harper & Brothers, New York, 1953, p. 195. Quoted from *Proc. Soc. Psych. Research,* Vol. 33, p. 255.

2. Wereide, Thorstein, "Norway's Human 'Doubles,'" *Tomorrow,* Vol. 3, No. 2, 1955, p. 23. One such variation is the socalled Vardøgr phenomenon, a form of nuclear psi entity observed only in Norway and Scotland.

For experimental references see: *A.S.P.R.,* XLVIII, No. 4, 1954, p. 126 (Table 1). Johnson, Raynor, *op. cit.* Tyrrell, G. N. M., *Man the Maker,* E. P. Dutton, New York, 1952. F. W. H. Myers, *Human Personality,* Longmans, Green & Co., London, 1907. Sylvan Muldoon and Hereward Carrington, *The Projection of the Astral Body,* 1929; *The Phenomenon of Astral Projection,* 1951, Rider & Co., London.

3. Tyrrell, G. N. M., *The Personality of Man,* Pelican Books, Baltimore, 1948, pp. 197–98.

4. Tyrrell, G. N. M., *Apparitions,* Pantheon, New York, 1953, p. 36.

5. Miller, Paul, *Science in the Seance Room,* Psychic Press, Ltd., London, 1945, p. 121.

6. Pawlowski, F. W., *Zeit. f. Parapsychologie,* "The Medium Kluski," 1926, pp. 5–22. *Ibid.,* "The Medium Mirabelli," 1927, pp. 450–62.

Lambert, Helen C., *A General Survey of Psychical Phenomena,* The Knickerbocker Press, New York, 1928.

8

Shamanism: The Biology
of the Ritual of
the Irrational

We have considered in the last two chapters the descriptive basis of our belief in the existence of an independent state of the nuclear mental self. If such exists, and if we are to accept the many experiences and experiments cited in this direction, we should seek to gain an understanding of the techniques which have been used to activate the psi plasma in the achievement of telepathy, and to isolate the nuclear psi plasma for the purpose of achieving the state of a mobile center of consciousness. Primitive and ancient man has left us a large legacy of crude experimentation whose purpose was to achieve these objectives. There is a world-wide distribution of such experiences, but for the purpose of clarifying the issue I am going to cite only one class of experience which I believe will advance our understanding.

Fundamental to all these practices is the phenomenon of Shamanism.[1] The term *Shaman* was introduced into the Western world by the Russians, who first met with certain Siberian tribes known as the Tungus in the seventeenth century. During the following centuries several travelers, for instance, Gmelin, Georgi, and Pallas, and the historian Miller gave descriptions of the practices performed by the tribal specialists known among some Tungus groups under the names Šaman, Saman, and Haman. In Europe it made its appearance a little later than in Russia. Indeed, the Shaman was first understood as a kind of pagan sorcerer, which meaning has persisted up to our day among laymen and was partly responsible for the delay in the understanding of the phenomenon itself.[2]

In all Tungus languages Shamanism refers to persons of both sexes who have mastered spirits and who at their will can introduce these spirits into their power in their own interests, particularly for helping other people who suffer from the spirits; in such a capacity they may possess a complex of special methods for dealing with the spirits.[3] The following description is based principally on the extensive researches of Shirokogoroff, who spent many years living with and observing Shamanism in Siberia. The Tungus whom he has studied and with whom we are concerned in this description are the northern Tungus of Siberia inhabiting the basin of three great rivers, namely, the Enissy, the Lena, and the Amur.

Most Shamans become aware of their calling after the age of fifteen and rarely after reaching full maturity. A person of either sex in his development first shows signs of being nervous or hysterical, often with trembling. He then either leaves the clan or is driven out and retreats to the woods for a solitary life, braving all the elements. This retreat is of variable duration. He then voluntarily returns to the clan when he feels he has some mastery over the spirits.

In order to be elected a Shaman he must first pass a test wherein he recites a list of the spirits by heart and answers questions concerning the details about the spirits in order to prove his familiarity with them. Then he must pass a trial of which the forms are many.[4]

One trial is the ability to walk on hot coals without being burned. This form of trial by fire is known the world over. Hindu ordeal books, for example, prescribe the rite of carrying red-hot iron a specified distance of seven steps, after which the hands are examined for burns. An African rite requires a stone to be plucked from a container of boiling oil. And a similar ordeal is carried out with melted lead in Burma. Among the Bedouins, disputing witnesses may be tested for their veracity by being required to lick a white-hot spoon, the liar presumably emerging with a charred tongue. In the most juridical form, particularly that prescribed by old Scandinavian and Anglo-Saxon laws, the witness is required to walk barefoot over glowing plowshares, generally nine in number.

There are many contemporary instances of individuals who have gone through the ordeal of fire. Joseph Campbell, the eminent scholar, related to me that he experienced fire-walking in the great Shinto temple in Kyoto, Japan. He was observing monks performing the fire-walking ceremony, standing in his bare feet while the ceremony was going on. He relates that one of the monks took him by the hand and requested him to walk over the glowing coals. Following the monk and stepping quickly, and as he thought, lightly, over the coals, he was able to pass through the long pit without suffering any burns. In fact, he says that the sensation on the soles of his feet was one of coolness, rather than of heat.

Mayne Reid Coe, Jr., a doctor of philosophy from Riviera Beach, Florida, has published his own experiments with fire-walking in *True* magazine (August 1957 issue). He was able to hold to his tongue for a brief period a steel bar heated to 2000 degrees F. He was able to place molten lead upon his tongue and spat it out in the solidified form. He has been able to heat iron to its melting point of 2795 degrees F., and plunge his fingers into it without suffering any burns. He has been able to heat sheet metal to a cherry-red heat and step on it without suffering any burns. Coe has the theory that moisture secreted by the sweat glands forms micro-globules on the surface of the skin, and this serves as a barrier to heat penetration. This idea can be easily illustrated by heating a frying pan to six or seven hundred degrees F. and placing a few drops of water in it. The drops of water will not vaporize immediately, but instead will form globules which spin around and dance over the surface of the heated pan. They retain their globular identity for some seconds before evaporating.

If this theory is valid it would be of great interest to our present discussion. The sweat glands are regulated by a cholinergic chemical. The tongue and other mucous-membrane surfaces of the body are also covered with moisture and this secretion is principally regulated by the cholinergic system. A person in the proper state of cholinergia would therefore secrete adequate moisture on these surfaces to form globules of liquid which either by reflection or by creating an insulating vapor barrier protect the skin from heat. Conversely, as in the fire ordeals, a person who is guilty would presumably have the usual symptoms of adrenergia, consisting of a dry mouth, decreased mucous-membrane secretion, and dry skin.

The second trial undergone by the candidate for Shamanship is of the opposite nature in that it tests his ability to withstand extreme cold. The candidate is taken out on a frozen river, and several holes are cut in the ice at a distance one from another. The candidate is required to dive through one hole, pass under the ice, and come up at the next hole; come out, dive again, and come out the third hole, and so on, all together nine times.[5] In Tibet the candidate for initiation undergoes a similar trial, sitting by a hole cut in a frozen lake. He sits absolutely naked and water-soaked sheets are thrown over his body. Because of the extreme cold, the sheets freeze immediately. The candidate must then generate enough body heat, called *Tumo*, to dry out the sheet. Success in this test is measured by the number of sheets which the candidate can dry. Some candidates have been reported to dry as many as nine or ten sheets under these frigid environmental conditions.

If the candidate for Shamanship survives these ordeals and the trial is considered satisfactory by the jury of the clan, he gains recognition and becomes a Shaman. In most cases the trial and the act of recognition must last nine days.

The tools of the Shaman's trade can be divided into two classes. The first is familiarization with many different devices such as feathers, bones, knuckles, various plants, mineral paste, etc. These, most of us are familiar with from the American Indian medicine man. The other tools of the Shaman can be considered as arising strictly out of mental operations. Shirokogoroff characterizes the psycho-mental[6] art of the Shaman under four aspects:

The Shamanistic practices, which presume the existence of Shamans, may originate only on the susceptibility of falling into the state of ecstasy under trance.[7] Ecstasy is used in the original Greek sense of "being outside of one's self," rather than the current use of ecstasy as being a state of thrill or excitement.

Shamanism may exist only in ethnical units among which there is a need of treatment of harmful mental conditions in a particular form affecting a great number of people. This could take the form of acute depression, great excitement, or even mass fear or hysteria.

Shamanism then is defined as the mechanism of a self-regulating psychomental complex. It is essentially a group phenomenon. Yet still more narrowly it is an ethnical phenomenon on which depends both the variable psychic conditions and the theoretical background which exists in the given social units.

Shirokogoroff goes on to say that the Tungus maintain what we would call a hypothesis about the ability of the Shaman. That is, they ascribe to him certain ability and powers.

The most important characteristic condition which makes of an ordinary man a Shaman is that he is a master of spirits, or at least a group of spirits.

He can perform healing on the sick.

In a state of great concentration the Shaman may come into telepathic communication with other Shamans and ordinary people who are at a great distance from him.

Divination of the future.

Doubling of the personality,[8] or what we have described as the mobile center of consciousness.

These are what we might call the fabulous powers of the Shaman. Of course, the Shaman uses common methods to exercise his leadership, that is, simple logic and intuition. However, he also uses special methods for an intensification of perception, imaginative thinking, and for an intensification of his intuition. Shamans all use telepathy and communication at a distance to a greater or less degree, but use different methods to attain it. Some may do it in their dreams, during ecstasy, or in a normal state of concentration or "desire" in which they simply think strongly upon the object of their intent. The interesting point in these cases is that the Shamans say they "send the soul" with a communication. They believe that this can be better done during the night. Shamans also believe that they can more easily attain ecstasy in the dark.

The methods of dreams and ecstasy are of a special character, but they serve the same purpose and are a perfection of a means of cognition. As a rule, the Shamans have recourse to dreams when they have difficult cases or when they have to perform Shamanizing. However, Shamans sleep with different purposes. It has been shown especially in the case of Manchu Shamans, and also of Goldi Shamans, according to the descriptions of I. A. Lopatin,[9] that they go to sleep before the performance, and the spirits are supposed to come into them during the sleep. The northern Tungus Shamans also sleep, but ecstasy comes later. However, the awakening in a state of ecstasy is also not a pure and simple ritualism (though it may be included in the ritualism as well), but the reaching of ecstasy in a half-conscious state is easier, and therefore the Shamans sleep before the performance. These half-conscious states are probably what Western mediums experience as light trance.

The methods used by the Shamans can best be illus-

trated by describing their ritual. The following is quoted
from Shirokogoroff.[10]

PART ONE

"When everything is ready and there is no longer light
in the western sky where the sun sets the clansmen come
to the wigwam.[11] Outsiders are not allowed to be present.
Together with the other people the Shaman arrives, and
his paraphernalia are also brought into the wigwam. After
taking some tea, the Shaman puts on his headdress and
apron. In the meantime the drum is dried on the fire. The
drum is usually a loop of wood which has the general
shape of a frying pan including the handle. Over the
looped portion is stretched tightly a skin membrane. The
drum is then handed over to the Shaman who begins slowly
and not too loudly to drum. Soon after this he begins to
sing. In the song-declaration the statement is made of the
reason of the sacrifice, to which spirit it is made, and what
kind of sacrifice is offered. The tempo and rhythms vary
greatly. One of the women continually produces smoke
of a certain resinous plant,[12] and brings the plant near
the Shaman, that he can breathe the smoke. Such a smoking is used in all forms of Shamanizing. This part of the
performance is concluded by a divination with the drumstick or a cup.

PART TWO

"Part A.   A reindeer is sacrificed in the wigwam by
a certain ritual. The whole preparation takes about an
hour.
"Part B.   During this part the Shaman must exteriorate
his soul and take the immaterial substance of the sacrifice
to the lower world. The Shaman sits, drumming and sing-

ing. He rises, hands the drum to the assistant and takes out the reindeer staffs. He begins to sing, to move rhythmically and from time to time make short leaps, while his assistant is drumming. On every strophe the assistant and the other people reply by repeating either the last words, or special words—the refrain. The tempo gradually increases and the replies become more and more persistent and louder.

"The Shaman takes a big cup (about 100 cc.) of Vodka about 40% strong and smokes several pipes of tobacco. Singing, jumping and general excitement increases. Gradually the Shaman brings himself into ecstasy. When this happens, the Shaman falls down on a raft and remains without moving. Now the drumming is slow and the singing stops. If the Shaman remains motionless for too long a time he is sprinkled with blood three times. If there is no effect the Shaman is recalled by singing. Then the Shaman begins to reply in a weak voice to questions asked (in singing) by two or three people at his side. Then the Shaman rises. This evolution is repeated four times in the same order.

"After this performance the Shaman sings a rather long time. In the meantime the drumming assumes a very fast tempo and the singing becomes very loud. Finally the Shaman throws himself on the reindeer skin and for a long time remains motionless and silent. Light drumming with singing continues, then the people begin to call back the Shaman. If he does not reply they sprinkle blood on him and direct sparks of fire (produced by flint and steel) at him. If there is no effect, the people who are present get very nervous, for the Shaman may not return at all and thus die.

"When the Shaman's consciousness returns, the people lift him up, pass around him, produce sparks with flint and steel, ring the bell and beat the drum. They express their joy that the Shaman has returned from Buni—the world of the dead. The Shaman sits down seemingly exhausted, and lightly drumming, sings. A divination with a drumstick is once more performed. This second part of the performance is over, which takes about two hours and sometimes may last longer. The people and the Shaman drink tea and eat boiled meat.

PART THREE

"After an interruption lasting two or three hours, that is, already at daybreak, the third and last part is performed which is carried out in the same way as the first part."

Shirokogoroff says that one does not very often get the opportunity to see this form of Shamanizing because the traveling to the lower world is considered such a dangerous and difficult operation for a Shaman that it is rarely performed. Now there are many points of interest to our inquiry in this description of the Shaman ritual. The subjective experiences of the Shaman are undoubtedly of the same nature as already described in Chapters 6 and 7. There is not only the sense of leaving the body as a nuclear mobile center of consciousness, the sense of travel, the knowledge of events going on at a distance, but there are also the real or imaginary encounters with entities of the lower world and of the animal world. Very often during the second part of the ceremony the Shaman acts out the combat from which he has just emerged victoriously with some demon or denizen of the underworld. In the description of the performance, we have seen that the Shaman may start the ritual after a sleep, during which the spirit comes into him, evidently as a continuation of his state during this sleep when elements which constitute his normal state were at least partially eliminated. In this condition the Shaman believes that the spirit is in him and he acts, talks, and thinks as though the spirits were acting. Such a state is known to all those who can assimilate a different personality to such a degree that they may be able to live it in great detail and to actually behave as the person who has this complex. Great dramatic and operatic artists as well as musicians assume the complexes of either the creator of the work of art which they are performing or of the character which they are to live.

Psychiatry is certainly familiar with pathological cases of doubling of the personality. Such states presume that the individual can assume and maintain a personality form different from his own, and maintain it in the face of, or in the presence of, other and often conflicting personalities. The condition of abnormality consists in the fact that these people do not assume such complexes at their own will nor do they change them at their will, but the complexes come by themselves. Often in exaggerated cases this has been called "possession." Primitive societies believe that possession occurs by the action of spirits and they have evolved a multitude of techniques for exorcizing such malignant spirits.

In the Shaman's ecstasy the degree of doubling and elimination of normal elements of consciousness, as well as the breaking of the existing norm for behavior, are variable. However, there are limits on both sides, namely the Shaman's state must not turn into an uncontrolled hysterical fit,[13] and he must not suppress ecstasy; in fact, hysterical fits and suppression of ecstasy do not permit involuntary self-expression of the doubles (spirits)[14] nor render a freedom to intuitive thinking. Within these limits various degrees of intensity in effectiveness of ecstasy must be distinguished. For producing such a state the Shaman must possess special psychomental conditions. First of all, he must have the ability of doubling, even perhaps splitting, personality, he must have a certain power of controlling his thinking mechanism, he must know the method of bringing himself into this state, and methods maintaining and regulating this state as long as it is required for the practical purposes of the performance, always considering the presence of an audience and considering the aims of the performance.

These mental controls constitute an art private to each

individual, and differ perhaps very little from the ordinary and extraordinary methods of mind control that each of us, either consciously or unconsciously, uses in his daily life. There are some interesting physiological conditions of the Shaman during ecstasy which we will examine in greater detail. As we have seen, ecstasy usually starts during sleep, so that we evidently have a case of strong self-suggestion bringing about an action during this state of partial unconsciousness. Some Shamans practice preliminary acts before sleep for bringing themselves into ecstasy. These have to do with the drumming and the singing carried on by the Shaman in which he continually increases and decreases the tempo and the intensity in order to find a physiological rhythm that will lead him in the desired direction. The direction of course is that in which the coming of a spirit can be attained. And of course as soon as he achieves this, that is, as soon as the complex of the spirit appears, the Shaman must only maintain his state. This is usually maintained by the assistant who is in such rapport with the Shaman that he manages the drums in such a way to keep the Shaman in the proper framework. Shamans believe that the influence of the audience is helpful and their emotional sympathy with the state of the Shaman helps him to continue. Shirokogoroff states that several Shamans have told him that they cannot perform if there is no audience. One of them has formulated it more specifically: "All people present help me to go over to the lower world."[15]

We have seen that the audience is also influenced by the Shaman so that a cyclical current of influences, first radiated by the Shaman, then reflected back by the audience, is intensified until it reaches a level maintaining the proper state of excitement. Whether we understand this state of the Shaman and his relations with the audience as mutual hypnosis or suggestion, the direct mutual influence of a continuous excitement is such that the Shaman and his audience become a complex emotional, mental, and telepathic network, and thereby the Shaman's ecstasy is maintained. For this reason a Shaman does not like the presence of spectators who do not participate in this action. However, they do not object to persons who do not belong to the Shaman's clan, even to such as belong to other ethnical groups, provided they do not destroy the harmony of the Shaman's audience.

Shamans use special techniques not only to bring on the state of ecstasy but to maintain it. Three methods are widely used, namely, smoking tobacco,[16] drinking wine or other alcoholic beverages, and the use of inebriating mushrooms.[17] However the Shaman usually neither smokes nor drinks before the performance; but it is done when they change spirits and additional excitability is required or when the Shaman is tired. The smoking may be with an ordinary tobacco pipe, several of which the Shaman may smoke quickly and without interruption.[18] Shirokogoroff has seen five and even six pipes smoked one after the other. The Shaman may also breathe the smoke of resinous conifers,[19] or even incense, the latter being more common among the Tibetan oracles. The same effect is produced by the taking of alcoholic drinks such as Russian vodka or Chinese wine.[20] A strong person may drink more than a bottle of vodka during his performance. In some cases the Shamans abstain from drinking, for they say that drinking does not help but makes them weaker. This is probably a constitutional idiosyncrasy, as I have seen both extremes in individuals with high telepathic ability, namely those who are very sensitive to the effects of alcohol and those who seem to be insensitive and can consume large amounts of alcohol. It is a known fact that if the Shaman oversteps the limit of drinking needed for obtaining ecstasy or as a stimulant, he may be intoxicated to such a degree that no ecstasy can be maintained. In this case audiences laugh when they see a drunken Shaman.

The weight of the Shaman's costume is usually thirty to forty kilograms and in Tibet a headpiece of this great weight is carried throughout the performance, including the dancing. The carrying of such heavy weights either on the head or the body requires great strength, and requires the output of additional effort in order to carry on the performance. If the Shaman is so weak that he cannot continue to carry the costume it is assumed that he is tired and must cease.

Shirokogoroff says, "If we leave aside doubtful facts, there will remain my own observations which clearly show the physical power of a Shaman increases enormously, that his physiological state is not like that of normal people. Ecstasy requires enormous energy so that all Shamans whom I have observed and who really have been in ecstasy, were unable to move after the performance and were covered with perspiration. The pulse was weak and slow, the breathing was rare and shallow. Some of them were in a state of half consciousness, while at certain moments they might have been 'unconscious.' "[21] This is a state which we have already recognized as being due to extreme cholinergia.

The analysis of the Shaman's psychology during the ecstasy and in ordinary times shows that in so far as the Shaman is concerned, the performance is only a special means to create a special condition which liberates the Shaman's "mental self" from the influence of his normal mode of thinking. However, the Shaman must remain on the dividing line between the state of "nervous fit" and perfect consciousness. He must, in fact, remain balanced on a razor's edge of consciousness. The function of the assistant can now be better understood. The assistant really helps direct the Shaman's mental process by asking him questions which are only partially perceived by the Shaman, who must not be brought back to complete consciousness. The assistant must also interpret, for the Shaman does not remember what he has said when the ecstasy is over, and the persons who are not experienced cannot understand him. This is particularly true in Tibet, where the utterances of the state oracle often are incoherent and a special secretary is used to interpret his statements to the audience.[22]

This cursory review of the principal elements of Shamanistic psychology and technique could be repeated many times over from other cultures and other places. But essentially, disregarding superficial cultural factors, the physiology and psychology of the Shaman is essentially the same wherever one operates. I have abstracted from these many accounts those elements which I believe are important in the understanding of the physiological and psychological methods which can be developed and exploited to expand or isolate the nuclear psi plasma from the body.

In general we can say that the candidate for Shamanship is what we would call psychologically a "jumpy" type. His instability is not necessarily that of an epileptic, but is the kind often found in brilliant minds which emotionally and mentally leapfrog from one state to another, very often to the discomfiture of those associated with them. In spite of this unstable psychology he must be extremely stable physically and athletically vigorous.

It is apparent that a general conditioning of the body over a period of time must occur. This is best exemplified by the kind of resistance the Shaman develops to cold and other stress.[23] This is equivalent to a high degree of effective adrenergic response to stressful situations. The resistance to heat which the Shaman evidences by feats of fire-walking appears to be at an opposite pole from his resistance to cold. In general this latter condition combined with athletic power can be viewed as an effective degree of cholinergic response.

Fasting is common not only to Shamanship, but to almost any ascetic practice in the many religions which seek to attain a higher state of mental evolution.[24]

It is apparent that the level of the carbon-dioxide content of the blood is an important factor. The Shaman increases the carbon-dioxide content of his blood by his dancing and exercise, and by special means of breathing.[25]

He probably not only maintains a high level of carbon dioxide in his lungs and blood, but also maintains a relatively increased pressure of the carbon dioxide in his system. Not only is the carbon dioxide carefully regulated within the body, but the burning plants which produce carbon dioxide in great amounts are consciously and purposefully inhaled by the Shaman.

A number of stimulants are used by a Shaman to increase his central-nervous-system excitability and general emotional excitement. These are provided by the burning of resinous compounds and we would use camphor as an example of this class of compound.

The Shaman also uses certain drugs[26] which are known to be depressants of the central nervous system. Representative of this class is the use of tobacco and alcohol.

The use of a drum seems to be universal in Shamanism. The drum beat creates a pulsed sound wave which exercises rhythmic auditory stimulation and its accompanying rhythmic pulsing of the central nervous system.[27] Very often the use of the drum is modulated by hand clapping, singing, or other forms of interrupted sound.

There is a phase of the Shamanistic performance where dancing, leaping, and the burden of the heavy costume leads to maximum muscular exertion. In terms of our general concept this is a mixed form of stimulation which is characterized in the early phases by adrenergic excitation, and in the later phases by cholinergic stimulation.

All of the above techniques, if used in serial order, lead to one end result, namely exhaustion. In the state of exhaustion the Shaman is probably under the dominance of cholinergia, and this is of such a nature that it leads to decreased frequency of neural electrical discharge.

The state of exhaustion is followed by sleep. This may be or may not be true sleep in that some residuum of consciousness may still be present which allows the Shaman to consciously enter the state of doubling of consciousness or a mobile center of consciousness. This is the goal of the Shaman's performance, namely, to be liberated from time and space restrictions of the body in the form of a nuclear mental entity.

In order to know more about this mental stage that the Shaman enters, it is necessary to go to the study of Yoga. There is a large, poorly explored area of relationship between Shamanism and Yoga. Yoga presumably had its origin in the Vedic times of India. The Vedic religion was characterized principally by a ceremony in which a plant called *Soma*[28] (not identified with certainty) was the principal sacrifice or sacrament in the ceremony. Whatever the plant was, it certainly induced the state of ecstasy as exhibited generally in Shamanism. Some individuals have theorized that Yoga arose when the supply of the plant *Soma* decreased and ultimately disappeared, the theory being that an ecstatic state was originally realized with the help of *Soma,* and once without it the Vedic Indians tried to duplicate this experience. Ultimately they were able to work out psychological, mental, and spiritual exercises which not only carried them into ecstasy but through it and beyond to realms of experience not known in Shamanism.

In Eskimo Shamanism the decisive experience is not getting out of the body as in the Tungus Shamanism, but it is the production of an inner heat which leads to a state of inner illumination. While the Shaman also develops this "inner heat," it is not the ultimate goal of his practices. However, in Yoga, as practiced in India, "inner heat" is definitely cultivated and used to reach a stage of luminosity in which the mind is flooded with the glory of colorful experiences. There is another peculiarity of Yoga which distinguishes it from Shamanism; after spiritual ripening, the Yogin remembers his previous incarnations. This characteristic is not encountered anywhere in Shamanism. The one ultimate common denominator between Shamanism and Yoga is the fact that both seek to escape the restrictions and limitations of the time and space world in which the body lives. They seek an emergence from time in the form of a nuclear mental entity. The Shaman uses the

techniques of ecstasy to achieve this end. The Yogin by
sheer mental effort, which Eliade has called enstasis, seeks
to achieve such time and space autonomy. There is no
question that the techniques of Yoga are far advanced
beyond the crude techniques of Shamanism. While Shamanistic practices illuminate the basic physiological changes induced in the body, we must turn to Yoga to
understand the mental dynamics of autonomy.

NOTES   Chapter 8

1. I refer specifically to that type of ritual as exemplified by
the Tungus Shaman. The essence of this type of ritual is that it
aims to alter the normal state of consciousness by various forms
of exercise or drugs so that consciousness enters a new state of
awareness wherein it can carry on communication processes in
the absence of the usual sensory or instrumental basis of communication. This ritual is to be distinguished from that type in
which certain external systems (as for example, cards, symbols
[astrological], etc.) are manipulated, rather than the state of
consciousness, in order to achieve communication or intelligence.
The earliest reference to this practice is to be found in the
Sumero-Akkadian culture (3rd millennium B.C.), where of the
thirty or so known classes of the priesthood, one class specialized
in foretelling the future. Consult these authorities: Bedrich
Hrozny, *Ancient History of Western Asia, India, and Crete,*
Philosophical Library, New York, 1953. W. Kroll, *De Oraculis
Chaldaicis,* Breslauer Philologische Abhandlungen VII, i, 1894.
Marcelle Bouteiller, *Chamanisme et Guérison Magique,* Press
Universitaires de France, Paris, 1950. Mircea Eliade, *Le
Chamanisme et les Techniques Archaïques de l'Extase,* Payot,
Paris, 1951. Ruben Walter, *Schamanismus im Alten Indien,* Acta
Orientale, Lugduni Bata vorum, Vol. 18, Pt. 3–4, pp. 164–205,
1940.

For other cultures where this hypothesis was apparently maintained see: David Blondel, *A Treatise of the Sibyls,* London,
1666. Johannes Greber, *Communication with the Spirit World,*
Macoy, New York, 1932. Paul Christian, *The History and Practice of Magic,* 2 Vols., Forge Press, London, 1952. Eugene Osty,
Supernormal Faculties in Man, Methuen & Co., London, 1923.

Bernard Bromage, *Tibetan Yoga*, 1952; *The Occult Arts of Ancient Egypt*, 1953, The Aquarian Press, London.

2. Shirokogoroff, S. M., *Psychomental Complex of the Tungus*, Kegan Paul, Trench, Trubner & Co., London, 1935, p. 268. Printed in Peking, China.

3. *Ibid.*, p. 269.

4. *Ibid.*, p. 351.

5. *Ibid.*, p. 352.

6. *Ibid.* "By the term 'psychomental complex' I mean here those cultural elements which consist of psychic and mental reactions on milieu."

Shirokogoroff uses the word *psycho* in the sense of psychical: "Of the soul or mind, of phenomena and conditions apparently outside the domain of physical law" (*Oxford Concise Dictionary*). By "complex" Shirokogoroff refers to the total constellation of ethnographical factors in a group or society.

7. Ecstasy is usually thought of as a state of madness in which an individual is "beside himself." This means that the locus of consciousness is no longer strictly centered in the body. "A trance-like state in which the mind is fixed on what it contemplates or conceives" (*Webster's New Collegiate Dictionary*). "Our greatest blessings come to us by way of madness, provided the madness is given us by divine gift," says Socrates in the Phaedrus. Madness is here used in the sense of ecstasy just defined. Socrates goes on to distinguish four types of "madness": 1) Prophetic madness, whose patron god is Apollo. 2) Telestic or ritual madness, whose patron is Dionysus. 3) Poetic madness, inspired by the Muses. 4) Erotic madness, inspired by Aphrodite and Eros.

For descriptions of the content of ecstasy see: Aldous Huxley, *Perennial Philosophy*, Harper & Brothers, New York, 1945. Evelyn Underhill, *Mysticism*, E. P. Dutton, New York, 1931. William James, *The Varieties of Religious Experience*, 1908.

For the technique of ecstasy see: W. Y. Evans-Wentz, *The Tibetan Book of the Great Liberation*, Oxford University Press, 1954. Alexandra David-Neel, *Magic and Mystery in Tibet*, Claude Kendall, New York, 1932. Osterreich, T. K., *Possession, Demoniacal and Other*, Kegan Paul, Trench, Trubner & Co., London, 1930.

8. Doubling of the personality is best expressed formally in the German language by the term *Doppelgänger*, which means the wraith of one alive. This is best illustrated from common ex-

perience where one sees oneself acting out a part in a dream, but one views oneself as from the outside. Thus one consciousness observes the other consciousness of one's self. In the case of the *Doppelgänger* the wraith of one's self may become visible to another person. Thus we can distinguish between a doubling of the personality that is known only to the individual privately, and another which can be known publicly.

9. Shirokogoroff, *op. cit.*, p. 361.

10. *Ibid.*, p. 305.

11. The wigwam used by the Tungus is similar to the familiar cone-shaped wigwam of the American Indian. The wigwam of the Algonquin Indians is identical in construction to that of the Tungus.

12. The Tungus believe that smoke or vapor is a form of matter that is easily assimilable by the spirits, and hence the most suitable form in which to offer different types of sacrifice (meat, vegetable matter, etc.) to the spirits. The use of resinous plants of many species is found in many other cultures for this purpose.

13. The use of the term "hysterical fit" simply denotes that the Shaman loses the *technique* and the *aim* of the ritual of the irrational, and since he is under severe stress he may have a true conversion hysteria. This can take any of the bizarre forms known from modern clinical psychiatry.

14. Shirokogoroff, *ibid.*, p. 55. The idea of the soul, or spirit, is very very old. Even *Homo neanderthalensis* presumably had this idea, since he buried his dead. When the idea of the spirit and its *possible exteriorization* first illumined the human brain is unknown. "According to the Tungus idea, the spirits are immaterial, they cannot be seen unless they take a special form, they may influence physical bodies, they produce various sounds, they possess all human characters, including the feeling of temperature, hunger, anger, gratitude, emotional excitement, etc. Thus the spirit is like the human being."

15. *Ibid.*, p. 363.

16. Shirokogoroff does not give us any information as to the drug that may have been used before the introduction of tobacco. The best guess that one can make is that *Amanita muscaria* must have preceded the use of tobacco.

17. The use of this mushroom in the ritual of the irrational in Siberia was first mentioned by Philip Johan von Strahlenberg, *An Historical and Geographical Description of the North and*

Eastern Parts of Europe and Asia, Particularly of Russia, Siberia, and Tartary, London, 1736 (English translation), First Edition in German in 1730, Stockholm. Marco Polo does not mention it in his travels. The earliest reference to this mushroom is by Albert Magnus, *De Vegetabilus,* in the thirteenth-century work. See: W. W. Ford, "The Distribution of Poisons in Amanita," *J. Pharm. & Exp. Therap.,* 1: 275–87, 1909; "The Distribution of Hemolysins Agglutins, and Poisons in Fungi, Especially the Amanitas," *ibid.,* 2: 285–318, 1911. M. M. Metcalf, "Amanita Muscaria in Maine," *Science,* 61: 567, 1925. A. H. R. Buller, "The Fungus Lore of the Greeks and Romans," *Brit. Mycol. Soc. Trans.,* 5: 21–26, 1914.

The active principle of this mushroom is "muscarine," a substance whose precise chemical formula has not yet been unraveled, although many attempts have been made to do so. However, the pharmacological and psychological actions of this "poisonous" mushroom are well known. See: Sir Henry Hallett Dale, *Adventures in Physiology,* Pergamon Press, London, 1953, p. 201 *et seq.*

It is the opinion of the author that the early stimulating effects of alcohol and tobacco represent that phase of the ritual where adrenergic and cholinergic stimulation and output is at its peak. It is believed that adrenergic and cholinergic substances in excessive amounts pass from a purely excitatory effect on ganglionic transmission to an inhibitory effect. See: Marrazzi, A., *Fed. Proc.,* 12: 338, 1953.

18. The use of tobacco smoke in the ritual of the irrational presents us with one of the knottiest of problems. There are several reasons for this. The first is that tobacco smoke contains many active substances other than nicotine, and the action of these substances and of nicotine is complex. The second reason lies in the fact that in the ancient tradition and practice of the ritual of the irrational, the use of tobacco is a relatively new innovation (not introduced into Eurasia until the sixteenth century) and therefore we can receive little or no illumination from analogical practices in the older traditions.

The following quotation is from Monardes' work entitled *Segunda Parte Del Libro, De Las Cosas Que Se Traen De Nuestras India Occidentales,* printed at Seville in 1571.

"This plant, which is commonly called tobacco, is a very ancient herb and known among the Indians, especially those of New Spain. . . . One of the marvelous things about this plant, which excites the most wonderment, is the manner in which the Indian priests use it. When there is important business among the Indians and the caciques or chiefs of the village think it necessary to consult with the priests, they go to them and state the problem. The priests, in their presence, take some leaves of the tobacco, throw them on the fire, and receive the smoke of it into their mouths or nostrils, by means of a cane. After taking it they fall down upon the ground as if dead, and remain thus, according to the amount of smoke they have taken. When the plant has done its work they recover and give answers, based on the visions and illusions they had while in the trance, and interpret as seems best to them, or as the devil advises them. . . ."

Let us now turn to the effects of tobacco smoke and its chief alkaloid, nicotine, quoted from Erich Hess, *Narcotics and Narcotic Addiction,* Philosophical Library, New York, 1946, Chap. 9.

"Tobacco smoke is the product of a dry distillation with steam distillation. A quantity of one gram of tobacco yields two liters of smoke. One part thereof, the main current, gets into the mouth, the rest escapes into the air. In this so-called secondary smoke current, the nicotine is contained in its free form; the smoke gives an alkaline reaction. In the main smoke current, which mostly has an acid reaction, the base is contained in salt form. Just how much nicotine goes up in the smoke when the tobacco is burned depends on the alkaloid content of the tobacco, as well as on the speed of its burning. At a slow smoldering, 0–4% of all the nicotine is found in the smoke, at a medium speed of burning 28–33%, at a quick burning 40–55%. Heavy smokers consume more than 60 mgm., even up to 200 mgm. of the base daily, which represents triple to quadruple of the lethal dose, and its tolerance can only be explained by habituation. In addition to nicotine, the smoke also contains other toxic matters, created through the decomposition of the vegetable substance. . . .

"When smokers and non-smokers are given nicotine salts, it becomes evident that these possess no subjectively stimulating influence. They produce only an unpleasant effect. They interfere with mental capacity quite considerably. (Wahe) Even the impression of whether a cigar is strong or mild has no causal connection with its nicotine content. The sensations which the smoker experiences as pleasurable must be the products of different factors. Hull observed an increased steadiness of manual movements, and increased speed in continual addition after the smoking of a pipeful of tobacco. In general, the frame of mind of the smoker determines the effect of the smoking. If he is over-excited, the tobacco has a soothing effect; if he is in a depressed mood, smoking excites him."

The pharmacological effects of nicotine are abstracted from Gaddum, J. H., *Pharmacology,* 4th Ed., Oxford, 1953, p. 182.

"Since nicotine first stimulates and then depresses both the sympathetic and the parasympathetic ganglia, the peripheral response to nicotine is complex. Nicotine imitates the effects of muscarine by stimulating the ganglia from which cholinergic nerves arise. It imitates the effects of adrenaline by stimulating sympathetic ganglia, and also by causing a liberation of adrenaline from the adrenal glands.

"The picture is complicated still further by the fact that nicotine first excites and then inhibits most of the central nervous system. The vagus, vomiting, and vasomotor centers are all subject to this double effect and salivation and vomiting are prominent features of early nicotine poisoning. Spinal reflexes are depressed. Respiration is stimulated, but this effect is largely due to an action of nicotine on the carotid sinus. After large doses the respiratory center is depressed, and with larger doses is the cause of death. If two drops of pure nicotine are placed on a dog's tongue he drops dead in a few seconds. Smaller doses have an initial stimulant action and convulsions may be a prominent feature of the response.

"The toxicity of tobacco smoke, too, is determined by this base (nicotine). But the by-products such as collidine, pyridine, hydrocyanic acid, ammonia and methyl alcohol may disguise and modify the pure alkaloid effect. Alessio observed that injections of medium quantities of cigar-smoke saturated Ringer solution caused an increase of the blood pressure and an accelerated pulse rate (adrenergia). Whereas high doses caused a drop of blood pressure and slowed down the pulse rate (cholinergia)."

In order to ascertain what effects the tobacco produces in the Shaman it will be necessary to restate the cycle of behavior that he exhibits after taking the alcohol and tobacco. It was stated: "Singing, jumping and general excitement increase. Gradually the Shaman brings himself into ecstasy. When this happens, the Shaman falls down on a raft and remains without moving." Thus the (adrenergic) stimulating effect of the alcohol is quite apparent in the first phase of this cycle. The Shaman reaches a climax of excitement and it can be assumed that the nicotine produces a balanced cholinergic and adrenergic excitatory effect both peripherally and centrally. These effects have been described above.

The induced central-nervous-system excitability would maximally activate the ascending reticular activating system and the medullary centers as well as the cortex. The question then arises as to what are the nervous-system shifts that account for the transition from extreme excitability to an immobility leading to sleep? One line of explanation lies in the autonomic and central-nervous-system paralyzant action cited for nicotine. Another line of explanation lies in the known inhibitory effect of an excess of either acetylcholine or adrenaline. Another line of explanation would arise if an actual epileptic discharge occurred as a result of the excitement, and if such a discharge were of the type described by Wilder Penfield as "Cortical inhibitory seizures." See: *Epilepsy and the Functional Anatomy of the Human Brain,* Little, Brown, Boston, 1954, p. 654. I quote:

"The arrest of pre-existing sporadic epileptiform discharge and reduction in voltage of all forms of electrical activity at the outset of a clinical seizure must be explained on a different basis. The interseizure EEG of certain of these patients showed sporadic spikes and slow waves from one or both deep anterior temporal regions.

"Even though the patient does not respond to questions during the suppression of the EEG, there were a few who reported afterward having had an aura at the onset of the attack. This raises the question of the *Apparent suppression* being an attentive or arousal response, especially since the aura may be accompanied by an emotional disturbance. The mechanism would then be analogous to the blocking of the occipital alpha rhythm with attention to visible stimuli.

"It would seem that an epileptic discharge may cause true inhibition and suppression of the electrical activity of the cortex, though further studies are necessary to clarify the neurophysiological mechanisms involved."

In view of the fact that alcohol is known to increase the permeability of blood vessels and of the hemato-encephalic barrier (Gaddum, *op. cit.,* p. 111), we might expect some penetration of the cerebrospinal fluid by either a cholinergic substance or nicotine. If such occurred the following effect might follow:

"Injection of cholinergic substances and of pituitrin in the lateral ventricles of the brain produces marked parasympathetic stimulation, by excitation of the hypothalamic centers in front of the optic chiasm. Stimulation somewhat posterior to this area excites sympathetic responses. Cushing, 1931, observed that the introduction of pituitrin into the lateral ventricles produces marked vasodilatation, sweating, lachrymation, salivation, vomiting and fall of temperature. Pilocarpine produced similar effects in doses which would be ineffective hypodermically. The effect is arrested by atropine, injected either into the ventricles or hypodermically. Intraventricular injection of 0.1 to 0.5 gamma (0.0000001–0.0000005 gram) of acetylcholine produces prolonged sleep, disturbed respiration, and cardiac irregularities similar to vagus stimulation, but no fall of blood pressure. These effects are not prevented by atropine. Similar effects are produced by intraventricular injection of nicotine or caffeine, or by clamping both carotid arteries." Sollman, T., *Pharmacology*, Saunders, 1948, p. 290.

One might have to consider a synergistic action of some or all of the effects cited above, the end result being cholinergia.

19. I have not been able to positively identify the species designated by *Laedum palustrum*. It is apparent, however, that it is a conifer. Hence, I designate this part of the performance by a class of chemical substances derived from conifers, namely, the Terpenes. It is believed that this is permissible since the same practice is found in many other cultures that use different forms of the terpenes. The Tibetans burn juniper.

20. When the Shaman raises the cup of vodka (ethyl alcohol) to his lips, he has reached that stage of the ritual where his organism is approaching a peak of activity and excitement, and the alcohol adds one more pulse to bring him to the peak before its depressant effects close in on him. We have been told that the Shaman's performance will have failed if he gets drunk; but we will consider primarily the "stimulant" effect of the alcohol on his performance.

Unlike most other substances, including water, alcohol is rapidly absorbed from the stomach. If any reaches the small intestine it is rapidly absorbed from there. It soon becomes evenly distributed throughout the body water. Small quantities are excreted in the breath and urine, but most of it is metabolized. The normal human being can burn about 10 c.c. of alcohol per hour. The body can derive up to one-quarter of its energy from alcohol, so that alcohol is a food which can be used as a source of easily available energy.

In the body all other effects are generally overshadowed by its action on the nervous system. In defiance of general opinion, careful analysis shows that this effect is primarily a depressant one. Experiments with conditioned reflexes have shown that inhibitory reflexes are depressed more easily by alcohol than excitatory reflexes. The effect is particularly marked on the highest centers. These highest centers normally exert an inhibitory influence, enabling the organism to behave sanely and sensibly, weighing crude instincts against one another, and counting the final cost. When these centers are paralyzed, the cruder instincts have their way, and behavior becomes more spontaneous, more childlike, and less critical. The effect of the loss of both frontal lobes of the cerebrum is curiously like that of alcohol, though this latter effect is, of course, permanent.

"Human alcohol intoxication is commonly divided into four stages:

1 A large whisky (30 c.c. of alcohol) reduces the average person to the first stages of intoxication, which is the only stage in which he really feels pleased with himself. His loss of efficiency is still so slight that he can hide it from himself, since his critical faculty is dulled. The extra self-confidence may actually increase his efficiency in simple tests, such as the working of an ergometer, but higher accomplishments such as walking straight, standing still with the eyes shut, or saying 'British Constitution' are never improved and often impaired. Spinal reflexes are measurably slower and weaker.

2 In the second stage of intoxication the novice loses all self-control, and the experienced drunkard consciously pulls himself together and speaks and moves with exaggerated care.

3 In the third stage he is dead drunk and unconscious.

4 In the fourth stage he is in danger of death from paralysis of the respiratory and vasomotor centers in the medulla.

"Concentrated, but not dilute, alcohol taken by mouth, causes a reflex stimulation of the medulla by irritating the mouth and throat." Gaddum, *op. cit.*, p. 113.

"Kaufman and associates (1947) administered 40–150 c.c. of 10% alcohol over a period of two to three minutes in sixteen patients. All became clinically intoxicated. In four non-epileptics no EEG changes appeared. In the epileptics there was an increasing prominence of alpha activity and a diminution of the amplitude of prior abnormal potentials." Strauss, *et al.*, *Diagnostic Electroencephalography*, Grune and Stratton, New York, 1952, p. 128.

First, it must be assumed that the Shaman does not go beyond the second stage of intoxication (if he is successful). Second, he gets a great deal of easily assimilable energy in order to achieve the final spurt of excitation, and he is aided in crossing this barrier by a certain loss of inhibition. Third, these measures increase the amplitude or frequency of the alpha rhythm (augmented by the alcohol), and further protection is afforded by alcohol against epileptic seizure (by diminishing the spike potentials). In addition, alcohol at first markedly increases the oxygen consumption of the brain and improves the circulation by dilating the pial vessels. See: Page, Irving, *Chemistry of the Brain*, Williams & Wilkins, Baltimore, 1935, p. 325.

21. Shirokogoroff, *op. cit.*, p. 364.

22. De Nebesky-Wojkowitz, Rene, *Oracles and Demons of Tibet*, Mouton & Co., The Hague, 1956, Chap. XXI.

23. The extremes to which cold adaptation is carried can be seen in the following quotation: "To spend the winter in a cave amidst the snows at an altitude that varies between 11,000 and 18,000 feet, clad in a thin garment or even naked, and escape freezing, is a somewhat difficult achievement. Yet numbers of Tibetan hermits go safely each year through this ordeal. Their endurance is ascribed to the power which they have acquired to generate *tumo.*" David-Neel, *op. cit.*, pp. 198–210 (Penguin Ed.).

24. For effect of fasting (hallucinogenic) see: D. H. Rawcliffe, *The Psychology of the Occult*, Derricke Ridgway, London, 1952.

25. There are a number of facts which point to the conclusion that in the Shaman, during the ritual of the irrational, there is a marked increase in the pulmonary alveolar carbon-dioxide tension and an increase in the blood carbon-dioxide content. The hypercapnea is also evidenced by the fact that the smoke of a burning resinous plant is administered to the Shaman throughout the performance. The great exertion of dancing under the weight of a heavy costume increases his carbon-dioxide production, which is not blown off as a result of the grunting form of

breathing used. Assuming that the carbon-dioxide concentration is increased both in the alveoli and the blood, what effect will this have on the central nervous system?

Using the inhalation of 30% carbon dioxide and 70% oxygen as a therapeutic measure, Meduna has made the following clinical observations: Meduna, L. J., *Carbon Dioxide Therapy*, Charles C Thomas, Springfield, Ill., 1950, p. 18.

MOTOR RESPONSES		SENSORY RESPONSES	
Number of CO_2 Inhalations	*Effect*	*Number of CO_2 Inhalations*	*Effect*
2–3	Fluttering of eyelids starts. After 8–10 inhalations, this is constant.	About 20	Colored figures, patterns, lights *Presque vu.**
10–30	Psychomotor excitement takes many forms.	Past 30	*Presque vu*—if pronounced has the import of divination.
30–50	Seizures may occur with: —conjugate deviation of eyes. —torsion of body-homolateral. —pupils react to light. —rhythmic movements of limbs.		
60–90	Pupils fixed. Opisthotonus. Tonic extension. After the seizures the patient at once regains consciousness.		

* *Presque vu*—The phenomena and events in the visual field point in a certain direction, and suggest an end which is not quite reached, or they lack the proper completion or resolution. A form, a movement, a pattern, etc., is almost complete, but since it is never completed, a characteristic *presque-vu* experience arises.

Using the same gas mixture in man, Meduna and Gibbs (*ibid.*, p. 9) have demonstrated the following alterations in cerebral physiology (20 to 35 inhalations were given):

1. The A/V oxygen difference decreased from 5.90 Vol. % to 2.86 Vol. %. This result was due to an increase in venous oxygen content from 13.43 Vol. % to 17.0 Vol. %, indicating that the utilization of oxygen by the brain was inhibited.

2. The carbon dioxide of both the carotid artery and the internal jugular vein was doubled.

3. The R.Q. of the brain was raised from .95 to 4.46. This figure is based not on an increased utilization of oxygen by the brain, but rather on the increase in carbon-dioxide content.

4. Blood sugar—arterial and venous unchanged.

5. Lactic acid content of the venous return doubled. This indicates an anerobic catabolism.

The psychological experience that goes along with carbondioxide and oxygen administration can best be illustrated by one of Meduna's subjects. *Ibid.*, pp. 28–29.

"After the second breath," reported a twenty-nine-year-old healthy female nurse who had taken a treatment, "came an onrush of color, first a predominant sheet of beautiful rose-red, following which came successive sheets of brilliant color and designs, some geometric, some fanciful and graceful—purple and rose coloring predominant. As these sheets came toward me they seemed to engulf me and leave me breathless in the mad rushing sensation. Then the colors left and I felt myself being separated; my soul drawing apart from the physical being, was drawn upward seemingly to leave the earth and to go upward where it reached a greater Spirit with whom there was a communion, producing a remarkable, new relaxation and deep security. Through this communion I seemed to receive assurance that the petit problems of whatever was bothering the human being that was me, huddled down on the earth, would work out all right and that I had no need to worry. In this spirituelle I felt the Greater Spirit even smiling indulgently upon me in my vain little efforts to carry on by myself and I pressed close the warmth and tender strength and felt assurance of enough power to overcome whatever lay ahead of me as a human being." (End of case report.)

"In this beautiful experience we can discern almost all the constants of the carbon dioxide experience: 1) Color; 2) Geometric pattern; 3) Movement; 4) Doubleness of Personality; and 5) Divination, or feeling of esoteric importance." (Statement of Meduna.)

It should be pointed out that carbon-dioxide inhalation can also produce feelings of nameless and shapeless horror and terror in some individuals. Of particular importance to this analysis is the fact that though the subject may pass into unconsciousness or sleep, a vivid memory of the experience remains. This fact argues for a retention of a form of consciousness in the memory area of the temporal lobe.

26. Shirokogoroff tells us (page 9): "The Shaman may also breathe the smoke of Laedum Palustrum, or any plant with a pleasant smell (all conifers are used), or even Chinese incense." The burning of resinous plants and their juices and gums has an ancient history in many forms of ritual. The ancient Egyptians used frankincense (*Boswellia carterii*) in their temple rituals since the beginning of their recorded history. Frankincense gum was employed almost exclusively in the sacrificial service of the Tabernacle and the Temple until the time of Solomon's reign (Exodus 30:1, 7–9, 34. Songs 4:6, 14). The Chinese, East Indians, Greeks, and Romans all used various resinous plants and their gums were burned as incense to increase the power of prophecy of their oracles and soothsayers. It is difficult to find any common chemical basis for the many substances so used, but it appears that the traditional usage centers around substances that chemically are terpenes. Of the many substances in the terpene group it is the impression of the author that camphor is the most efficacious in the ritual of the irrational. The discussion in this note will be centered around camphor, because its effects on the central nervous system have been thoroughly studied by modern techniques.

"The odorous components of essential oils are not unfamiliar to us. They are chiefly esters, alcohols, aldehydes, ketones and hydrocarbons. The hydrocarbons and, indeed, many of the other compounds, by reason of their derivation from them, have a peculiar architectural structure and are known as terpenes. There are cyclic, dicyclic and open-chain terpenes, all having the empirical formula $C_{10}H_{16}$ and then there are the sesquiterpenes, $C_{15}H_{24}$. . . .

"In the dicyclic terpenes we have pinene, camphor, camphene, borneol and fenchone. . . ."

Camphor, $C_{10}H_{16}O$, is a derivative of terpene, and is therefore allied to the volatile oils. Large doses produce convulsions, similar to those of metrazol, but much more persistent. In mammals the location of the convulsant action is chiefly above the optic thalami, for section below these abolishes or greatly diminishes the convulsions. The motor cortex participates, for the direct application of powdered camphor to this region results in Jacksonian and generalized epileptic spasms. Adriani states that the primary site of action of camphor is a slightly stimulating effect on the cerebral cortex and the medulla when used in small doses subcutaneously.

If our surmise is correct that camphor is representative of this step in the technique of the ritual of the irrational, we must assume that, like some of the other techniques already mentioned, its purpose must be to activate epileptiform electrical discharge without the clinical manifestations. That this deduction is not without foundation can be seen in the fact that it would tend to augment the excitatory effect of interrupted auditory stimulation on the temporal cortex. Furthermore, the Jacksonian convulsant effect of camphor is blocked by carbon dioxide. In cats, the administration of 15% carbon dioxide increases resistance to camphor convulsions, and if camphor convulsions are already under way the carbon dioxide will stop them. The stimulant effect of camphor on the medulla and respiratory center is good insurance against the depressant effects of the alcohol and nicotine.

For further information see:

Wallis Budge, *The Mummy,* A Handbook of Egyptian Funerary Archeology, Cambridge University Press, London, 1925. See esp. p. 34 *et seq.* Sir Henry Yule, *Travels of Ser Marco Polo,* 3 Vols., John Murray, London, 1921. This latter book gives the details of the cultivation and trade in frankincense in the Red Sea coastal areas, presumably the source of supply for the ancient Egyptians—their land of "Punt" is allegedly Somaliland.

Moldenke and Moldenke, *Plants of the Bible,* Chronica Botanica, Waltham, Mass., 1952, p. 57.

Moldenke, *ibid.,* p. 124.

The basis for my impressions about camphor has come from information furnished me by Dr. D. G. Vinod of Poona, India. His vast experience with the ritual of the irrational in Tibet and India led him to the conclusion that some form or other of the terpenes is used in these cultures, and that the most efficacious is camphor.

Moncrieff, R. W., *The Chemical Senses,* John Wiley & Sons, New York, 1944, p. 329.

Sollmann, Torald, *Manual of Pharmacology,* Saunders, 1948, p. 209.

Adriani, John, *The Pharmacology of Anesthetic Drugs,* Charles C Thomas, Springfield, Ill., 3rd Ed., 1954.

Meduna, *op. cit.,* p. 6.

Some of the better known of such drugs are: *Soma*—see: K. M. Mushi, *The Vedic Age,* George Allen & Unwin, London, 1951. Tobacco—see: *Panacea or Precious Bane,* Sarah Augusta Dickson, The New York Public Library, New York, 1954. Parica (*Pipdadenia peregrina*)—see: Dickson, *ibid.* Fumes of burned barley, laurel leaves, and hemp seed as used in Grecian times—see: A. C. Bouquet, *Comparative Religion,* Penguin Books, 1942.

Among other drugs that may be mentioned are coniine, ololiuqui, peyotl (mescaline), *Peganum harmala, Yage,* Deadly Nightshade, strychnine, and various mushrooms such as *Paneolus, Psilocybe, Amanita, Stropharia,* etc.

27. The drum is the single most important physical technique in the ritual practice by the Tungus Shaman. Since recordings of the Tungus Shaman drum are not available to the author, he analyzed the sonic properties of a drum identical in construction to that used by the Tungus from recordings made of the Eskimos of Southampton Island to the north of Hudson's Bay by Laura Boulton. Frequency analysis of such recordings (with both the drum and singing going on) reveals the following facts: The drum rhythm is 2/4. The tempo in this recording is four beats per second. For the drum and singing combined there is represented the complete range from 80 cycles per second (the lowest limit of the frequency analyzer's output) to approximately 7000 cycles per second. This frequency distribution shows two main power peaks—the drum has a peak output of 35 decibels at ap-

proximately 1400 cycles per second, and the singing has a peak output of 40 decibels at approximately 3500 cycles per second. A continuous sonic output is maintained at about 35 decibels with peak outputs marking each drumbeat. These figures give us an approximation of the tempo, energy and frequencies stimulating the Shaman in the early stages of the ritual.

It would not be an exaggeration to say that the Shaman sets the tempo of his entire organism by the pacemaker of the drumbeat. Through his dancing the tempo of the entire proprioceptive discharge into the ascending reticular activating system is synchronized with the drumbeat. Analysis of the Eskimo recordings shows that the respiratory cycle is paced by the drumbeat. Apparently an inhalation is taken for an eighth note at the end of each two measures, in some cases this inhalation may be of a quarter-note duration. Inhalation occupies one-eighth of the respiratory interval, and seven-eighths of the interval are used for slow exhalation associated with the singing. This kind of respiratory cycle would serve to maintain a high pulmonary alveolar carbon-dioxide tension and high blood pCO_2.

In the ritual the tempo of the drumbeat increases as the stage of ecstasy is approached. In order to determine how fast a tempo can be achieved by a drum the author analyzed a number of recordings of cult drumming of the Yoruba of Nigeria. The fastest tempo found for a single drum was fourteen beats per second, although there is no reason to assume that faster tempos cannot be achieved; and the slowest was that of a dundun drum at a tempo of approximately six per second.

Some idea can be gained of the effect of such fast drum tempos on the central nervous system from the experiments reported by Gastaut, *et al.* These authors used intermittent auditory stimulation as a provocative test for epilepsy. They found that effective auditory stimulation has the following characteristics:

1) Using the range of 1000 to 5000 cycles per second a maximum response was shown at 2–3 kilocycles. 2) The range of interruption of the above frequency output was eight to twenty times per second. 3) Optimum response was obtained at the same frequency (of interruption) range at which intermittent photic stimulation was effective.

They report that the effect on the subject is the same as with photic stimulation, i.e., showing the appearance of EEG spikes in the absence of clinical symptoms. But auditory stimulation differs from photic stimulation in the following sense: 1) It is much more rare to provoke the EEG picture of epilepsy in a normal person with auditory stimulation than it is with photic stimulation. 2) When an infra-clinical attack is provoked there is seen a brief outburst of electrical activity predominantly in the temporal cortex with the character of a "K" complex. In the cases described by Gastaut an intermittent auditory frequency of eleven per second was sufficient to provoke the EEG picture of epilepsy in the temporal lobe.

The role of the drum in the ritual of the irrational now becomes clear. It can set the tempo of a massive auditory and proprioceptive pulsed-discharge through the centrencephalic-temporal-lobe circuit at a frequency that matches the alpha frequency of eight to fourteen cycles per second. In addition profound biochemical changes result which protect against an epileptic seizure. The correlation of such a drum tempo in the temporal cortex with the alpha tempo (range 8–14 c.p.s.) in the occipital cortex will be discussed in Chapter 10.

For further information see:

Boulton, Laura, and the Hudson's Bay Company, *The Eskimos of Hudson Bay and Alaska,* Ethnic Folkways Library, Album No. P444, 1954, N.Y.C.

Boulton, Laura, *ibid.,* Side 1, Band 1. Analysis made with Sonograph Frequency Analyzer with the co-operation of Capt. Blair Headley, Acoustical Laboratory, Army Chemical Center, Md.

Bascom, William, *Drums of The Yoruba of Nigeria,* Ethnic Folkways Library, Album No. P444, 1953, N.Y.C. Analysis of dundun drum recording made with Sonograph Frequency Analyzer with the co-operation of Capt. Headley.

H. Gastaut, J. Roger, J. Corriol, and Y. Gastaut, *"Les formes expérimentales de l'épilepsie humaine induite par la stimulation auditive intermittente ou épilepsie psophogénique,"* Rev. Neurol., 80: 633–34, 1948.

28. History and tradition also throw some light on this problem. One of the oldest recorded chemical techniques in the ritual of the irrational is to be found in the Rig-Veda, and the ritual of Soma. The soma is a plant that has never been positively identified, but Geldner opines that all the available evidence points to its being either the Ephedra plant, or a species of Ephedra now extinct. The descriptions given in the Rig-Veda of a soma intoxi-

cation certainly match very closely the traditional picture of ecstasy. The active principle of the Ephedra is ephedrine, which has been shown to have an adrenergic inhibitory effect comparable to that of adrenaline. It is my belief that there is some evidence in the Rig-Veda that the *Amanita muscaria* may have been used in the ritual of the irrational to produce ecstasy. That this mushroom disappeared from use is suggested by the paucity of reference to it in the literature.

For further information see:

Geldner, Karl Friedrich, *Der Rig Veda, Aus dem Sanscrit ins Deutsche uebersetzt und mit einem laufenden Kommentar Versehen,* "Harvard Oriental Series," Vol. 35, Cambridge, Mass., 1951, p. 4 *et seq.*

Geldner, *ibid.,* p. 6.

Petrullo, *The Diabolic Root,* University of Pennsylvania Press, 1934. Edwin D. Barvey, *Shamanism in China, Studies in the Science of Society:* Presented to Albert Galloway Keller, New Haven, 1937, pp. 247–66. Nora K. Chadwick, "Shamanism among the Tartars of Central Asia," *Journal of the Royal Anthropological Institute of Great Britain,* 66: 291–329, 1936. Nora Chadwick, *Poetry and Prophecy,* Cambridge, 1942. K. Meuli, *Griechschen Opferbrauche,* Phyllobodia für Peter von der Mühl, 1946.

9

Yoga: The Psychology of
Autonomy for the
Nuclear Mobile Center
of Consciousness

Yoga is a doctrine and a practice that originated in India.[1]
Its main purpose is to gain for the individual complete independence. This is not only an independence from the
external influences of nature and man, but also an independence from the internal emotions, tensions, and
other impediments to what we might call an ideal state
of self-sufficiency. The doctrine is so widespread that it
permeates every religious school in India and surrounding
countries.[2] Such widespread influence of a basic doctrine
is naturally bound to give rise to many different schools
of Yoga and if we were to arrange them in a scale, at
the one end would be that Yoga which is solely concerned
with physical well-being and physical health, running
through intermediate stages concerned principally with
emotional and mental health, and ascending to areas where
the principal concern is spiritual perfection and individual
independence qualified by the desire for a union with God.

However, we are principally concerned with Yoga technique and not its ideological evaluations. The Shaman and
the Yogin start essentially from the same point, personal
physical hardihood and athletic vigor. The Yogin also subjects himself to great extremes of cold in order to condition
his body to this form of stress. Under the pressure of ex-

ternal cold he also seeks to liberate that "inner heat" which is thought to be the fuel and energy for spiritual liberation. This is not strictly speaking one of the techniques of Yoga, it is merely a foundation for any future development in Yoga, and it is assumed that the Yogin achieves such physical hardihood and the ability to create "inner heat." From here on there is a single-pointed technique which is followed throughout all subsequent stages of development. This can be summed under the heading of "Concentration."

The beginner in Yoga assumes one of the traditional sitting postures, and placing a candle before him, attempts to gaze at it with fixity and steadfastness. He seeks to keep his attention unwaveringly fixed upon the candle as long as possible. This develops control of the tides and fluxes of the mental stream of association. The Yogin may dispense with an external object to exercise the power of concentration, he may in fact, simply pick a point between his eyes, an imaginary point, and concentrate upon it just as he would upon the candle. Basic to the exercise of mental concentration is the act of visual concentration. Later on such concentration may be extended to other sensory systems.

The psychological conditioning based upon concentration takes two different forms. The first one is the one called "restraint," and this is concerned with those things which one is not to do, and this is in the area of personal hygiene, abstinence in sex, food, and of course mental and emotional restraint. The other form is that called "disciplines" and these are more in the direction of achieving moral purity.

In striving to achieve mastery over the random internal mental noise of the mind, and the random external noise of the mind whose origin lies in physical sensations, the Yogin moves through a gradation of controls. He begins with the control of sensory perception. He learns to look upon the candle for what it is. From this factual perception he learns to draw the correct inferences. And from his precise perception and correct inferences he learns to give what is called reliable testimony about his perception. In other words, he tries to see things as they are, and not as his mind would color them or preconceptions interpret them.

The Yogins have a term for the random noise of the senses, and the noise of the subconscious mind, it is called *Cittavrti*. This term has a rather interesting meaning— whirlwinds. The Yogins look upon the unrestrained and uncontrolled activity of the senses and the subconscious mind as whirlwinds without purpose which must be harnessed and brought under control.

The Yogin goes from the control of his senses and his understanding of the information gained therefrom to studying the internal activity of his own mind. In our day we can illustrate this by examples from studies made on what is called the restricted environment.[3] Here an individual is placed in an environment that reduces the amount of physical stimulation to his sensory system. The flow of energy from the outside world is cut down to an absolute minimum. In this state the subject lies in an environment without sound, without light, with temperature fixed, and with all the other physical sources that make for sensation controlled. When the noise of the outside world dies down he suddenly becomes aware of the internal noise of his body. He hears in an exaggeratedly loud fashion the beat of his heart, the rumble of his intestines, the noise of respiration, etc. In addition to these noises of purely physical origin in the body he becomes aware of the background noise of his own mind. He begins to hallucinate, strange creatures float through his imagination, some of them terrifying, some of them benign, the form of these images being dependent upon the nature of his mind and his psychological history. Some people can stand such an environment for only a short time, say an hour, and others of greater courage and control can stand it for as long as twenty-four hours. In either case the ghosts of one's mind rise to haunt one and often the experience can be highly unpleasant.

It is with such delusions and hallucinations of the mind that the Yogin works. He too achieves a state similar to that of the subject in the experimental restricted environment. However, when he has reached this state of development he is in considerable control of himself. He is not aware of, or bothered by, the noises of the body. These have been brought under harmonious control. His mind, as a result of concentration exercises, is not disordered, and therefore he can allow a single hallucination to appear in his mind and manipulate it and control it as though it were a puppet. He controls it; it does not possess him. These exercises are long and arduous but in them the Yogin learns not only to control delusion and hallucination but he also learns how to manipulate the "stuff" of the mind.

Having conquered the random flow of all forms of hallucination in his mind he then goes on to more fruitful endeavors and develops his abstract imagination. By this is meant that he no longer deals with the primordial images and stuff which arise in hallucinations, but looks beyond and through these for their abstract meaning. This process can be illustrated from laboratory experiments which I carried out, and which have been done by others, using the stimulation effect of a flashing light.

This consisted of a million candle power stroboscopic light. The subject, in this case a telepathic receiver, looked through his closed eyelids (at a distance of about nine inches) into this powerful light. The light was so controlled that it could flash within a frequency range of two times per second to forty-eight times per second. The subject while looking into the light controlled the frequency of the flash with a knob and adjusted it to that point which pleased him the most. I worked at this phenomenon most intensively with Peter Hurkos. Hurkos found that at a frequency of nine cycles per second he would have the following experience.

As he looked into the light his whole mental field became illuminated with a multiplex geometrical pattern. Very often it was like looking at a brilliantly colored mosaic made up of small regular geometrical figures. As Hurkos carefully adjusted the frequency of the flash, the brilliantly illuminated and colored geometrical pattern in his mind began to slowly revolve in a clockwise direction as he viewed it. The clockwise motion increased and gave him a feeling of being whirled outward, in other words, a centrifugal mental effect. By sharply controlling himself he was able to ignore the sense of being whirled outward and concentrate on the center of the pattern, finding therein what appeared to him to be a long tube which gave him tranquillity. At the end of the tube he suddenly saw distant visions. While gazing into this tranquillity he could accurately describe by extrasensory perception physical scenes going on thousands of miles away, as was demonstrated in many different experiments with him.

The important finding in this study was that it was possible to artificially induce a hallucinatory mental experience which resolved into an outward reach of the mind such as had been found earlier in an association with a state of cholinergia in Mrs. Garrett and Harry Stone. Accompanying this verifiable heightened telepathy and/or clairvoyance was a feeling of great relaxation and peace. Hurkos best described it when he said, "Looking into the light makes me forget all of my personal problems; I get out of myself completely, and easily look into whatever it is that I wish to concentrate upon." Immersed in this stroboscopic light, Hurkos undoubtedly experienced the peace and relaxation that the Yogin finds after mastering restraints and disciplines.

In addition to controlling the external and internal noise of the body and the mind the Yogin spends a great deal of effort in exercising his memory functions. He is very well aware of the close linkage between the memory function and the essence of mind itself. Therefore control of memory is an absolute necessity before any higher development can occur. He exercises such memory concentration both in the wide-awake state and in the sleep state. A Yogin does much of his exercises in what we call the sleep state. However, for the Yogin, sleep is not a state of unconsciousness, he is under all of the influences that we each personally know during sleep, with the one exception that he maintains an alert consciousness within this state of "sleep."

However, the true Yogin does not begin with the stages and exercises which we have just described. These are common to many different aesthetic, ascetic, and religious exercises. True Yoga begins with the study of the so-called postures.[4] Physical posture is a fundamental technique in Yoga. The simplest posture is one in which the Yogin sits on a mat or an animal hide on his haunches. His back is straight and his legs are crossed in the traditional lotus posture. His neck is bent forward so that his chin touches his chest. His tongue is bent backward so that the tip of it enters into the posterior portion of the nasal passage. His hands are relaxed across his knees and various positions are assumed by the hands themselves, the basic one being with the palms placed upward. In this position the Yogin carries out the exercises for concentration cited in the previous paragraph. The Yogin then goes through a long stage where he develops mental control over every one of the voluntary muscles of the body. For example, one of the simple controls is the ability to be able to tense the right rectus abdominal muscle, while the left one is relaxed. Or he may tense one rectus abdominal muscle and have the other one undergo rhythmic contractions. Or both abdominal muscles may alternately contract rhythmically to produce a churning motion on the intestines. The chief purpose of these exercises on the voluntary muscular system is not so much the athletic feat itself, but to guarantee that the mind at least can be the absolute master of its own means of locomotion. The end purpose of such exercises is to induce a state of complete relaxation of every muscle in the body.

Basic to such voluntary muscular control is the doctrine that this should be done under complete mental control at every step of the way. This is unlike the Shaman's doctrine, where rapid and violent movements are unconsciously carried out. Such movements are entirely against the tradition of Yoga. Having mastered the voluntary muscular system of the body, the Yogin turns his attention to mastering the involuntary muscular system of the body, the smooth muscle system. These are the muscles in the bronchi of the lungs, the muscles that control the blood vessels, the muscles that control the gastro-intestinal organs and the excretory organs. The first system that gets attention is that which controls to a great extent the rhythm of respiration, the diaphragm. In general the Yogin tries to achieve both maximum tenseness and maximum relaxation of the diaphragmatic muscles in preparation for his future exercises on the control of respiration. In general, during rhythmic Yogic breathing, the diaphragm is kept at a tense level.

The Yogin achieves remarkable control over the gastro-intestinal tract. One of the oft-quoted examples is that of swallowing a long bandage and propelling it through the entire twenty-eight feet of the gastro-intestinal canal and having it emerge at the rectum. While this may appear to be exhibitionism, the Yogin develops this technique in order to "clean out" his gastro-intestinal tract. In my opinion the primary purpose of these exercises is to gain complete mental control over the autonomic functions, but the Yogin makes use of each of these exercises for hygienic purposes.

Not only does the Yogin gain complete control over the normal functions of the involuntary muscular system, but he in fact reverses the rhythms of nature. For example, one of the simpler feats of the Hatha Yogin is the ability to draw fluid up into the bladder to the extent of a liter, and to use this fluid to flush the bladder. More remarkable is the ability that the Yogin develops over controlling his heart rate. Reliable witnesses and scientists[5] have actually measured the fact that the Yogin can so slow down his heart rate that it approaches the rhythm normally found just prior to death. The Yogin aims to accelerate or slow down his heart principally to exercise his new-found mental control against something. However, the Yogin's long exercises to gain complete mastery of the voluntary muscular system and the involuntary muscular system are all aimed at gaining perfect rhythmic control over his respiration. Control of respiration is one of the fundamental techniques of Yoga and from it are believed to stem many of the higher mental and spiritual powers which are necessary in order to attain personal independence.

It must be emphasized that in carrying out such exercises, particularly on the autonomic nervous system, the Yogin is able to release adrenergic chemicals at will and to the degree he desires, as well as to release the cholinergic chemicals to any degree necessary for his purposes. I believe that this is one of the great achievements of the technique of Yoga, this power to place the body at any required balance between adrenergia and cholinergia or a preponderance of one system over the other.

Yoga calls the control of respiration *Pranayama*.[6] This comes from the word for breath, *Prana,* and the word for pause, *Ayama.* The essential meaning of pranayama is mental control over respiration with the object of slowing down the normal respiratory rhythm, or even stopping it for long periods of time. It is the belief of the Yoga doctrine that rhythmic respiration serves to unify consciousness itself with breathing. This is based on the assumption that the act of breathing supplies the fuel of consciousness. We might say, in terms of the concepts developed here, that breathing is a vehicle for building up the power of the psi plasma.

Respiratory exercises are always carried out in one of the traditional Yogic postures. Respiratory exercise is divided into three phases. The first is that of inhalation, called *Puraka.* The second phase is that of holding the breath at the top of inhalation and this is called *Kumb-*

haka. The word *kumb* comes from an old Sanskrit root which means pot or a vessel, and in this instance pictures an inverted bowl. The holding phase is followed by the exhalation phase, called *Rechaka.* Holding is not only holding the breath within the lungs but is conceived of as a definite phase outside of the lungs. In this latter case holding would follow the exhalation phase where the holding refers to holding back air from the lungs themselves. There is a definite ratio between these phases which can be expressed in time, 1 : 4 : 2. This is the traditional ratio although many other variations have been worked out.

In the beginning of pranayamic exercises the holding phase is usually set at the lowest limit for about 12 seconds, and the practitioner works up to an upper limit of 108 seconds. The other ratios then have a corresponding value. In the next higher stage of the development of pranayama these ratios are multiplied by a definite factor (usually 12). Then the new lowest limit for the holding phase becomes 144 seconds, and the upper limit for holding becomes 1296 seconds, or 21.6 minutes. The respiratory rate of the Yogin therefore moves in the direction of becoming slower and slower, while he still maintains the same high level of consciousness and mental control over all the functions previously cited. In fact, the ultimate aim of the pranayamic exercises is to achieve that state of slow respiration which is found in hibernating animals. Yogins and Fakirs have been known to publicly demonstrate this ability by performing the feat of being "buried alive" and in some instances such burials have lasted as long as thirty days. When the Yogin arises from his long deep sleep, although dehydrated and having lost considerable weight, he nevertheless is in good health.

One of the many respiratory rhythms used by Yogins is called Ujjaye, and Behanan[7] has done some oxygen-consumption measurements on this form of breathing at Yale University. When using the Ujjaye technique of breathing, his respiration rate was 76 cycles per hour. During this exercise his oxygen consumption was measured. It was found that in spite of this slow rate of breathing, his oxygen consumption increased 24.5 per cent over that of control levels. Behanan also reports on his subjective experiences during such breathing exercises. He points out that the first fifteen to twenty minutes of the Ujjayic breathing exercises results in a sense of tingling all over the body, and mental excitation and exhilaration. This we have come to recognize as being based on a state of adrenergia. Following this early excitatory phase, the Yogin then passes into a state of deep relaxation. Although he is sitting up straight and his mind is intensely alert, all his muscles both voluntary and involuntary feel at perfect ease and are relaxed. This state of deep relaxation leads the mind to an inward turning, or toward the center of the mental field, and results in increased concentration of the type peculiar to Yoga. This state we recognize from our previous discussions as a state of cholinergia.

I have made some personal experiments on the mental effects of various degrees of cholinergia. For this I used extracts from the mushroom *Amanita muscaria*, whose chief constituent is muscarine, a powerful cholinergic drug. Different doses of muscarine show a wide spectrum of effects. A very small dose of muscarine produces a feeling of relaxation, well-being, an increase of muscular strength, and as shown earlier, a facility for telepathy. The consciousness is scarcely altered with such small doses. With massive doses which lead to poisoning there are of course all the symptoms of massive activation of the parasympathetic nervous system, nausea, vomiting, diarrhea, etc.; the mental state is that of extreme hallucination (the kind depending on the psychological history of the individual) and this can lead to the subjective experience of a mobile center of consciousness. I was seeking to find a state of cholinergia intermediate between these two extremes.

When I found the proper dose the following effect occurred. The first was that of a state of inebriation unlike anything I have experienced from any other chemical, including alcohol. It was a highly poised, calm, and ecstatic state. There was no effect on the voluntary muscular system in the way of imbalance, staggering, or other such dysfunction. I sat perfectly still for about an hour in one of the simpler Yogic postures. I then passed through this state of inebriation, which is comparable to the state that Behanan describes as exhilaration and excitement. Thereafter I lost consciousness for about an hour; observers tell me that I sat motionless throughout this period with a pulse rate of 36 and very slow respiration. I did not seem to be in any serious difficulty, and even responded to their questions, but I have no remembrance of this. When I came out of this state, that is, recovered consciousness, I had a singular experience. I felt that I was absolutely and unconditionally detached from "everything." In short, I was the only existence. I was aware that something else existed, but I can only describe this as "everything" else, the primary reality was the knowledge of self.

I cite this experience merely to illustrate what I believe the Yogin attempts to achieve by the exercise of concentration and rhythmic breathing, which I believe culminates in the proper state of cholinergia. The entire mental flux reduces to a single point, i.e., Self. I noticed after I passed this point of being aware only of self that I gradually related other things to myself. First I related myself to my body. Then I related myself and body to the floor on which I sat. Then I related to the walls, then to the other people in the room. In this way I took new elements into my consciousness, one at a time, and was able to relate them with a clarity which I have not known before.

There are other concomitants of Yogic pranayama. It has been reported by Floyd[8] that every inspiration of the breath in the human being is accompanied by a marked change in the electrical potential of the skin. This can take the form either of an increase in potential or a decrease. The order of change is about 10 millivolts D.C. It is also known that such breathing increases the carbon-dioxide content of the alveolar tissue in the lungs, as well as in the blood. Both of these effects result in an increased pressure of carbon-dioxide gas upon the nerve cells of the brain. Carbon dioxide when administered in such increased pressure is known to result in hallucination, feeling of expansiveness, and eventually leads to unconsciousness.

However, the Yogins themselves state that the chief purpose of perfected pranayama is to release a latent mental energy in the mind which they call kundalini. The Yogins conceive of kundalini as being latent in the body and it has its origin at the base of the spinal column in the form of a tightly coiled vortex of energy. The Yogin looks upon this as the ultimate energy, therefore extremely powerful, and its release can be accompanied by serious danger to the individual; therefore this must be done with absolute control and caution.

Yoga conceives that the physical source of prana comes from the air and this is filtered out by the process of pranayama. Therefore, in spite of the fact that the Yogin attempts to cut off all physical energies that come through the sensations, he nevertheless does draw upon one physical source, the air, for his mental operations. We are not told whether the filtered air is directed to the kundalini center, or whether the filtered air simply serves to release the kundalini energy.

Air, as is well known, is composed of 20.9% oxygen, 79% nitrogen, some rare gases, and some pollutants. Of these the body utilizes only oxygen. We have not as yet mentioned the intimate dependence of consciousness on the chemical oxygen. There is no question that the Yogin makes maximum use of the consciousness-maintaining properties of oxygen. How oxygen is transformed by the Yogin for special use we do not know.

It is well known that oxygen under the impress of a given amount of energy (for example, a few thousand volts D.C. potential) converts easily to the ionized state and to higher polymers of which the first is ozone. Under the influence of such electrical fields the oxygen in the air gains a negative charge (ionized). Many workers have shown that negatively ionized oxygen exerts a beneficial effect on the organism, such as slowing respiration,[8a] and lowering of the blood pressure,[8b] and a feeling of mental alertness and general well-being.[8c] Negative oxygen ions increase the action of the cilia in the respiratory passages[8d] which are responsible for keeping it free of dust and other noxious particles. Positively charged carbon-dioxide ions on the other hand slow down the ciliary beat. Positively charged atmospheric gas ions, in general, do not have the salubrious effect shown by negatively charged ions.[8e] In my own researches I have found that an excess of negative ions breathed by a sensitive definitely increases ESP-test scores for telepathy. (See Appendix A.)

The relationship between the ionized states of oxygen, ozone, and carbon dioxide in the central nervous system during pranayamic breathing is not known. This is a ripe area for research. It might provide a further chemical basis for understanding some of the phenomena associated with higher states of consciousness.

Up to this point the Yogin has reached the stage where he can consciously release the kundalini energy. Prior to this he has been able to focus his mind on specific points throughout his anatomical system, and particularly those centers which control autonomic function. He now consciously directs the kundalini energy to each of these autonomic centers. In the technique of Yoga these are not precisely identified with the autonomic centers, but are spatially in the same area, and are called chakras. The addition of the kundalini energy to each of these chakric centers is the next step in the development of mental control by the Yogin. The kundalini energy added to these centers moves him into a higher dimension of personal control and toward his goal of complete independence.

This leads to the stage called abstraction, and is properly speaking the fifth stage of the Yoga technique. Here the purpose is to completely dissociate sensations in the mind from their physical origin in the sensory receptor system. The Yogin manipulates sensations in his mind just as though they had their origin in the physical world. For example, he creates the image of a tree in his mind from memory. He not only sees the image of a remembered tree, but begins with the seed of the tree and watches the dynamics of the evolution of that seed through the various stages of growth into the completed tree. In this process it is most important to note that he avoids illusion and hallucination completely. He believes that he is actually reconstructing the idea forces of nature and is studying their dynamics. He does this in isolation from the physical origin of such sensations and therefore the process is called abstraction.

In order to achieve this type of power he uses one principal technique, which is the control of consciousness through its four stages. Yoga defines the stages of consciousness as: 1) The awake state of consciousness. 2) The state of consciousness in sleep when one has dreams. 3) The state of consciousness in sleep when there are no dreams. 4) The cataleptic state of consciousness. This latter must not be confused with hypnosis or what we normally call trance. The essential feature of the passage of the Yogin through these four states of consciousness is that he never loses consciousness; he maintains in what appears to be normal sleep a thoroughly alert consciousness. This also holds true for what is known as the cataleptic state of consciousness, and this is the one exercised in the state of being buried alive. In going through the various stages of consciousness his principal aim is to be able to master these states so that he can go to a higher state of consciousness called samadhi.

The state of samadhi is the end goal of the Yogin efforts.[9] There are three stages associated with attaining samadhi which cannot very sharply be differentiated from one another, which are called, 1) (stage six) True concentration. 2) (stage seven) Meditation. 3) (stage eight) Samadhi. We must remember that up till now the Yogin has brought under complete control sensory noise from the physical world, internal noise of the body and all that this implies, and has achieved complete control over the states of adrenergia and cholinergia both in regard to specific organs and with respect to his general mental state. He furthermore has found ways of extracting energy from the world around him through pranayama and has learned to direct and localize this energy from the kundalini center. He now works his operations solely by mind control of what I have termed the psi plasma. I believe the psi plasma could be identified with the kundalini energy. With the beginning of true concentration we can no longer find physiological, chemical, or physical foundations for the operations of the Yogin. We are now in the realm of unconditioned mental dynamics largely unknown in the world of Western science and psychology.

Having learned to control the substance prana by mental operations alone, the Yogin goes on to the state called meditation. Here his goal is to actually control the realm of the physical by virtue of his control over what I believe to be psi plasma. There are a number of ways to illustrate such control. We have all heard of levitation, but very few people have ever seen it. I myself have not witnessed physical levitation, and have to rely on the testimony of others.

Experiments have been done in psychology laboratories to show that when an individual is placed in an isolated environment he may very often have the illusion of being levitated. For example, one experiment[10] with twenty subjects showed that eight of the subjects very definitely had the sensation that they were physically rising in the air, although the observers were quite aware that the individuals did not leave their chairs. The Yogin has learned to avoid these pitfalls of the mind.

Sir William Crookes has given us the best scientific studies of levitation in his researches on the famous medium D. D. Home. Crookes measured the levitation powers of D. D. Home and confirmed by means of a spring balance that (without physical contact) Home could create both an increase and a decrease in gravitational force on objects. Then Crookes attested to the most striking phenomenon of all. The instance in which Home was levitated and carried through a window at a point eighty feet above the street and then returned into the room. Crookes makes this affirmation.

"The phenomena I am prepared to attest are so extraordinary and so directly opposed to the most firmly-rooted articles of scientific belief—amongst others, the ubiquity and invariable action of the force of gravitation—that even now, on recalling the details of what I witnessed there is an antagonism in my mind between reason, which pronounces it to be scientifically impossible, and the consciousness that my senses, both of touch and sight—and these corroborated by the senses of all who were present—are not lying witnesses when they testify against my preconception."[11]

Another example of such control, even though it is on a smaller scale, has been furnished by Wiener.[12] He cites the case of a Yogin in the state of meditation whose electrical brain waves were being recorded. The ordinary individual, when he has his eyes wide open and the electrical brain activity is being registered, does not show the presence of alpha waves, these being slow sinusoidal waves of the order of eight to fourteen cycles per second.[13] The Yogin, however, was able to demonstrate prominent alpha-rhythm frequency with his eyes wide open. This means that he is able to control the molecular and electrical activity of his brain to such an extent that external light energy was not able to cause the disappearance of the alpha frequency. This type of control is developed to higher and higher degrees by the Yogin. The purpose actually is not to demonstrate control over physical nature, but rather to give the developing mind something greater to pit its energies against. The mind can only develop in the face of the proper degree of resistance, and at this stage it is the physical realm that provides the proper degree of resistance.

Having achieved this power, the Yogin now prepares to enter the state called samadhi. We have no equivalent term in the Western world to describe it. It is based upon all the factors already cited, but it is not a state of consciousness per se. If there is any description that is adequate it is that the Yogin now realizes himself as a nuclear mental entity which is able to control the physical dynamics of his body, control physical objects and energies at a distance from his body, and is able to move freely as a mobile center of consciousness independently of his body. This is the true meaning of the independence and autonomy that is the goal of all Yogins. However, this is not the end in that the Yogin goes on to a state that we can scarcely comprehend but which can be faintly described as merging his liberated nuclear self with that of a greater entity, namely God.

Eliade[14] describes samadhi as having two different conditions. The first is samadhi "with support," and this means the nuclear mental entity is still dependent in some way upon either the physical world as form or energy, or upon the physical basis of sensations, ideas, and memories. The Yogin seeks to go past this state where there is no association with the world of physics, and this is called the state of samadhi "without support." In this state the Yogin enters into a state of being that has no foundations or connections with any other form of human consciousness. It is in this state that he merges with the Absolute. We cannot in our Western way of thinking expect to follow with any clear understanding the realm which the Yogin has now entered.

It is a curious fact that the Yogins who have achieved this stage of experience and who have returned to speak about it are not able to give us an adequate description of where they have been. The language used to describe this experience is couched in terms of color, radiance, and light. It seems as though the language that we have and use was devised to describe the physical world in which we live and is inadequate to describe this other world. Anyone who has read these accounts by Yogins themselves has a great feeling of disappointment in not being able to truly understand what it is they are talking about. The feeling is almost equivalent to the void that the Yogin claims to have entered.

Since we cannot follow the Yogin in this experience we can at least retrace the means by which he reaches this realm. In retracing his steps we will in the following chapters go into some of the minutiae underlying the practices of both the Shaman and the Yogin. By such a survey we hope to arrive at some general concept of the biological dynamics, mental dynamics, and physical dynamics employed in order to be better able to ask the proper questions of nature so that we can eventually understand and control the personal psi plasma.

NOTES Chapter 9

1. *The Yoga Sutras of Patanjali,* Tr. by Rama Prasad, Sudhindranath Vasu, Allahabad, 1924. Bailey, Alice, *The Yoga Sutras of Patanjali,* Lucis Publishing House, New York, 1949.

2. For India see: Behanan, K. T., *Yoga: A Scientific Evaluation,* Macmillan, New York, 1937. For Tibet see: David-Neel, *op. cit.* W. Y. Evans-Wentz, *Tibet's Great Yoga Milarepa;* also *Tibetan Yoga and Secret Doctrines,* Oxford, 1935.

3. Heron, Woodburn, Doane, B. K., and Scott, T. H., Selection 23, "Visual Disturbance after Prolonged Perceptual Isolation," p. 328, *Readings in Perception,* Beardslee and Wertheimer, Eds., Van Nostrand, New York, 1958. Additional references found here.

4. See Behanan, *op. cit.* Also *J. Yoga Institute,* Bombay. Rawcliffe, *op. cit.* Shri Yogendra, *Yoga,* The Yoga Institute, Bombay, 1952. Alain Danielou, *Yoga: The Method of Re-Integration,* Christopher Johnson, London, 1949.

5. See Parts 1 and 2, pp. 1–282, *Forms and Techniques of Altruistic and Spiritual Growth,* Ed. by Pitrim A. Sorokin, The Beacon Press, Boston, 1954.

6. Rama Prasad, *Nature's Finer Forces,* Theosophical Publishing House, Madras, India, 1947. Charles Johnson, *The Yoga Sutras of Patanjali,* John M. Watkins, London, 1949.

7. Behanan, *op. cit.,* Chap. 11.

8. Butler, J. A. V., *Electrical Phenomena at Interfaces*, Methuen, London, 1951, p. 265.

8a. Ferrannini, L., *Revista de Meteorologia e Scienza Affine*, Roma, julio-agosta, 1939.

8b. Augusto M. Robles Gorriti and Antonio Medina, "The Application of Ion Therapy in Hypertension," National Ministry of Public Health, April 12, 1954, Buenos Aires.

8c. Curry Manfred, *Bioklimatik*, 2 Vols., American Bioclimatic Research Institute, 1946.

8d. *MD* magazine, October 1958, Report on the work of A. P. Kreuger and Richard A. Smith of the University of California.

8e. H. H. Skilling and John C. Beckett, "Control of Air Ion Density in Rooms," *J. of the Franklin Institute*, 265: 423–34, 1953. W. W. Hicks, US Patents No. 2,594,777; 2,640,158.

J. C. Beckett, "Air Ionization as an Environment Factor," *Applications and Industry*, September 1954.

John L. Worden, "The effect of air ion concentration and polarity on the carbon dioxide capacity of mammalian blood plasma," Lecture before the American Physiological Society, April 12, 1954, at Atlantic City, N.J.

Christen B. Nielson and Harold A. Harper, "Effect of air ions on succinoxidase activity of the rat adrenal gland," *Proc. Soc. Exp. Biol. & Med.*, 86: 753–56, 1954.

Yaglou, C. P., Benjamin, L. C., and Brandt, A. D., "The influence of respiration and transpiration on ionic content of air of occupied rooms," *J. Ind. Hygiene*, 15: 8, 1933.

Howard C. Murphy, "How ion density affects comfort," *Heating, Piping & Air Conditioning*, October 1954.

Yaglou, C. P., Benjamin, L. C., and Brandt, A. D., "Physiologic changes during exposure to ionized air," *American Society of Heating & Ventilating Engineers*, 39: 965, 1933.

9. For a complete description of the technique of this process see: W. Y. Evans-Wentz, *The Tibetan Book of the Great Liberation, or the Method of Realizing Nirvana through Knowing the Mind*, Oxford, 1951.

"The Voidness—in all Tibetan systems of yoga realization of the voidness (Tib. Stong-pa-nid); (Skt. Shunyata) is the one great aim; for to realize it is to attain the unconditioned Dharma-Kaya, or 'Divine Body of Truth.'" *Tibetan Book of the Dead*, Oxford, 1951.

10. Horton, Lydiard H., "The Illusion of Levitation," *The Journal of Abnormal Psychology*, Vol. 13, 1918–19.

11. Quoted from Paul Miller, *Science in the Seance Room*.

12. Wiener, Norbert, *Cybernetics*, Wiley, New York, 1948.

13. It is to be noted that the Shaman exposes himself to maximal auditory stimulation, and minimal visual stimulation. Visual stimulation is received on the occipital cortex, while auditory stimulation is received on the first temporal convolution in a narrow zone that borders the posterior third of the fissure of Sylvius. Lying between these two poles is the memory area of the temporal lobe. Since there is a close relation between light stimulation, the occipital cortex, and the alpha rhythm, let us analyze this aspect of the problem.

W. Grey Walter states:

"In most people the alpha rhythms, prominent when the eyes are shut and the mind is at rest, disappear whenever the eyes are opened or when the subject makes a mental effort—for example, while doing a sum in mental arithmetic. Exceptions had of course been noticed; entire absence of rhythms in some cases. But it was only in the course of war services at the Burden Neurological Institute that we were able to designate some of these exceptions as a stable group with definite characteristics. It was shown in 1943 that individuals with persistent alpha rhythms which are hard to block with mental effort, tend to auditory, kinaesthetic or tactile perceptions rather than visual imagery. In this group of persons the alpha rhythms continue even when the eyes are open and the mind is active or alert.

"The group with persistent activity is known as P for short, while the larger group, whose alpha rhythms are responsive, are known as R. A third group was further definable as those people in whose EEG's no significant alpha rhythms are found, even when taken with the eyes shut and the mind idle. This group is known as M, for minus, and consists of persons whose thinking processes are conducted almost entirely in terms of visual imagery.

"Several surveys have been made to find out how these types are distributed in the population; groups comprising more than 600 persons have been studied for this purpose. The proportions vary a good deal according to occupation, but, in general about two-thirds of an ordinary normal group of people selected at random are found to be of the R type, and the remaining third are about evenly M and P. The proportion of M types is usually rather higher in science students than in art students.

"Occasionally disorders of thought are found associated with wildly exaggerated alpha characteristics, but mental illness is usually accompanied only by the most subtle and evanescent changes in the EEG. An alpha rhythm which persists when the eyes are open and the subject is apparently fully occupied—reading aloud for instance—is usually suggestive of some isolation from reality. In a few cases absurdly persistent alpha rhythms have been the first clear indication of something wrong, that what seemed unintelligible or eccentric brilliance was really lunatic delusion."

W. Grey Walter, *The Living Brain,* W. W. Norton & Co., New York, 1953, p. 222.

It is known that the absence of visual stimulation, lack of mental concentration, and alcohol increase the prominence of the alpha rhythms in the occipital cortex; and that an increase in body temperature, adrenocortical and thyroid activity tend to increase the alpha frequency. The Shaman and Yogin in the adrenergic phase are believed to undergo physiological shifts in the same direction. The idea seems unavoidable therefore, that one of the major purposes in the initial phases of the ritual of the irrational is to increase the amplitude and frequency of the alpha rhythms. Later, the amplitude remains high, but the frequency is decreased.

For further information see:

Penfield and Rasmussen, *The Cerebral Cortex of Man,* Macmillan, New York, 1950. Morris B. Bender, *Disorders in Perception,* Charles C Thomas, Springfield, Ill., 1952.

Gerhard von Bonin, *Essay on the Cerebral Cortex,* Charles C Thomas, Springfield, Ill., 1950.

Strauss, *et al., Diagnostic Electroencephalography,* Grune and Stratton, New York, 1952, p. 128.

14. Mircea Eliade, *Yoga, Immortality and Freedom,* "Bollingen Series LVI," Pantheon Books, New York, 1958.

10

The Biological
Foundations of
Psi Plasma

Our description of the preparatory exercises and techniques of the Shaman and the Yogin need not be confusing to the Western mind. The practices of the Shaman with his exaggerated kinetics, and the Yogin with his exaggerated quietude, appear to be two opposite approaches to autonomy. However, if we analyze the underlying physiological processes we will find equivalent strata in these techniques.

We see that both techniques require extremes of stress for developing physical and psychological toughness. We see that this is followed by a phase which leads to an excitatory state which we have categorized under the term adrenergia. In the case of the Shaman this excitatory phase is of rather long duration as evidenced by the singing, dancing, and drum beating. In the Yogin it is of relatively short duration and is illustrated by the first twenty minutes or so of a breathing exercise.

Both the Yogin and the Shaman then go into a phase of relaxation coupled with an unusually alert state of mind which we have described under the term cholinergia. This phase of great relaxation and intense concentration is characterized by exhaustion in the case of the Shaman, and a slowing down of all the rhythms in the body of the Yogin. This latter is the key to the direction taken physiologically both by the Shaman and the Yogin.

The Yogin, for example, is capable of slowing his heart rate from a normal seventy-two beats per minute to a frequency of one beat per minute, or less. He slows his respiratory rhythm from the normal rate of eighteen respirations per minute to extremes of one to three respirations every hour. The most significant slowing down observed is the rhythm of the electrical waves of the brain. These are slowed down from a normal rate of approximately thirty beats per second to an alpha frequency of eight to ten beats per second. It has further been noticed that in the Yogin the slowed-down alpha frequency has the characteristics of a sine wave.

In order to understand what is going on physiologically we shall have to analyze what happens to a single nerve cell when its frequency of electrical impulse is slowed down. Although the single nerve cell is a very complex chemical, physical, and electrical system, we can make some generalizations which will give us a simplified model for the purpose of our understanding. We can imagine a nerve cell as being constituted of a long tube with a bulb on the end. This would look somewhat like a thermometer bulb and stem. The surface of this bulb-ended tube is the all-important functional component of a nerve cell and is called the plasma membrane. The plasma membrane is the surface which is responsible for carrying the electrical waves of the nerve impulse.

The plasma membrane must not be thought of as an electrical conductor like a metal such as copper. Rather it must be conceived of as a nonconductor, a dielectric, like paper or plastic. Let us imagine that a thin layer of a nonconductor is coated around the entire thermometer-bulb-shaped structure. The thin dielectric then has a conducting medium on the inside of it and on the outside of it, and these are the tissue fluids of the body. The inside conducting layer of the dielectric has the properties of a cathode, that is, negative charges will migrate toward it.

The outside conductor has the properties of an anode, that is, positive charges will migrate toward it. Thus the plasma membrane can be conceived of as a simple sandwich with two conductors separated by a nonconductor. This is what is known as a capacitor in electrical terminology. A capacitor has the property of being able to hold a certain quantity of electrons, that is, it is a reservoir for electrons.

The plasma membrane in addition to being a capacitor is also a rectifier. A rectifier is an electrical element which allows charges of a certain sign to pass through in one direction but not in the other. In the case of the nerve plasma membrane it will allow electrons to flow from the outside to the inside. The rectifier function and the capacitor function are lumped into the physical structure of the thin dielectric. The capacitor-rectifier also has a high electrical resistance across it, that is, it offers resistance to the flow of electrons across it. In addition to its properties as a capacitor, rectifier, and resistor, the plasma membrane has the property of magnetic induction. Inductance can best be thought of as a coil of wire helically wound around some magnetic material such as iron. The change in magnetism that the current in the coil generates is called its inductance. In the case of the inductive component of the plasma membrane, it is not possible at this time to assign any definite spatial localization to it.

The amazing thing about the nerve plasma membrane is that the values for each of the components listed are unusually high. The capacitance is of the order of one microfarad, the resistance can reach values of the order of a million ohms, and the inductance has the value of 0.2 Henrys. All these high values are lumped in the thin membrane of the surface of the nerve. It has been calculated by Aschheim[1] that the effective thickness of the plasma membrane is of the order of 1.367 Angstrom units, or a centimeter divided by one hundred million. This makes it an extremely thin membrane.

In general the plasma membrane has a large concentration of potassium ions, K^+, on its inside surface, and a large concentration of sodium ions, Na^+, on the outside surface. However, the concentration of K^+ on the inside is about ten times greater than the concentration of Na^+ on the outside. It is this difference in ion concentration that gives rise to the voltage difference across the plasma membrane, called the resting potential. The resting potential across the nerve membrane is of the order of sixty millivolts, and the inside of the nerve is negative in sign, electrically speaking. Therefore the inside of the nerve is negatively charged and the outside of the nerve is positively charged, the entire arrangement being very much like the electrical potential that exists between the two terminals of a battery.

When a nerve is stimulated an electrical impulse travels from one end to the other. The single electrical impulse starts from a resting value of negative sixty millivolts, goes to zero volts, reverses in sign to reach a value of sixty millivolts positive, and this potential then falls to zero again, and the potential becomes negative sixty millivolts when the nerve comes to rest again. The shape of this electrical wave is that of a spike with the point straight up, and a line drawn through the center perpendicular to the vertical axis of the spike represents the zero voltage level.

Therefore we can imagine that the nerve impulse starts from its resting potential of minus sixty millivolts at the bottom left-hand side of the spike, runs up through the zero point to positive sixty millivolts at the peak of the spike, and then drops down again through the zero point to reach its resting potential of minus sixty millivolts. Because of its similarity to the shape of a spike this component of the electrical impulse is called the spike potential. The spike-component duration is about a thousandth of a second, and nerves can conduct such impulses at a maximum frequency of about five hundred pulses per second. When a nerve is stimulated either by a sensory stimulation or by an action of the will, such a train of electrical spikes can be visualized on an oscilloscope.

We see that the nerve cell through its plasma-membrane shell is an electrical generator and that the wave form, frequency, voltage, and other electrical characteristics have been thoroughly measured. In addition to being an electrical generator of pulses the nerve cell is also a generator of certain chemicals involved in nerve conduction. These chemicals are many, such as adrenaline, serotonin, histamine, acetylcholine, etc. There is much debate among neurophysiologists as to whether the nerve impulse is primarily an electrical conduction phenomenon or a chemical conduction phenomenon.

In order to include the role of the chemicals generated by the nerve we will now have to complicate our simple nerve model. Instead of dealing with a single bulb-ended tube we now have to bring two of them into our picture, by placing the bulb end of one against the tubular end of the other, because we have now to consider the method of transfer of the nerve impulse from one nerve cell to another. The natural mode of nerve stimulation would start in the bulb, travel down the tube and then jump a short distance to the next bulb element. The gap between the two nerve elements, that is, where the tubular end of one nears the bulb end of the other, is called the synapse.

It is at the tubular synaptic end of the nerve that the chemicals are produced. It is known that in cholinergic nerves the substance acetylcholine is released and it in turn stimulates the bulb end of the next nerve across the synapse. The duration of action of the acetylcholine is limited by a substance called cholinesterase. Cholinesterase allows the acetylcholine to stimulate the bulb end of the second nerve for a fraction of a second and then it chemically neutralizes or inactivates it. When a nerve secretes acetylcholine, it is called a cholinergic nerve. When a nerve secretes adrenaline or its synapse is stimulated by adrenaline, it is called an adrenergic nerve.

Now there are some peculiar properties of the synapse

which are different from that which we ascribe to the nerve cell as a whole. It is known for example that the membrane on the bulb end of the cell (which is called the post-synaptic membrane), facing the tubular end, is not excitable by electricity, but only by chemicals. This is the origin of the debate as to whether a nerve is principally an electrical phenomenon or a chemical phenomenon.

Now we have to complicate our two-cell model a little further, and add a third nerve element to the picture. The first nerve element, let us say, will excite the succeeding cell, which is number two; we add a third cell parallel to the first and its function will be not to excite the number-two cell across the synapse, but to inhibit it. In other words, the function of cell number three will be to produce the usual electrical impulse, produce a chemical substance at the synapse, but this in turn will inhibit the second cell from firing a nerve impulse. The function of inhibitory and excitatory nerves is very complex in the brain itself, and often what is interpreted by us subjectively as an excitatory effect is really an inhibitory effect. This can be illustrated in the case of alcohol. When we take a drink of alcohol our initial reaction is one of excitement. But this is due to the fact that alcohol is a nerve-depressant and the inhibitory cells are more sensitive to the action of alcohol than are the excitatory cells. Therefore the alcohol will depress the inhibitory cell number three, and thereby release its braking action on cell number two. This allows cell number two freedom from restraint, so it becomes more sensitive to excitatory impulses from cell number one.

Now in the case of some of the chemical compounds which we have noted that the Shaman uses, we have to clearly distinguish between those which have an excitatory effect and those which have an inhibitory effect. For example, the alcohol consumed by the Shaman first depresses the inhibitory cells, which results in a certain amount of excitation. If too much alcohol is consumed not only are the inhibitory cells depressed but also the excitatory cells, and this leads to staggering, incoherence, and the familiar stupor associated with drunkenness. On the other hand, when he uses certain compounds—for example, the mushroom which has muscarine (an acetylcholine effect)—this initially increases the activity of both the excitatory and inhibitory nerve cells, resulting in a greater over-all sense of power and control.

Adrenaline we normally think of as an excitatory agent. However its action can be compared in many ways to that of alcohol. Adrenaline, when introduced into our three-celled system, works principally as an inhibitor of nerve-impulse transmission across the synapse. Its effect is principally on the inhibitor cells (number three), and therefore its initial effect is one of apparent excitation. If large amounts of adrenaline are released at the synapse it will block conduction of both the inhibitory and excitatory cells. From time to time we will refer to the effects of adrenergia and cholinergia as to whether they are exerted on the plasma membrane itself, on the synapse, or on the post-synaptic membrane.

We can simplify our entire problem of understanding the biology of the ritual of the irrational of the Shaman and the Yogin by considering what happens to the electrical characteristics of the plasma membrane on the assumption that the principal goal is to decrease the frequency of biological rhythms. We have observed that the normal nerve impulse has the form of a sharp spike, and that its frequency is of the order of 500 cycles per second at a maximum. In the very advanced stages the ritual of the irrational tends to alter the nerve wave form from a spike to that of a smooth sine wave, and tends to decrease the frequency of the cell elements of the brain to a uniform 8 to 10 cycles per second.

Now the frequency characteristic of a single nerve cell is principally a function of two of the electrical constants of the plasma membrane, the inductance and the capacitance. If we take the value of the normal inductance, 0.2 Henrys, and multiply it by the value of the capacitance, 1 microfarad (1 millionth of a farad), and then take the square root of this product, we establish the period or duration, T, of each single nerve pulse. If we take the reciprocal of this value, that is, $1/T$, we get the frequency of the nerve impulse. If we carry out this calculation for a normal person who is in a normal physiological state, we find that the resonant frequency of his nerve impulses is about 360 cycles per second[2] (which can of course attain a maximum of about 500 cycles per second).

If we examine the relationship between the inductance and capacitance in this equation we find that an increase in capacitance will be the principal factor which will lower the frequency. If we increase the normal capacitance of the plasma membrane by a factor of about four hundred and introduce this into our equation, we will find that the frequency of the nerve cell comes out to 8 cycles per second, and that it is a sine wave.[2a] This is the essence of the change induced in the nerve-plasma membrane by the prolonged exercises and techniques which go to make up the ritual of the irrational.

This is a most important clue in our basic understanding of the relationship of the electrical constants of the human body to the problem of the expansion or separation of the nuclear mobile center of consciousness from the body. An increase in capacitance of the plasma membrane means that each individual nerve cell is capable of carrying more electrical charge and releasing this in a slower graded rhythmic form. The increased capacitance and the rhythmic sine oscillation of the electrical potentials of the nervous system as a whole are the keys which will eventually clarify our understanding of this most important problem.[3] Having established this hypothesis we will now examine the physical and chemical changes that occur in the long-term preparatory phase of the ritual of the irrational.

Essentially, the difference in conditioning between the Shaman and the Yogin is only one of degree and their separate approaches can be lumped under one heading, namely that of stress. Thanks to the work of Selye and many others there is emerging a sound concept of what occurs to the body under the impact of either physical or psychological stress.

Selye has shown that under stress the human body undergoes a process of general adaptation to the new loads and strains which it must bear. The most important manifestations of this response of the body to stress are an enlargement of the adrenal glands, which have two components, the adrenal cortex and the adrenal medulla. The adrenal medulla is the source of adrenaline and related compounds, and the adrenal cortex is the source of a large group of compounds generally called corticoids. The second change is that there is an involution or decrease of the thymus and lymphatic glands, and this is reflected in the distribution of the cells found in the blood. This manifests principally as a decrease in eosinophils, lymphocytes, and an increase in the polynucleocytes. When stress is extreme there is a third effect, a degenerative effect, which shows up as ulcers of the gastro-intestinal tract. However, in our discussion we will not be concerned with these pathological aspects, since they are avoided by the Yogin and the Shaman.

The general adaptation to stress undergone by the body has three principal phases. The first is called the alarm reaction, in which we get the effects of adrenergia which parpare one for fight or flight, and in this stage adaptation of the organism to the new stresses has not yet been acquired. Under stress the individual goes through repeated episodes of alarm and if the organism responds properly without breaking down it will reach what is called the stage of resistance, in which the adaptation to the new load is optimal and adequate. If the stresses are carried on beyond the capacity of the body, then the third stage is reached, which is called the stage of exhaustion, in which the acquired adaptation is lost. We will not be concerned with this third stage in our discussion either, because the Yogin and the Shaman build up their physical resistance to the point where they do not suffer from a breakdown, but are capable of reaching short-term periods of exhaustion from which they recover rather readily.

The body reacts to stress in a rather simple way. The pituitary gland under the pressure of nonspecific agents such as cold, tension, etc., releases a hormone known as the adrenocorticotropic hormone, abbreviated ACTH. ACTH in turn stimulates the adrenal cortex to produce a group of compounds known as steroids, which fall in two groups, mineral corticoids and glucocorticoids. The mineral corticoids are such compounds as desoxycorticosterone and electrocortin. Examples of glucocorticoids are compounds such as cortisol and cortisone. The effects of these two groups of compounds are many and complex on the body. For example, it was found that either glucocorticoids or mineral corticoids in large dosages possess the property of producing a state of great excitation followed by confusion, and if the dose is large enough followed by marked depression of all muscular and reflex activities and eventually deep anesthesia. As is well known, the corticoid compounds have now found a wide use in treating many different illnesses and diseases. But in general we can say that the preparatory stresses of the ritual of the irrational lead to markedly active production of the adrenocorticotropic hormone which leads to a strong and efficient organism.

We have suggested earlier that the state of deep trance of the Yogin was compared by the Chinese to the state of hibernation of animals. However, if we compare the physiological changes[4] that go on in hibernation with those that occur during the stage of resistance of the general adaptation syndrome in the Yogin, we find that the two states are quite unlike. For example, in hibernation the basic metabolic rate is low, whereas in the Yogin it is high. In hibernation the blood sugar is markedly reduced, whereas in the Yogin it remains normal or may be elevated. The state of hibernation shows a pronounced increase of the thymic and lymphoid tissue in the body, whereas the stage of general resistance to stress shows a marked involution or decrease of thymicolymphoid tissue. The principal similarity between the state of hibernation and the stage of resistance is that the pH of the blood is lower, that is, its acidity is increased. As is shown in Appendix D, Table I, this condition holds during the later phases of the ritual of the irrational. Therefore, although trance and hibernation may appear to an outside observer to be very much the same condition, it must be emphasized that they are, if anything, physiologically speaking, directly opposite conditions.

For the reader who is interested, I have prepared a table (Appendix D) of the general biochemical changes that occur in the body as a result of certain stresses such as cold adaptation, fasting, and exercise during the ritual of the irrational.[5] These biochemical changes give us a clue as to the effect of the body chemistry on the state of the plasma membrane. In general we can state that the biochemical shifts are all in the direction of increasing the electrical capacitance of the plasma membrane and changing its properties in the direction of slower and more powerful electrical nerve pulses.

There are some general changes that occur in the ritual of the irrational (after having reached the stage of general resistance), following exercises such as we have indicated the Yogin does.

The first change is known as metabolic acidosis and this results from excess production of certain organic acids such as acetone bodies and lactic acid; and from excess loss of base, such as sodium, from the body.

This is compounded by retention of certain acids such as the phosphates and sulphates. This condition of metabolic acidosis is generally found in adrenal cortical overactivity, starvation, and following violent exercise. The effect of acidosis on the state of the nervous system can be illustrated by its reverse condition, namely, where there is a condition of alkalosis or excess alkali in the body. This can very easily be initiated by incorrect breathing. If one takes in a very short shallow breath and quickly thereafter exhales with a long sighing breath, one has set the stage for the rather rapid production of alkalosis in the body. The alkalosis in the body is caused by blowing off excess carbon dioxide, which is the source of carbonic acid in the blood. As the carbonic-acid content drops, the acidity of the blood is lowered, resulting in a net alkalinity. The first symptoms of this are a tingling in the extremities; such tingling is due to rapid and erratic firing of the nerves in the skin at a high frequency. The next feeling is one of mental agitation, fear, often confusion. This again is the result of an erratic and high-frequency discharge of nervous impulses in the brain. If the condition persists long enough, in some cases this may be as short as a few minutes, the individual becomes unconscious. Metabolic acidosis on the other hand serves the opposite function of decreasing spontaneous firing of nerves, thereby increasing the threshold to physical stimulation, giving a slower rhythm and a feeling of calmness and relaxation.

The next factor that we have to consider is the amount of heat production during the ritual of the irrational. Heat production is usually measured under two basic concepts, the first being the basal metabolic rate, or BMR, and the calorigenic output of the body. The BMR is usually expressed as the amount of energy produced per unit of surface area of the body per hour when the subject is in the basal state (twelve hours after the last meal and after a night's sleep). This value is calculated from the amount of oxygen consumed during a fixed period. An increased calorigenic output usually refers to an increase in the heat production of the body without an accompanying increase in the basal metabolic rate (although the term calorigenic refers to an increased heat production without reference to the accompanying change in the basal metabolic rate).

We know that in general both the Yogin and the Shaman practice for long periods the ability to withstand cold and to increase the heat production of the body. The principal factor in increasing the heat production of the body is the elevated thyroid function which accompanies the stress production of ACTH. The increased calorigenic output can be attributed to the great activity of the adrenal cortex as well as the adrenal medulla, both of these organs being stimulated as a result of the pressure of stress. The function of the increased heat production by the body cannot be too clearly rationalized in the picture that we have presented. However, we must think of the increased rate of oxygen consumption as being basic to both an increased metabolic rate and an increased calorigenic output.

As is well known, consciousness is intimately dependent on the presence of oxygen in the nervous system. If the oxygen supply to the nerves or the brain is stopped for a matter of a few minutes, nerve function and consciousness are both lost; and if the oxygen deprivation is continued for a few more minutes, the nerve structure itself suffers irreparable damage. Individuals who have been subjected to prolonged oxygen deprivation may suffer a loss of mental capacity and become, from the point of view of consciousness, mere vegetables thereafter. In this light we can assume that the heat production generated (based on oxygen consumption) during the long-term and the short-term phases of the ritual of the irrational are vital elements in building up the fine structure of the plasma membrane, as well as maintaining consciousness at a very high level of awareness.

Along with the factor of increased heat production we must consider whether or not the body temperature also rises. The evidence favors a slight rise in body temperature rather than a fall in body temperature during the ritual of the irrational. It is well known that cold adaptation, exercise, and dehydration elevate the body temperature. It is also interesting to note that many individuals during febrile states, as in the Geddes case cited earlier, experienced either hallucinations or genuine telepathy, and in certain rare cases, the mobile center of consciousness.

In addition to the dependence of consciousness on the

presence of oxygen in the nervous system, the brain also requires, as its principal fuel, sugar. We have noted that fasting is an important part in all rituals of the irrational. One would assume that fasting would lead to a lowered blood sugar. The evidence, however, shows that cold adaptation and generalized increase of thyroid and adrenal functions tend to elevate the amount of sugar present in the blood. Certainly in the short-term phase of adrenergia and particularly during dancing and exercise, the blood sugar would definitely tend to rise. As in the case of oxygen, lowering of the blood sugar definitely leads to a decrease of mental control and will power and can lead to unconsciousness. We must recognize the necessity of maintaining either a normal or an elevated supply of blood sugar to the brain during the ritual of the irrational.

One might assume that the slowed respiratory rhythm in the case of the Yogin and the breathing of large amounts of smoke in the case of the Shaman would result in a decrease in the oxygen supplied to the brain. The evidence is all to the contrary and there does not appear to be any factor of hypoxia, that is, lowered oxygen supply, as being a vital factor in the ritual of the irrational. All the evidence indicates that oxygen supply is maintained at a normal or even increased level.

Along with the problem of the oxygen supply to the brain we must consider the factor of carbon-dioxide supply to the central nervous system. We have earlier stated that a deficiency of carbon dioxide in the blood leads to an alkalosis of the blood. An excess of carbon dioxide is definitely developed in the blood by both the Yogin and the Shaman. In the case of the Shaman it is the result of external supplies of carbon dioxide in the form of smoke, and in the Yogin it is the holding of the breath which insures that the lungs do not lose carbon dioxide.

Carbon dioxide has another effect besides maintaining a certain level of acidity in the blood and the central nervous system. This is the effect of the pressure of carbon dioxide in the blood stream, and on the nerve cell itself.

Loomis[6] has shown that there are remarkable changes in cell function as a result of increased carbon-dioxide pressure, or as it is more formally called pCO_2. He has shown that an increase in pCO_2 will completely change the sexual nature of small organisms called hydra. When the pCO_2 is increased, the hydra changes from asexual reproduction to sexual reproduction. This is a profound biological change induced by the simple factor of carbon-dioxide pressure.

Carbon dioxide in modern psychiatry is also used therapeutically, especially in the neuroses and some of the milder psychoses. The carbon dioxide is administered as a mixture of 30% carbon dioxide and 70% oxygen. The patient breathes this mixture under slight pressure. In the average individual five to fifteen breaths of such a mixture leads to a rapid sequence of events. The first is a gasping feeling as though one cannot catch one's breath, followed immediately by rapid and deep respiration. This is accompanied by a tremendous feeling of excitement and even agitation. This is immediately followed by vivid mental hallucinations which usually take the form of precise geometrical patterns of brilliant color and of great complexity of movement. This is soon followed by unconsciousness. Meduna, who developed this technique, claims that a series of such treatments restore highly neurotic individuals to a stable, relaxed, and useful state of being. In general we can say that carbon dioxide in certain concentrations has a remarkable restorative power on the individual nerve cell,[7] and this must be looked upon in somewhat the same light as the structure-maintaining function of oxygen cited earlier.

We have seen that fasting is a fundamental practice in the ritual of the irrational. In general either prolonged fasting or even short-term severe fasting leads to what is known as a negative nitrogen balance. This is the difference between the nitrogen gained from food and that excreted in the gastro-intestinal system and the urinary system. If the output that is excreted exceeds the intake, the balance of nitrogen is said to be negative, that is, the body is losing nitrogen. On a low protein intake, starvation, or severe exertion the individual excretes nitrogen derived from the dissolution of his own protoplasm and so goes into negative nitrogen balance. The nitrogen consumed is a principal building block for amino acids and proteins. The depletion of one's amino acids and body proteins again must have a fundamental tonic and restorative effect on the structure of the plasma membrane of the nerve cell, even though we do not know the precise mechanism involved.

In general both the Shaman and the Yogin dehydrate their body before any great excursion into their unique mental or spiritual world. In order to understand the effects of dehydration we must realize that the water in the body is distributed between three compartments. These compartments are separated by membranes similar to the plasma membrane described earlier. The plasma membrane regulates fluid transport in both directions across its surface.

The first compartment is that of the tubular system of the blood stream. This is where water accumulates after oral ingestion. The water then diffuses across the blood-vessel membrane of the first compartment into the second compartment, which is essentially the fluid medium which exists between the vascular system and individual cells. The third compartment is the fluid system within each cell itself. In general the fluid tends to remain at a constant level in the intracellular or third compartment.

Initial dehydration shows up first in the blood compartment since it tends to keep the second compartment, the intercellular space, well hydrated. When dehydration proceeds still further, both the first and second compartments become dehydrated. In extreme dehydration the third compartment, that is, the intracellular fluid itself, becomes depleted.

Dehydration is accompanied by a loss of sodium chloride, and this loss of base further increases acidity. In general, when a protoplasmic system is dehydrated, we can say that the capacitance of the plasma membrane tends to be increased. This can be illustrated by a simple example. When a person is quite dehydrated, as, for example, after two or three days of abstinence from water, the body becomes so dry that it builds up a high surface charge of electricity. In this condition one can lay one's hand on a piece of paper and lift it up by simple electrostatic attraction.

As a result of stress and as a result of certain exercises we can say that the sympathetico-adrenal system is capable of meeting sudden demands in order to put out the necessary amounts of adrenergic compounds. This initially tends to increase central-nervous-system excitability by the mechanism cited earlier for the inhibitory synapses. When the concentration of adrenergic substances is further increased, the post-synaptic threshold is raised for both the inhibitory and the excitory fibers. Therefore in order to get nerve conduction across the synapses a number of mechanisms have to be altered in the plasma membrane.

The first is that the absolute value of the voltage across the plasma membrane must be increased so that it can have more energy in order to break the adrenergic barrier placed across the post-synaptic membrane. This can be most simply visualized by imagining voltage as a pressure. This is comparable to having water in a tank at an elevation exert a pressure through a pipe at a lower point; the pressure in the water pipe is in direct proportion to the height of the water tank. In the case of the inhibitory effect of adrenergia we can imagine that this exists as a water dam interposed between two nerve fibers at the synapse. As the inhibitory effect of adrenergia increases, the height of the dam increases; therefore in order for water to be able to pour over this dam from one nerve to the next the height of the water level behind the dam must be increased. This raising of the height of the water level is analogous to the increase in voltage pressure that must occur in order to overcome the synaptic barrier. And as we have shown earlier, an increase in capacitance of the nerve membrane means an increased capacity to hold more electrons. In this sense the increased capacitance is very much like increasing the height of a water reservoir, thereby gaining more voltage pressure.

In order to get this increase in voltage pressure behind a synapse we need, in addition to increased capacitance, an increase in the amount of cholinergic substance to stimulate the synapse. There appears to be some direct correlation between certain types of nervous activity and the production of cholinergic substances. For example, Richter and Crosslin[8] have shown that an animal, when at rest or asleep will produce larger amounts of acetylcholine. Conversely, the amount of acetylcholine in the brain is decreased during emotional states or in convulsions induced by electrical stimulation. The greatest increase is found during sleep and in certain states of anesthesia.

It is known that the sleep state is associated with an increased amplitude of the slow alpha rhythm. Since the Yogin tends to bring his neuronal rhythms to the 8–10 cycles per second of the alpha rhythm, it is apparent that the acetylcholine content of the brain must increase. This would then provide the necessary motive power to overcome the increased adrenergic thresholds at the synapses. It is also a fact that an increase in the potassium ion surrounding the nerve will increase the rate of acetylcholine production.[8a] The stress functions we have cited show that certain of the mineral corticoids tend to increase the loss of potassium by the body. In general we can say that the Yogin must develop processes which tend to conserve potassium ions, and lose sodium ions, although this mechanism is unknown. As we have noted earlier, an increased potassium concentration on the inside of the plasma membrane is a vital factor in maintaining the voltage potential of the nerve at a high level. It is also interesting in this connection to note that ethyl ether[8b] in small quantities markedly accelerates the production of acetylcholine.

This may throw some light on the experiences of Bob Rame cited earlier. Cholinergia, as we have said many times, now finds some rationale as being a vital factor in the regulation and control of the biological state leading to a mobile center of consciousness.

In general we can say that if the correct amounts of potassium, carbon dioxide, and acetylcholine are added to the nervous system, these definitely produce an increase in the amplitude of the wave forms, or voltage increase. However, if these agents have a prolonged action on the nervous system or are given in high doses, there is a decrease in the electrical activity of the brain, principally a decrease in frequency. These facts accord well with our hypothesis that the aim of the last portion[9] of the ritual of the irrational is to decrease the frequency of the nerve elements in the brain toward the rate of the alpha frequency, 8–10 cycles per second.[10] Having now outlined the general physiological condition necessary for the control of the plasma membrane, we turn in the next chapter to a more detailed analysis of the relationship between the plasma-membrane state, and the psi-plasma state.

NOTES Chapter 10

1. Aschheim, Emil, "Ion Adsorption and Excitation," *Science*, March 20, 1959, p. 779.

2. Frequency of an electrical oscillation:

$$v = \frac{1}{2\pi\sqrt{LC}}$$

For plasma membrane:

$$L = \quad 0.2 \text{ Henry} = MQ^{-2}L^2$$

$$C = 1 \text{ Microfarad} = M^{-1}Q^2L^{-2}T^2$$

Taking these values we find the resonant frequency of normal nerve by the above equation to be approximately 360 c.p.s.

2a. It is known that the form of the oscillation is dependent on the dielectric constant ϵ. In this circuit $\epsilon = \alpha LC$ where:

$$\alpha = \text{damping constant}$$
$$L = \text{inductance}$$
$$C = \text{capacity}$$

For large values of ϵ we get waves of the form seen from the heart and the nerves—which is called a relaxation oscillation by Van der Pol. Pender-McIlwain, *Electrical Engineers Handbook,* Wiley, 1950, pp. 7–85. For small values of ϵ the waves become sinusoidal. In general, if α decreases, the frequency increases. We know that in the Yogin the electrical waves decrease in frequency and become sinusoidal. Therefore we expect to find in his plasma membrane a general decrease in α, an increase in capacitance, with L remaining constant, or showing an increase, if there is an increase in the paramagnetism of oxygen.

Thus to get a sine wave in the Yogin we increase the capacitance to 4×10^{-4} Farads, and increase L to 1 Henry.

$$v = \frac{1}{2\pi\sqrt{LC}} = \frac{1}{2\pi\sqrt{1\text{H} \times 4 \times 10^{-4}\,\text{F}}}$$

$$= 8 \text{ cycles per second.}$$

3. Lancelot Whyte has presented us with a most lucid statement of the problem involved. Lancelot L. Whyte, "A Hypothesis Regarding the Brain Modification Underlying Memory," *Brain,* 77: 158–65, 1954.

"Most biological structures, in the course of their function, undergo cycles of electrical, chemical, and structural changes. They suffer rhythmic pulsations which display electrical, chemical, and structural aspects. We may therefore expect to find that the structural basis of memory lies in *pulsating* modifications of cortical material.

"Again, most biological structures tend to develop in the course of their function. We should therefore look for a *self-developing pulsating structure,* i.e. one which is extended or strengthened in the course of the potential cycles which it records and facilitates. . . .

"The question then arises: On this assumption *What kind of pulsating structural modification of the cortical cytoplasm, largely independent of its division into cellular units, can be produced by its pulsations so that the modification facilitates their repetition? . . .*

"The oscillations of electrical potential which constitute these pulses may be due either to the displacement of individual mobile charges or to changes in the total polarization of an extended structure considered as a unit. In either case the electrical cycles will be associated with structural cycles, the molecular structure of the protein or the arrangement of the fibrils undergoing cyclic changes. Thus in the course of the electrical cycles, the protein structures will be worked to and fro along an axis coinciding with the direction of the changing action potential. . . .

"We thus reach the following working hypothesis:

"A polarization pulse passing through a region of cortical cytoplasm in a given direction may produce a cumulative residual effect by introducing an element of long-range anisotropic ordering into previously disordered protein chains or fibrils, or by increasing an existing element of such order, of such a kind that the region thereafter responds more easily to a repetition of the same stimulus."

It can be assumed that the use of interrupted sonic stimulation sets up a polarized pulsation in the neuronal soma (a volume transmission in addition to the surface transmission) which facilitates a memory function. In addition to this effect of direct stimulation, the chemical adrenergic blockade of post-synaptic transmission would tend to conserve the energy of the cell, and thus augment the stage of self-excitatory synchronous discharge. Self-excitatory discharge of single cells can lead to a synchronous discharge of many cells on the basis of volume transmission. It is here suggested that the same process which brings about self-excitatory discharge in the neuronal cells of the temporal cortex may be responsible for augmenting the alpha activity of the neuronal cells of the occipital cortex, or whatever structure is involved. In any case, the evidence seems to point in the direction of an increased amplitude of alpha activity during the latter phases of the ritual, and it is here proposed that after the direct sonic stimulation of the temporal cortex has ceased, the alpha rhythm (of the occipital cortex?) takes over the task of maintaining the pulsed polarization of the self-excitatory activity of the temporal cortex soma. This is an effect which goes on in addition to the self-excitatory activity and the two become synchronized. W. Grey Walter has made an interesting analysis of such an activity of the alpha wave from his studies of the effects of intermittent photic stimulation: W. Grey Walter, *The Living Brain,* W. W. Norton & Co., New York, 1953, pp. 106–9.

"Considering now these hallucinations in their simplest manifestation, how does it happen that the precise repetition of a flash, making a field of light on the retina without pattern in it, is seen as a moving pattern? The light is stationary; the eyes are shut and do not move; the head and the brain are still. Yet something must move to produce moving patterns. . . .

"The imaginary patterns provoked by flicker in conjunction with alpha rhythms are produced in the brain. Their movement is the movement of some hitherto unsuspected mechanism of the brain. What is this mechanism?

"Put in this attenuated form, and given the proviso that the required mechanism has to be contained in the human head, a communications engineer would jump to the only conclusion which would seem possible to him; A scanning mechanism. . . .

"There is much to be said for the hypothesis. It is necessary to assume some mechanical principle which could be incorporated in apparatus compact enough to be carried about in the head, and no other principle of this character is known. Also, both equations are satisfied by $x =$ scanning mechanism."

If we follow his process to its logical conclusion in the case of the self-excited temporal soma rhythm in synchrony with the alpha rhythm, we must conclude that there is produced an "image" that is motionless and without content—a *tabula rasa.* This is curiously like the stage of "abstraction" that the Yogin seeks to attain, and which Wiener has described as being associated with an almost perfect rhythmicity of the alpha rhythm. This is the cognitive mechanism of the Yogin's mind endlessly scanning for nonsensory data to be recorded in memory.

4. Morgan & Stellar, *Physiological Psychology,* 2nd Ed., McGraw-Hill, New York, 1950, p. 407.

5. Because it is known that the Shaman and Yogin undergo the long-term stress of cold adaptation and fasting and short-term stresses of maximal intensity (dancing or breathing), we can extrapolate from classical physiological investigations in each of these fields and in a rough way deduce the possible major biochemical shifts that may occur in a "model" candidate. These shifts are summarized in Table I (see Appendix D).

6. Loomis, W. F., "Sexual Differentiation in Hydra," *Science*, October 18, 1957, pp. 735–38.

7. The physiological changes induced by the administration of carbon dioxide have been ably analyzed by Gellhorn, and the following sections are quoted from his book, *Physiological Foundations of Neurology and Psychiatry,* University of Minnesota Press, Minneapolis, 1953, Chap. 19, p. 450 ff.

"The action of carbon dioxide on the cortex of the brain has been studied in man through the use of sensory tests. Thus it was found that visual functions decline reversibly in hypercapnea. This is indicated by the increase in the threshold for the discrimination of brightness and by the lengthening of the latent period of the negative afterimages. The effect occurs a few minutes after the inhalation of carbon dioxide in concentrations of 5–7%. Similarly the threshold for hearing rises under these conditions.

"It is well known that carbon dioxide increases the frequency and decreases the amplitude of cortical potentials as noted in the human EEG and direct recordings from the cortex of animals. This phenomenon is similar to the changes in the EEG seen during mental activity or sensory stimulation and appears to be primarily due to an excitation which results in a *decreased synchrony* of cortical potentials.

"Cortical excitability depends on at least two systems, the long efferent tracts, which send impulses to the specific projection areas, and the hypothalamus, which through its 'upward discharge' influences the cerebral cortex as a whole. The experiments already discussed, and the following observations show that these two systems are influenced by carbon dioxide in opposite ways. . . .

"1. The increase in frequency of cortical strychnine spikes occurring during the inhalation of 10% carbon dioxide is due to subcortical discharges.

"2. If subcortical discharges are eliminated, the effect of carbon dioxide on the cortex results solely in a decrease in excitability.

"3. Subcortical discharges account for the increased responsiveness in hypercapnea of the cerebral mantle to nociceptive and proprioceptive excitation."

The subcortical discharge responsible for these phenomena originate in the posterior hypothalamus, since lesions in this area abolish increased spike frequency to carbon dioxide and reduce or eliminate the generalized excitation of the cortex following nociceptive stimulation.

Two facts stand out from these investigations. First carbon dioxide has at least two points of attack in its action on the brain; it diminishes (in concentrations of 10–15%) cortical excitability, as indicated by the reduced responsiveness of sensory projection areas to specific afferent impulses and of the motor cortex to electrical stimulation, and it increases the discharges and reactivity of the hypothalamic-cortical system. This differential action of carbon dioxide is retained in anesthetic concentrations which eliminate spontaneous hypothalamic and cortical potentials, whereas the responsiveness of specific projection areas persists in a somewhat reduced degree.

Second, this work confirms, on the basis of different experimental procedures, the conclusions arrived at earlier: 1) That awareness is abolished when the hypothalamic-cortical system is anatomically or functionally eliminated. 2) That perception, which is absent in high carbon-dioxide as well as in barbiturate anesthesia, is only possible if afferent discharges to the cortex persist from peripheral receptors and from the hypothalamus.

Meduna, *op. cit.*, p. 14, describes the effect of CO_2 on a single nerve:

1 Raises threshold of stimulation (5% CO_2) and increases membrane potential (inc. membrane potential 5.3–6.6 MV)
2 Decreases speed of condition of impulses
3 Increases height and duration of action potential
4 Increases resistance to fatigue—CO_2 increases ability to perform work.

8. Elliott, K. A. C., Page, Irvine H., and Quastel, J. H., Eds., *Neurochemistry*, Charles C Thomas, Springfield, Ill., 1955, p. 155.

8a. *Ibid.*, p. 158.

8b. *Ibid.*, p. 161.

9. The abrupt termination of the Shaman's carefully built-up intense excitement just as he reaches "ecstasy" by a stage of "exhaustion," and the Yogin's transition to peace and relaxation, presents us with the greatest of paradoxes. This is not too unlike

the process following the climax of erotic excitement, and was probably the end-point of the Bacchanalian ritual in Ancient Greece. In the ritual of the irrational we will attempt to show that it is the commencement of the release of a "mobile center of consciousness."

Up to the point in the ritual that Shirokogoroff has called ecstasy the techniques used by the Shaman produce two different conditions which are not only mutually antagonistic but serve to build up an excruciating psychological tension. The first includes those techniques which activate adrenergic processes which would normally result in an epileptic seizure. The second includes techniques which activate cholinergic processes that normally serve to protect against an epileptic seizure. The epileptogenic techniques are aimed at what might be called a localized temporal-lobe activation. It can be seen from Table I

TABLE I

List of physiological changes in the brain which may influence (epileptic) seizures. (After Lennox and Cobb, from Best and Taylor, page 1037.)

	CONDITIONS WHICH MAY TEND TO:	
	Prevent Seizure	*Precipitate Seizures*
Oxygen	Rich Supply	Poor Supply
Acid-Base Equilibrium	Acidosis by means of fasting, fat diet Ingestion of acids or acid-forming salts Breathing high carbon dioxide	Alkalosis by means of ingestion of alkali Hypercapnea— "blowing off" carbon dioxide
Chemical Constituents	Low Chloride(?) High Calcium	High Chloride(?) Low Calcium (tetany)
Water Balance	Dehydration	Edema
Intracranial Pressure	Decreased	Increased
Intracranial Circulation	Unimpaired	Impaired

(Lennox and Cobb) that those physiological changes which prevent epileptic seizures are by far and large predominant in the Shaman according to the analysis herein presented.

On the other hand, the general intense excitement, interrupted auditory stimulation, camphor and nicotine are specific provocative agents that would normally precipitate seizures. One is assured by Shirokogoroff that if the Shaman goes into a seizure, or if he gets drunk, the performance fails, i.e., he does not achieve his purpose (contact with the spirits). What then is the resolution of this physiological and psychological complex that now teeters on the razor's edge between an epileptic seizure and the coma of drunkenness or unconsciousness?

First, it will be assumed that it is possible for the Shaman to induce in himself a localized electrical activation of the temporal lobes. That such a mechanism is possible can be seen in the following experimental evidence from Penfield:

"Electrical after-discharge may remain a local process, primarily involving those neurones in the immediate vicinity of the stimulating electrodes. Impulses are conducted from these neurones to bombard other neuronal groups connected to this area by projecting pathways. This may cause the neurones in the projection area to fire with each volley of discharges from the area stimulated, and to cease firing the instant they are no longer driven by the focus of after-discharge. If the process stops here, distant effects of a local after-discharge do not represent, strictly speaking, a *spread of epileptic* process, but simply a projection of its effects over directly connected anatomical pathways." (Penfield and Jasper, *op. cit.,* p. 202 *et seq.*)

The localized electrical activation of the temporal lobe occurs through a complex process. At the height of ecstasy, there is a maximal stimulation of the ascending reticular activating system (kinesthetic activity) in synchrony with the drum tempo resulting in a maximal stimulation of the auditory cortex and the temporal cortex. This phase corresponds to the period of "stimulatory" action of the alcohol and the nicotine. Then the period of exhaustion sets in whose dynamics can best be understood by a consideration of the phenomenon of Electrical After-Discharge, and I again quote (Penfield and Jasper, *op. cit.,* p. 200):

"A relatively intense repetitive electrical stimulus applied to a local cortical area for a few seconds is followed by a sustained local after-discharge which simulates in almost every respect the type of local discharge which occurs at the onset of a *focal corti-*

cal seizure in an epileptic patient. The chief difference is, of course, that in the patient the electrical stimulus and electrode are missing, and we are not sure what takes place.

"The electroencephalographic pattern of the local cortical seizure which follows electrical stimulation may be divided into five stages:

1 Asynchronous activation.
2 Synchronous rhythmic discharge.
3 Interrupted 'clonic' discharge.
4 Exhaustion.
5 Recovery."

In the light of these experimental facts we attempt to resolve the paradox of the stage of exhaustion. A model of the scheme of transformation is outlined in the following table.

According to the analysis presented in the scheme below, exhaustion must be considered primarily as a cessation of ganglionic and synaptic transmission which results from the combined inhibitory effect of adrenaline, and the paralyzing effect of alcohol and nicotine. The pattern of the ganglionic and synaptic inhibition is so widespead that only the basal brain respiratory and cardiac rhythms go on.

The role of the camphor can now be better understood. It is known to be a respiratory stimulant and a cardiac stimulant, and it is furthermore postulated here that it may act as a direct stimulant to soma (cell body and dendrites) cells of the temporal cortex. The postulated inhibition of the subcortical centers (ARAS and Posterior Hypothalamus) may be complete or partial, but in any case it seems logical to assume that their effect on the temporal cortex is removed, thus leaving "islands" of chemically blockaded temporal-cortex cells carrying on a self-sustained repetitive synchronous discharge. It is this latter phenomenon that the author believes is associated with the doubling of consciousness so often reported in cases of epilepsy, in clinical psychiatry, and in the ritual of the irrational. The pathological manifestations must be distinguished from the more rare phenomenon of a mobile center of consciousness.

The suggested role of camphor is put forward as an hypothesis; like all pharmacological agents such an effect would depend on the dose used. Since the convulsant action of camphor is believed to be chiefly above the optic thalami (Soll., p. 209), and since

TABLE II

Penfield's Model of "AFTER-DISCHARGE"	Stage of the Ritual	Events in the Temporal Cortex
1. Stimulation	1. Ecstasy. "Stimu-tion" phase of alcohol and nicotine. Adrenergia.	1. Maximum "epileptiform" activation of the temporal cortex by subcortical and sonic stimuli with the drum (6–14/sec.) as the pacemaker.
2. Asynchronous Activation	2. Exhaustion. "Paralyzing" phase of alcohol and nicotine.	2. Subcortical (ARAS) inhibition, and synaptic inhibition of the cortex, particularly temporal cortex. Synaptic transmission blocked by adrenergic* effect of alcohol and nicotine.
3. Synchronous Rhythmic Discharge	3. Light Sleep. Doubling of Consciousness? $\downarrow$ Mobile center of consciousness. Cholinergia.	3. Self-sustained repetitive synchronous discharge of chemically isolated temporal cortex.
4. Clonic Stage		4. Gradual slowing of the above synchrony (8–10 c.p.s.?).
5. Extinction	5. Nonarousal state of Shaman. Danger of death.	5. Cessation of temporal cortex after-discharge activity.
6. Recovery	6. Arousal of Shaman. Memory of experiences recounted.	6. Return to normal cerebral physiology.

* Inhibitory.

the direct application of powdered camphor to the exposed cortex results in generalized epileptic seizures (Soll., p. 210) we can look to a cortical level for the site of action. Because camphor and other terpenes when stimulating olfaction also have a powerful effect (as do most odoriferous substances) on activating memory, and since current thinking (see Whyte, *op. cit.*) looks to cortical cytoplasm as being associated with the memory function, I believe that there is some justification for this hypothesis.

10. The place of light sleep in the ritual of the irrational has already been touched upon in Table II. It only remains to elucidate the possible mechanism whereby it fortifies the stage of synchronous rhythmic discharge of the temporal cortex. The role of light sleep in this process must be considered as two-fold: 1) It serves to activate the after-discharge of the temporal cortex; 2) It imposes a definite rhythm on the temporal cortical discharge.

Natural sleep is the result of diminished activity of the posterior hypothalamic center of wakefulness, probably induced by increased discharges from the anterior hypothalamic sleep center. Diminished "downward discharges" of extrapyramidal origin lessen the muscle tone and thereby reduce the feedback to the waking center. The diminution of sympathetic "downward discharges" from the lateral hypothalamic area and the mammillary bodies leads to a shift in the autonomic balance maintained by the hypothalamus and the medulla oblongata. Patterns of parasympathetic innervation become more prominent, as indicated by the narrowing of the pupils. The disappearance in the early phases of sleep of sympathetic impulses of cortical origin may also contribute to the alteration in the autonomic equilibrium.

The electrical activity of the brain during progressing consciousness from deep sleep to the alert stage can be illustrated in groupings as part of a spectrum as follows:

1 Deep sleep: Predominance of slow waves of high voltage with a focus anterior to the vertex, above area 6, and another above area 9 (Brazier, 1949).

2 Light sleep: Slow rhythms of a smaller voltage, intermingled with short spindles—14 c.p.s. in the anterior and central regions of the brain.

3 Drowsiness (somnolence): Scarce slow waves interfering with alpha rhythm of low voltage.

4   Alert state: Great variety of high-frequency components,
    slight tendency to steady rhythm (alpha), and great de-
    pendence on afferent stimuli.

"If we follow a drowsy (somnolent) subject further along the
path to oblivion—slow irregular waves appear, and with them,
from time to time, bursts of smaller, faster, spindly waves with
a frequency of about 14 c.p.s. The subject is now asleep (light)
and if we waken him suddenly will start and look confused; he
may deny that he was sleeping, or he may say that he has just
had a dream. There is some evidence that the 14 c.p.s. spindle
rhythms are associated with dreams, but this is hard to prove:"
W. Grey Walter, *The Living Brain, op. cit.*, p. 241.

Experimental evidence has established the fact that light sleep
can have a provocative effect on seizures in the temporal cortex.
In the Shaman and Yogin this may well serve as a natural method
of sustaining the postulated synchronous rhythmic discharge of
the temporal cortex. The association of the 14 c.p.s. rhythm
(spindle) found in light sleep with dreams is intriguing in this
connection. In the light of the previously stated evidence for the
possibility that the Shaman's adrenergic state may increase the
normal alpha frequency (8–14 c.p.s.) it would be interesting to
know whether the alpha frequency matches the 14 c.p.s. "dream"
spindles thus leading to a hypersynchrony with the pacemaker
of the temporal cortex after-discharge. The hypothesis is offered
that in this stage of the ritual of the irrational a mobile center of
consciousness may appear. This hypothesis can be tested by a
correlation between ESP test results, the experience of an MCC,
and the electrical activity of the brain. (See Appendix C.)

11

The Physical
Foundations of
Psi Plasma

I have used the word *plasma* in its original Greek sense of "form." The noun comes from a Greek root, from which we get our word *plastic*. The word *plasma* is used in many different connotations. For example, we speak of the primary substance of biological life as being protoplasm, sometimes this is differentiated into the word *endoplasm*. In the field of psychical research we run across the word *ectoplasm*. Here it is used to describe a substance which can be seen, felt, and often has an odor that exudes from mediumistic individuals during the condition of trance. In physics the word *plasma* is used to describe a collection of electrons and ions which are formed into a shape by magnetic fields and are able to maintain that identity.

There are other uses to which the word *plasma* has been put, but I merely wish to indicate that *plasma* as I use it, as descriptive of one of the states of mind, does not stem from any of these usages. My usage stems from the observed fact that the individual experiencing a mobile center of consciousness feels directly, and often observes his *form* as being that of the normal human body. When individuals see an apparition they also see it in the form of the human body. These facts have one thing in common, whether looked at subjectively or objectively, there is form.

This is perhaps the only level at which we have any idea as to the nature of the psi plasma.

If we seek for the unit psi plasma we run into difficulties. We can conjecture that psi plasma in some unit form begins with the simplest atomic structure—hydrogen; or that it awaits the appearance of life itself, that is, at the single-cell germ plasma stage of biological existence. It will be more instructive, however, to examine some of the known or the conjectured properties and dynamics of psi plasma before we begin any attempt at seeking to define the basic unit of psi plasma.

We have seen that a mobile center of consciousness as a nuclear mental entity has all the characteristics that we ascribe to mind. These include perception, feeling, association, reasoning, memory, and even the creation of ideas.[1] When human consciousness is firmly rooted in its own body, we know, each of us from personal experience, that mind has these same characteristics. Therefore it would be most profitable to begin our inquiry by trying to understand the interaction of our own mind with our own physical body.

It is apparent our sensations of the physical world come through our special sense organs. These receive physical energy from our surroundings, and are converted into a code form by the nervous system which consists essentially of pulses of electricity, or electrons in motion. The pulses of electricity travel along the nerve plasma-membrane channels to the appropriate receiving cell or group of cells in the brain. The result is a conscious sensation of something that exists outside of us.

There may be other channels by which we receive signals from the outer world, but these are not known at the present time.

In order to better understand the problem, let us consider the transaction that goes on in a simple sensation such as vision. It is known that it requires a certain minimal amount of energy from a light source to get minimal sensation of light. It takes about one hundred to one hundred and fifty photons of blue-green light hitting the surface of the eyeball to get the minimal sensation of light. However, the one hundred to one hundred and fifty photons are absorbed to a large extent in their passage through the protoplasm of the eye. It has been calculated that approximately six to eight photons actually hit the receptor elements in the retina to give the minimal sensation of light.[2] Now each of these six to eight photons is apparently absorbed by an individual receptor cell in the retina. Proceeding from each receptor cell (in this case rods) is a single thin filament of a nerve fiber. Multiple fine filaments shortly branch together into a single nerve fiber. We can state that one photon striking one receptor cell liberates one electron from the fine nerve filament. This one electron is probably an orbital photoelectron of the element potassium contained in the plasma membrane. This displaced single electron is sufficient to start nerve conduction along the fine filament. However, since it is known that it takes six to eight such liberated electrons to give rise to a sensation, it has to be concluded that the six to eight electrons liberated in the fine nerve filaments summate in one nerve fiber to stimulate the optic nerve proper which leads to the occipital portion of the brain. Here the mind perceives the sensation of one pinpoint of blue-green light. If we examine the other sensory receptive systems that have been studied closely we find that in general they require energy of the order 10^{-11} ergs to stimulate the minimal sensation. The nervous system and the receptor organs are stable for energies below 10^{-11} ergs; and conversely any energy that exceeds this critical limit will excite a sensation.

Now we must ask, what does this mean? We can say that this amount of energy is required to open the door of the senses. We have to distinguish two factors here. The first is that the barrier between the physical world and the mind consists of six to eight electrons, or about 18 electron volts. This is the strength of the wall that keeps out the sights and sounds of the world around us. It represents less energy than that given off by a single hair tickling the skin. The second factor is that less energy than this— 1 electron or about 2.5 electron volts—can influence the nervous system; but multiple such weak energies have to combine to give rise to a sensation. The role of such single-electron effects in our mind and sensations is not too well known, and may be responsible for subliminal perception, i.e., where a weak sensation actually registers on the mind, but we are not aware of it.

But then we must ask, if all the energy is used to open the door, what energy is left to pass through the door? Fortunately this question is not as difficult as it appears. It is a fact that the nervous system at rest is actually in a state of potential energy, and this consists of an electrical potential, as already described, across the plasma membrane of the nerve. Therefore the opening of the sensory door is like tripping a bucket of water standing above the door, releasing potential energy. But if only potential energy from the nervous system is released, how can this show any correspondence to the original exciting energy in the world outside of our skin?

In other words, what is the relation between the electronic neural events and the object of our sensation?

In order to evaluate this problem we have to take up an elementary concept of physics, namely, the idea of group waves. The fundamental relativistic postulate states that no material particle can exceed the velocity of light. Accompanying every motion of a physical particle or wave, there is believed to be another wave which has been called the pilot wave.[3] The velocity of the physical particle or wave is usually denoted by the letter v, and the pilot-wave velocity is usually denoted by u. The product of v and u is always equal to the velocity of light squared, c^2: or, $vu = c^2$. We will consider the velocity of the nerve impulse as a group wave associated with the velocity of the electron, which we will call v. The pilot wave, u, whose velocity is always greater than the velocity of light, c, we shall equate with the psi plasma and the mind. This leads to our first postulate: The velocity of psi plasma is always greater than the velocity of light.

A consequence of this postulate is that we would expect under the conditions of normal consciousness to find the pilot-wave velocity, u, approximately equal to the velocity of light but always slightly greater than it. A further consequence would be that the stronger the coupling between the pilot-wave (psi-plasma fields) and the physical fields of the body—the condition of normal awareness—the more equal would we expect to find the velocities of v and u. We can calculate these velocities from the normal conduction velocity of nerves (which is approximately 120 meters per second). This shows that with this speed of propagation of the nerve impulse the velocity of u (mind) is slightly over that of the velocity of light.[4] However, if we calculate what happens in the advanced Yogin, we find that the induced decreased frequency of biological rhythms, and therefore the decreased velocity of the mass wave associated with the electron, namely v, leads to a marked *increase* in the value of u; the velocity of light is exceeded by a large factor.[5] If this hypothesis is correct, we begin to see some of the simple conditions underlying the ritual of the irrational which lead to the control and manipulation of the psi plasma.

The concept of group waves for material systems, and pilot waves for the psi plasma and mind, raises the problem as to the relation between these domains.

We will describe four domains of nature to encompass a hypothetical solution. We begin with the theory of Dirac[6] that the metrical physical world (material system) exists in the positive energy state. Here exist the particles and waves of physics—the electron, proton, quantum, radiation, etc. This is the first domain.

Polar to this metrical positive-energy state (Dirac originally theorized, and it was later proven), there is a negative energy state whose energy and particles are opposite to the electron, proton, etc. Here exist the positron, the antiproton, etc. This is a very queer world where everything works in reverse when compared to our common-sense notions. This is the second domain.

These two domains can be illustrated by an example from modern physics. When gamma radiation comes very close to the nucleus of an atom, it disappears as such, is annihilated. In its place there are created two particles—an electron and a positron. The electron normally exists in the metric positive energy state, and therefore continues its existence. The positron does not normally exist in the metric positive energy state and therefore its period of metric existence is very short, about a tenth of a microsecond. Dirac has stated that the positron emerges out of the negative energy state. The negative energy state is beyond measurement, but it is mathematically shown to exist. When the positron emerges from the negative energy state it leaves behind it a "hole" in this state. This hole must be filled according to the laws of nature; within a tenth of a microsecond the positron collides with another electron and goes out of metric existence to fill the hole left in the negative energy state.

When a gamma ray creates an electron and positron there is a leftover unit of energy called the neutrino. The neutrino is a unique particle. It has virtually no mass, no electric charge, but does have a spin. A neutrino, if we can compare it to the size of any other known particle, is so small that if one could hold it in one's hand and drop it, it would literally pass through the entire earth and come out the other side. It does not interact with any other particle and therefore passes through the space existing between such particles.

When the positron collided with the electron and went out of metric existence, the event was registered in a unique manner. The collision of an electron and positron means death in the metric world for the particles, but in this process they give birth to a gamma ray. These two examples of the relation between domain One and domain Two raises many problems. How does radiation (by annihilation) create particles? Why do particles in annihilation convert part of their energy into radiation? Where does the neutrino come from, and what is this chargeless ghost of energy? And where does mind enter these transactions between the positive and negative energy states?

I want to present a simple geometrical picture of these two domains, and these in turn necessitate two more domains. Let us begin with the fourth domain, which in the nineteenth century was called the aether. Let us imagine that the aether is a cosmic fluid, and we will henceforth refer to it as the plasma. In the beginning the plasma was at absolute rest. Not a ripple, current, or motion stirs in this vast body of plasma—the fourth domain.

Then, by means unknown, the plasma is set in motion. How the plasma was set in motion is not our problem here. Our problem is to define the kind of motion. I choose to go along with the nineteenth-century physicists[7] who described this motion as a vortex. This vortex of the plasma is our third domain.

Let us picture this vortical motion in the trumpet form of a whirlpool in water, or a cyclonic twister in the air. Better still, let us combine the two, and picture two straight trumpet horns placed bell to bell, or two funnels mouth to mouth. This shape is called a pseudosphere. The pseudosphere is now set spinning around the long tubular axis. Let us place a number of such pseudospheres parallel to each other, and all spinning. In order for the spin to continue we will find that only alternate pseudospheres will spin in the same direction, the ones in between will have an opposite spin. Let us consider only one set of pseudospheres—those which spin in a counterclockwise direction as we view them from above.

Since these are vortices, they pull everything into them by a powerful centripetal force. This would leave spaces between the pseudospheres and this would not be permissible. We surmise that the centripetal force is so great that the other set of pseudospheres (going clockwise) are drawn toward the first set. The nature of the vortical action and pull of the first set is such that it will break up the plasma of the second set into a group of spherical bubbles. We often see such bubbles attracted around a whirlpool. The spheres thus formed, we now find, will neatly fill up all the space between the pseudospheres.[8] The vortical spin of the pseudosphere will place these spheres into a spin whose axis is at right angles to the axis of the pseudosphere.

The space that existed around the first set of pseudospheres is most symmetrically filled by placing four spheres on the upper rim (the bell of the trumpet) and four spheres below it. (See Fig. 7, Appendix F.) We can give a name to each of the four spheres on the upper side—electron, proton, neutron, and neutrino. We imagine that the pseudosphere rotates, but that in reference to its axis the spheres spin in one place like a top. If we analyze the spin of the four spheres we find that the electron (nearest us) spins counterclockwise and has a negative charge; opposite (farthest from us) is the proton, which in reference to the electron has an opposite spin and a positive charge. Between the electron and the proton (on the right side) is the neutron, and it spins toward us and has no charge; opposite the neutron is the neutrino, and it is spinning away from us and it has no charge. These are the basic particles of the first domain, the metric domain of physics—a positive energy state.

Below these four spheres we have four opposite spheres spun by the underside of the rim of the pseudosphere. We immediately see that each of these is spinning in a direction opposite to the one above it, and therefore each will have the opposite charge. These particles are respectively the positron, antiproton, antineutron, and antineutrino. This is the negative energy state of Dirac, the second domain. (See Fig. 7, Appendix F.)

The energy of each of these particles is determined by the number of spins per second imparted by the vortical motion of the pseudosphere, which we will now call the psi plasma. Following our previous definition, we will denote the particle spin by a velocity, v; and the psi-plasma vortical velocity by u. The product of v and u is always c^2. If the spin of the particle decreases it means that the sphere has fallen lower, and farther out on the curve of the bell of the pseudosphere. Paradoxically, unlike an angular velocity on a trumpet horn, on a pseudosphere the spin will be less as the sphere goes down and out, and higher as the sphere goes up and closer to the axial center. As the sphere spin decreases it will give up its loss of energy to the psi plasma in little packets, or quanta of energy. Thus the relation between psi plasma and particle remains constant at c^2.

If the electron sphere falls too far down it will enter the spin field of the positron, and since their spin is in opposite directions, all spin will be stopped by the collision. The loss of spin converts this rotatory motion into a linear wave motion, the gamma radiation.

If the sphere ascends higher on the column of the pseudosphere, its spin increases. The gain of energy is a gain in quanta of energy from the psi plasma. Thus we see that an energy exchange between the psi plasma and the particles can occur in quantal units in the form of radiation. Whether a particle ascends or descends the column of the pseudosphere is dependent on a certain twist, or torque, that occurs in the psi plasma itself. An increased twist raises it. This twist expresses the fundamental relation between the third domain (psi plasma) and the second and first domains (negative and positive energy states). The degree of twist is usually expressed in physics by the frequency of the radiation exchange between domain Two and domain Three.

Although our model is necessarily oversimplified—and like all analogies, not exactly true—it has been presented in order to answer the problem with which this chapter began. The important point to remember is that all exchanges of energy in the physical world are governed by the psi-plasma properties. And we further postulate that the psi plasma records and in a sense remembers every such transaction.

In order to better understand the relationship of the psi-plasma field to the energy field of particles we shall have to make a further excursion into some of the elementary concepts of particles. We will consider some of the other properties of the electron which are pertinent to the general hypothesis developed.

We can best visualize the electron as a small sphere with a needle placed through the diameter, and the electron spinning on the point of the needle very much like a top. We recall that the axis of spin is at right angles to the axis of the psi-plasma vortex. The electron axis itself can be considered as a magnet with the top portion of the needle being the north pole and the bottom portion being the south pole. Therefore not only is the electron a spinning top but it is a tiny magnet.

The electron in an atom is generally pictured as having an orbit around the central nuclear mass, the simplified picture being that of a satellite whirling around the earth. The orbital velocity of the electron gives rise to a certain angular momentum, the mass of the electron multiplied by its velocity around the central nuclear core. The electron has a total angular momentum first, due to its spin; second, due to its orbital velocity; and third, due to any wobbling of the spin axis and this latter is called the precession of the electron. All of these quantities can be rather accurately measured.[9]

In addition to its properties as a magnet and those of total angular momentum the electron has a fixed electrical charge. The mass of the electron is also rather precisely known and is of the order of 9.1×10^{-28} grams. As an electron increases its linear velocity, approaching the velocity of light, its mass increases by a factor proportional to the velocity usually called the beta factor, $\beta = (v/c)$. It is curious that while the mass of the electron increases with increased velocity, its electrical charge does not change; however, its magnetism increases. The various motions of the electron in space give rise to electric and magnetic fields that radiate from the electron.

The motions of the electron give rise to many complex relationships between these various properties. One of the relationships of great interest to our inquiry is that which exists between the magnetic moment (the magnet spin properties of the electron) and its total angular momentum. A. Schuster has proposed a general equation that relates the values of these two quantities which holds as well for large planetary masses as for the particles of physics. This equation can be written as:[10]

$$G_c = c^2 \left(\frac{P}{U} \right)^2 \beta$$

This equation shows that the gravitational constant, G_c, which is a universally present weak field force, is a resultant of the proportion between P, the magnetic field moment, and U, the angular momentum (this ratio is multiplied by the velocity of light squared, or c^2). The relationship is such that the governing force between the magnetic moment and the angular momentum is the gravitational constant. According to Einstein, the gravitational constant is a tensor. A tensor is an abstract object specified by a certain set of mathematical rules which are too complicated to discuss here. We can best think of a tensor with a very crude analogy. It is known that in the training of animals, particularly horses, the trainer conveys his command to the horse by a very slight, almost imperceptible, motion of his body. The horse immediately reacts to these slight motions by carrying out a certain act for which he has been carefully trained. This same conveyance of commands by simple motions of the body also extends to a large group of horses. We can picture the trainer standing at the center of his group of horses and making a slight motion, let us say leaning forward. The horses immediately respond by a certain act, let us say rearing up their front legs. This response of the animals can be thought of as a field change dependent upon the trainer. The trainer himself, by crude analogy, can be thought of as a tensor. Therefore the essential property of the tensor is such that any change in the tensor is immediately reflected by a change in the total system around it, proportionate to the change in the tensor.

In this equation we interpret c^2 as a constant for the velocity relationship between the electron and the psi plasma. P represents the magnetic field moment of a particle, the proton, around which an electron orbits in the atom (rather than the electron itself).

U represents the energy of the electron, hv, in quantal units expressed as total angular momentum. The electron, being in oscillatory motion (as in the nerve impulse), has a period, T. Therefore, $U = hv \cdot T$.

β is an expression of the velocity of the electron as the ratio v/c. Normally $c^2 (P/U)^2 \beta$ is a constant, the gravitational constant, G_o, a tensor. The tensor expresses a constant relationship between the vortical psi plasma and the mass of the particle it governs. The critical factor which can change the value of the constant is the period, T.

We can check this equation by slightly rearranging it to show that the velocity of light is also dependent on the same relationship.[11] If we apply this equation to an electron present in the plasma membrane of the nerve we can use known and accepted values in order to compute whether or not there is a possibility of changing the value of the gravitational potential in this small volume. If we carry out such a computation, leaving c^2 and P, the magnetic moment, constant, then any change in the gravitational potential must be due to changes in the angular momentum, U.

The angular momentum as already described is the product of three distinct factors. The first is Planck's constant of angular momentum, denoted by the letter h, whose value is 6.624×10^{-27} erg seconds. The second factor is the angular velocity of the quantum around the axial center of the electron. This we can state as the number of revolutions per second (the frequency) of the "mass" of a quantum, h, under a given velocity. If we then take the product of h and the frequency, v, we have a value for the energy of the electron, that is, a potential energy. If we then multiply this energy by a time period, T, which corresponds to the duration of a single nerve pulse, we get the total angular momentum of the electron during a given time period.

If we take the standard value for h, the normal duration of a single nerve pulse at approximately 400 pulses/sec, and multiply this by the number of revolutions of a quantum (within the electron), which is 8.08×10^{19} cycles per second, we get a value for U. This result for U will give us a satisfactory numerical value for both the velocity of light, c, and the gravitational constant, G_o. If we examine the relationship between the total angular momentum and the magnetic moment a little further, we will see that within one electron the relationship between P and U will remain constant as a result of the gravitational tensor. However, if we examine the relationship between the magnetic moment of a proton in the nucleus of a potassium or oxygen atom present in the nerve plasma membrane, and an ionic electron whirling around it, we will see that it is possible to get a significant change in the value of the gravitational constant. This change in the value of the gravitational constant, we will find, is principally a function of the period or duration of the nerve impulse. It immediately follows that as the rhythm of the nerve impulse decreases, its time period increases. The normal value of 2.45×10^{-3} seconds for a nerve frequency of approximately 400 cycles per second drops to a period of 0.125 second for a frequency of 8 cycles per second. The net result of such an increase in the duration of the time period as a result of a drop in frequency will be a lowering of the force of the gravitational potential within the volume of the electron.

Since this is an extremely radical conclusion, we must further justify it. We return to a consideration of the plasma membrane to determine the changes in the electrical field value that occur under the special conditions cited in the previous chapter. This shows by simple calculation for an ordinary potassium ion in the plasma membrane that the electrical field intensity surrounding it in a small space (whose radius is approximately 11×10^{-8} centimeters) reaches a value of 150,000 volts per centimeter.[12]

We further calculate that an increase of acidity, dehydration, and dielectric constant, which occurs during the ritual of the irrational, results in a decrease in the effective thickness of the plasma membrane which can reach a value limited by the diameter of the oxygen molecule, namely 2.2 Angstrom units, or 2.2×10^{-8} centimeter. When we calculate the electric field intensity surrounding a single potassium ion under these conditions, we find that it can reach the enormous value of approximately 3.6 million volts per centimeter. This would appear to be an exaggerated value, but it is perfectly possible for electrical field intensities in small regions of space to reach such values. Electrons in such a potential field can reach velocities approaching 99% of the velocity of light, and in this case we speak of the orbital velocity, not a linear velocity. However, the proton at the center of the ionic nucleus will not be subjected to such an effect since the electric field intensity at the center is approximately zero. Therefore, we expect the magnetic moment of the proton at the center of the ionic nucleus to remain constant, and this corresponds to our value P in the Schuster equation. The angular momentum of the ionic electron will be profoundly influenced by the high electric field values in its immediate vicinity.[13] It is these high field values which primarily influence the angular velocity (expressed as orbital frequency, v) of the electron, thereby increasing its energy value according to the equation $E = hv$. When this energy value is integrated over a period, which corresponds to the rhythm of the nerve pulses, we then get the total angular momentum of the electron. The high electric fields plus the slow nerve frequency will result in a lowering of the gravitational potential in the decreased thickness of the plasma membrane of the nerve.

We know that every physical particle has a physical field surrounding it. This physical field (magnetic, electric) has a certain strength of coupling to the particle which we postulate is determined solely by the value of the gravitational constant. This physical field in turn is coupled to its isomorphic, although not necessarily identical, psi-plasma field. Therefore any lowering in the gravitational potential around the particle will also lower the coupling of the physical field to the psi-plasma field. Such decreased attraction will allow the psi-plasma field to expand. This effect is the opposite of the phenomenon of gas expansion, due to the geometry of the pseudosphere. What we have just said leads to the second postulate with respect to the relationship between the physical fields of the body and the psi-plasma field. The postulate can be briefly stated as: Psi-plasma fields are coupled to physical fields by a gravitational force governed by the value of the universal gravitational constant.

We are now in a position to analyze the problem that this chapter began with: the mystery of how an event in the physical world becomes faithfully portrayed in the human mind. Let us return to the case of visual sensation. All we have to remember is that in the object we view there is an electron that reflects light, and in our brain there is an electron that is set in motion as a result of the reflected light entering the eye. The object electron suffers sufficient elastic recoil to increase the stress or twist in its psi-plasma field resulting in contraction, and radiation of light. The contraction always sends a pilot wave, *u*, ahead of the radiation to the electron in the brain. The series of quantum changes outlined earlier for the nervous system will match those dictated by the pilot wave. The net result is a standing wave, a standing wave of psi plasma that now exists between the object electron, and the brain electron with an identity of content. The identity of content at both nodes of the standing wave is precisely regulated by the psi plasma due to the original perturbation in the object. The latter was a quantum change in the value of U resulting in a small increase in the gravitational potential causing a torsion and contraction of the psi-plasma field.

We can look at this phenomenon from the opposite point of view, namely where the light reflects from an electron on the surface of a person, enters a camera, and falls upon an emulsion. The photons striking the emulsion change the silver halide from the ionic form to the metallic form; and in the process the silver ion gains a photoelectron. The photoelectron had absorbed energy (reflected from the person being photographed) and hence it went to a higher energy level. Thus, this electron had a small increase in total spin and mass. This increase in energy is precisely reflected in the psi plasma surrounding the electron by an increase of stress or strain resulting in a small increase in the value of the gravitational constant in this small region of space. Such an increase in G_o will serve to couple more tightly the psi field to the physical field of the electron.

Now let us suppose that another individual observes the person being photographed from the same angle as the camera. He will obviously witness the same scene as did the camera. The reflected photon will likewise release an electron in one of his brain cells as just described. This electron will undergo an increase in energy level with the same effect as described for the photo emulsion with regard to the psi plasma. In short, both photo emulsion and the brain cell incurred equivalent psi-plasma field changes, and these are initiated in both instances by the frequency and quantity of light reflected from the subject. Not only does each reflected light ray set up a strain in the psi plasma in its passage, but the psi-plasma field accompanies the radiation as a pilot wave traveling at velocity in excess of the speed of light. The pilot wave will form a standing wave between point of origin and point of interaction with either the brain cell or the emulsion. Such a psi-plasma standing wave will create precisely the same quantum changes in both the emulsion and the person. If the evidence of psychometry is accepted, then these identical psi-plasma quantum states must be of a permanent or semipermanent nature by the standards of a biological life span, and their basic quality is that of memory. This is certainly true of the observer of the person being photographed.

Any energy leaving an object external to us and then exciting a sensation in us will suffer some attenuation as a result of distance. But enough of the energy usually gets through to establish a standing-wave psi-plasma field between the object and the cognitive attention process. Thus the psi-plasma field establishes an identity of content for object and percipient of the sensation. Without such an hypothesis to account for simple sensation, there could never exist public agreement on things viewed in common.

Our hypothesis stresses the remarkable fact that any exchange of physical energy between an object and the perceiving mind results in a memory record both for the seer of the object and the object itself.

NOTES   Chapter 11

1. There are two main sources of information concerning the fragments of the ritual of the irrational leading to the development of a mobile center of consciousness, and these are:

    a. A vast body of religious, literary, anthropological, and personal case-history literature.
    b. Experimental data from the field of parapsychology.

More pertinent to this discussion is the experimental data from the field of parapsychology. Prof. Hart uses the term "ESP-Projection" as an appellation for what we have chosen to call a "Mobile Center of Consciousness." Either term seems to be acceptable for the purposes of experimental method, and it is only on philosophical grounds that Prof. Hart's term shows certain advantages in usage. Prof. Hart, on behalf of The American Society for Psychical Research and the International ESP-Projection Project, has proposed a definition of this term. Such a definition is most timely and welcome, and we accept his definition for ESP-Projection as being synonymous with what we mean by a mobile center of consciousness. With due apology to Prof. Hart, we will continue to use our term in this book.

Prof. Hart offers the following formal definition (1954):[a]

"ESP-Projection is a purported phenomenon which may have two evidentially verifiable aspects. The first verifiable aspect consists in observing and operating, from a position outside the physical body of the observer-operator. . . .

"The second evidential aspect of ESP-Projection as thus defined consists in the observation of the apparition of the projectionist, perceived and independently reported by observers present at the location to which he was projected, and corresponding with his movements, appearance, costume, and so forth, as independently reported by the projectionist."

Prof. Hart presents a classification of ninety-nine evidential cases that he has analyzed into three main types, based on the experimental method used for induction:

I   ESP-Projection by means of hypnosis.
II ESP-Projection by means of concentration.
III ESP-Projection by complex methods.
    a. Modern mediums.
    b. Primitive mediums such as medicine men.
    c. Ordinary individuals using personal methods.

Prof. Hart lists eight characteristics of full-fledged ESP-Projection:

1   Detailed observations of objects and events.
2   His apparition observed by others in circumstances corresponding to events and places visited by the projectionist.
3   He was aware of being observed as an apparition, and responded to the one who observed him.
4   That he saw his own (physical) body from an outside viewpoint.

---

[a] Hornell Hart, "ESP-Projection: Spontaneous Cases and the Experimental Method," *ASPR*, 48: 121, 1954.

    5 He was aware of occupying a projected body.

    6 Projected body floated up in the air.

    7 Projected body passed through physical matter.

    8 That he was aware of traveling swiftly through the air.

Prof. Hart comes to the conclusion that Type I showed characteristic number 1 prominently, and was weak in numbers 2 to 8; Type II showed characteristic number 2 prominently, and was weak or lacking in the other seven characteristics. It is apparent that the three types of experimental method shown are all variations of the hypnotic process, i.e., auto-hypnosis, or exterohypnosis.

Björkhem[b] has found, after hypnotizing several thousand human subjects, a few exceptional cases that exhibit the phenomenon of doubling of consciousness leading to the ability to collect intelligence at a distance. This rare finding among hypnotized subjects again stresses the unique physiological, and more particularly the psychological, conditions that underlie the motivation factor.

2. We want to elucidate two facts: (a) The minimum physical energy required to yield a given sensation in a human being. (b) To localize the action of such minimal physical energy to a particular atom or molecule in a nerve cell.

The answer to (a) is given by the experimental work of Hecht, *Medical Physics*, Vol. I, Ed. by Otto Glasser, Yearbook Publishers, Chicago, Ill., 1944, p. 1659. His data shows that the minimal energy required to stimulate the sensation of light (bluegreen, wave length 5.0×10^{-5} cm.) in the human is in the range of 5 to 14 photons. Later work has reduced this range to 6–8 photons. The quantum energy acts on the photopigment (rhodopsin) of the retina, and must have enough residual kinetic energy to stimulate the fine retinal nerves to electrical conduction.

Workers in this field are in agreement that one photon is absorbed by one rod element in the retina. That it requires 6–8 photons to yield the sensation of light may appear puzzling at first. But this difficulty is resolved when we recall the anatomical arrangement of the cells in the retina. Each rod has attached to it a slender single nerve filament. This nerve filament synapses with a bipolar nerve cell (which has many dendritic branches), and each of the dendritic branches terminates in the nucleus of

[b] Björkhem, J., *Die Verborgene Kraft*, Walter Verlag, Olten und Freiburg, 1954.

the bipolar cell. Thus the bipolar cell summates the electrical impulses from many rod elements.

The energy of one photon of blue-green light is given by Planck's equation, $E = hv = 3.96 \times 10^{-12}$ ergs $= 2.47$ ev. Thus 2.47 ev. will create photon-excitation in the rod element, and in the same transaction initiate electrical conduction in the slender single nerve filament which synapses with the bipolar cell which in turn excites the optic nerve. But it requires 6–8 photons to yield the sensation of light. Thus the energy of 6–8 nerve filaments has to converge on and summate in one bipolar cell in order to give the sensation of light. This gives us the answer to (a) in two parts. The minimal energy required to excite a single nerve fiber (without the sensation of light) is one photon, or 2.47 ev. It requires 6–8 such simultaneous excitations impinging on one bipolar cell to yield the sensation of light.

Now we postulate an answer to problem (b). The initiation of electrical neural conduction requires the displacement of electrons. Neural conduction is intimately dependent on the presence of the alkali metals in the nerve-cell membrane. The alkali metal most susceptible to giving up an electron is potassium, K^{39}. It requires a minimum amount of energy to free, or eject, an electron from its orbital binding in the atom, and this is the work function, w. The work function, w, of potassium is 2.12 ev. A photon must have this minimal energy in order to eject an electron from potassium, and a greater energy than this is added to the electron as kinetic energy, T. This is given by Einstein's equation:

$$T = hv - w$$

Thus: $T = 2.47 - 2.12 = 0.35$ ev. kinetic energy, T. We postulate that one such photon will excite a single nerve-filament cell to electrical conduction by ejecting one electron from a K^{39} atom.

But it requires the excitation of 6–8 rod-element single nerve cells to stimulate the bipolar cell; or 6–8 electrons impinging on one bipolar cell to yield the sensation of light in human consciousness.

Proof of the Postulate

If the energy of the photon falls below 2.12 ev., an electron will not be ejected from a K^{39} atom. Therefore, according to our postulate, we expect to find the threshold for rod vision in the human eye at that point where the energy of the photon falls below this critical level. This critical level, or threshold, should occur where v is equal to 5.09×10^{14} c.p.s., and the wave length is 5.87×10^{-5} cm.

Experimentally, it has been found that the threshold of rod vision does indeed occur within the range 5.8 to 5.9×10^{-5} cm. This observation agrees well with the theoretical prediction of 5.87×10^{-5} cm.

However, the cones of the retina respond to wave lengths as long as 6.8×10^{-5} cm. Our difficulty is resolved when we recall that potassium when contaminated by oxygen responds to longer wave lengths than the pure metal. The curve for such contaminated potassium shows a threshold at 7.0×10^{-5} cm. See Figure 56, E. J. Bowen, *The Chemical Aspects of Light,* Oxford, 2nd Ed., 1946, for this curve.

Hence we assume that the potassium present in the cone nerve cells exists in the contaminated form. This assumption gives us fairly good agreement between experimental values for cone vision (6.8×10^{-5} cm.) and the theoretical threshold for contaminated potassium in cone nerve cells (7.0×10^{-5} cm.).

3. For a simplified explanation of group waves see: Sir Oliver Lodge, *Beyond Physics,* Greenberg, New York, 1931, pp. 115–49.

For the application of the pilot-wave concept to biology see: Gustav Stromberg, *The Soul of the Universe,* McKay, Philadelphia, 1948, 2nd Ed., p. 42 *et seq.*

4. We consider the psi plasma as a pilot-wave phenomenon; and we consider the nerve-conduction velocity as a group-wave phenomenon.

The psi-plasma velocity is denoted by u. The nerve-conduction "electron" velocity is denoted by v.

$$u = \frac{c^2}{v} \qquad \text{(the DeBroglie equation)}$$

This is written as:

$$u = \frac{hv}{m_0 v}$$

For hv we write the value of the absolute threshold of sensory stimulation (3.96×10^{-12} erg). m_0 is the rest-mass of the electron. v is the maximum velocity of nerve conduction $= 1.2 \times 10^5$ cm/sec.

$$u = \frac{hv}{m_0v} = 3.6 \times 10^{10} \text{ cm/sec.}$$

We see that u, under the most normal of physiological conditions, exceeds the velocity of light. We postulate that consciousness exists when u exceeds the velocity of light.

5. We can calculate the velocity of the psi field of the Yogin when he is in extreme cholinergia which implies: 1) His sensory threshold has been raised. 2) His nerve conduction velocity has decreased along with the decrease in frequency. 3) The plasma membrane under the high electric field intensity has become a super-dispersive medium for the propagation of waves moving faster than the speed of light.

$$u = \frac{hv}{m_0v} = \frac{4.35 \times 10^{-11} \text{ ergs}}{(9.1 \times 10^{-28} \text{ gm})(100 \text{ cm/sec})}$$

$$= 4.78 \times 10^{14} \text{ cm/sec.}$$

We conclude that the velocity of the psi field increases with the induced decrease in nerve-conduction velocity and frequency.

6. Margenau, Henry, and Lindsay, Robert Bruce, *Foundations of Physics,* Dover, New York, 1957, pp. 501–14.

7. Sir Edmund Whittaker, *History of the Theories of Aether and Electricity,* Philosophical Library, New York, 1951, Vol. I, Chap. VIII, p. 240 *et seq.*

Dirac, P. A. M., "Quantum Mechanics and the Aether," *Scientific Monthly,* March 1954, p. 142.

Stern, Alexander W., "Space, Field, and Ether in Contemporary Physics," *Science,* Nov. 7, 1952, p. 493.

8. Whittaker, *op. cit.,* p. 293.

9. Forces between the electron and proton in the ionic molecule (see Note 12, also): The ions will become highly oriented in the electrified transverse field of the plasma membrane. Let us consider the forces existing in one ion, say the $O_2{}^-$ ion, and more specifically, the relation between one proton in the nucleus and the orbital valence electron. The $O_2{}^-$ ion will be maintained in the ionic state by the high electric field forces and collisions, and may even polymerize to higher forms, such as O_3, O_4, etc. Due to the high electric field, the proton and the electron will be

oriented and show parallel spin angular momenta. However, the orbital angular momentum of the electron will increase directly as a result of the high field intensity. The oribital angular momentum vector will be perpendicular to the spin axis of the proton and the electron. We will first calculate the values for the normal state of the plasma membrane.

Frequency of the orbital angular momentum based on an electric field intensity of approximately 350,000 volts/cm.: Such a field will accelerate an electron to app. 2.07×10^{10} cm/sec., an orbital velocity. This corresponds to an increase in mass of the electron by a factor of 1.37. Thus:

$$v = \frac{m_0 v^2 \beta}{h} = \frac{(3.908 \times 10^{-7} \text{ erg})(1.37)}{h}$$

$$= 0.808 \times 10^{20} \text{ c.p.s., or quanta/sec.}$$

(h = Planck's const.)

We can check this value of the orbital angular frequency by making use of a modified form of the Schuster equation which is based on a proportionality between the angular momentum and the magnetic moment. The magnetic moment of the proton is the value used for a field of one gauss (which approximates that found on earth), $P = 1.41 \times 10^{-23}$ erg/gauss. $G_c^{\frac{1}{2}}$ is the square root of the value of the gravitational constant. The Beta factor is of the order of unity, and is based on the ratio v/c, where v is the orbital velocity of the electron. U, the angular momentum, is derived from the energy (potential) of the orbital electron, multiplied by the period of the nerve impulse. We set the period of the nerve impulse close to its normal value for a frequency of approximately 318 c.p.s. and this is equal to a period $\pi \times 10^{-3}$ sec. Schuster's equation is written as:

$$V = \beta \left(\frac{U}{P} \right) G_c^{\frac{1}{2}} \qquad (U = h v \cdot T)$$

$$= 0.69 \frac{(h)(0.808 \times 10^{20})(3.14 \times 10^{-3})}{1.41 \times 10^{-23}} (2.58 \times 10^{-4})$$

$V = 2.10 \times 10^{10}$ cm/sec.

This value checks with our previous value, and incidentally gives us a clue to the proportionality between the orbital angular momentum, U, and the proton magnetic moment, P, as applied to the problem of nerve physiology and the plasma membrane. We can now use Schuster's equation in its original form to determine the effect of changes in the proportionality between U and P on the value of the gravitational constant, G_o.

10. Normal value of the Gravitational Constant, $G_o = 6.67 \times 10^{-8}$. Schuster's equation is written as:

$$G_c = c^2 \left(\frac{P}{U}\right)^2 \beta$$

The value of U is derived from $h\nu \cdot T$, and we use the same values as in the previous example. (Note 10.)

$$G_c = c^2 \left(\frac{1.41 \times 10^{-23} \text{ erg/gauss}}{(h)(0.808 \times 10^{20})(3.14 \times 10^{-3})}\right)^2 \beta$$

$$= (8.98 \times 10^{20} \text{ cm}^2 \text{ sec}^{-2})(1.05 \times 10^{-28})(0.7)$$

$$G_o = 6.67 \times 10^{-8} \text{ gm}^{-1} \text{ cm}^3 \text{ sec}^{-2}$$

Since the value of G_c is dependent on the proportionality between P and U, and the forces between these two vectors are dependent on the direction of their axes (with the direction of P serving as the reference axis), it is apparent that G_o is a tensor force. U is critically dependent on the value of the biological frequencies. If the frequencies increase (as in adrenergia), the value of G_c will increase. If the frequencies decrease (as in cholinergia), the value of G_c will decrease.

The proportionality between P and U in the above equation appears to be governed by elastance:

$$S = \left(\frac{P}{U}T\right)^2 = M^{-1}LT^2 = \text{elastic constant}$$

where T is a period of precession, and empirically we give it the value $\pi = T$. The values for P and U are those given above.

$$S = \left(\frac{P}{U}T\right)^2 = 1.04 \times 10^{-27} M^{-1}LT^2 \text{ elastic force.}$$

P and U show a quantized elastance which is the reaction to $h/2\pi = 1.05 \times 10^{-27}$ erg sec. action, although S has a slower period than $h/2\pi$. The elasticity would appear to be a property of the psi plasma rather than that of the particle.

11. The value of G_o in relation to the frequency of the biological rhythm of the nerve cells:

We use the case of the Yogin in a state of extreme cholinergia where the biological rhythms reach the low frequency of 8 c.p.s., or a period, $T = 0.125$ sec. All the other values are left as in the last example.

$$G_c = c^2 \left(\frac{P}{U}\right)^2 \beta = 1.297 \times 10^{-11} \text{ gm}^{-1} \text{ cm}^3 \text{ sec}^{-2}$$

It is apparent that cholinergia produces a marked lowering of the nerve frequency, and a marked lowering of the value of the gravitational constant in the small region of space represented by the interionic dimension of the nerve plasma membrane. The lowering of G_o will allow the psi field to expand as a result of pseudosphere geometry. Conversely, an increase in biological rhythms as occurs in adrenergia is accompanied by an increase in the value of G_o in the plasma membrane. This will contract the psi field.

The adrenergic state is identified with the sender function in telepathy. The cholinergic state is identified with the receiver function in telepathy. The high G_o value of the sender will attract the expanded psi field of the receiver, and the two fields will merge into a common mental field as a resultant.

12. If we calculate the electric field intensity according to the method of Debye, $E_v = e/_e r^2$, there are surprisingly large voltages in the small space of the plasma membrane. The interionic electric field intensity for 11 Å is 150,000 volts per cm. If we assume that the oxygen molecule creates a limiting interionic diameter of 2.2×10^{-8} cm. between the $K+$ and the $Na+$ *during excitation,* then the electric field intensity becomes 3,600,000 volts per cm. within this small region of space.

13. The value of G_o with increased electric field intensity (T is constant):

We assume an interionic distance of $r = 2.236 \times 10^{-8}$ cm., and this is based on the effective diameter of the excited state of the oxygen molecule ($K+O_2-Na+$) in the plasma membrane. This gives an interionic electric field of intensity of 3.6×10^6 volts/cm. The rest-mass of the electron = $m_0 c^2 = 8.17 \times 10^{-7}$ erg. This corresponds to a frequency of:

$$v = \frac{m_0 c^2}{h} = 1.23 \times 10^{20} \text{ c.p.s., or quanta per sec.}$$

This corresponds to a wave length of 2.426×10^{-10} cm., which is the Compton wave length of the electron, as well as the wave length of the positron-electron annihilation radiation—an extreme value.

$$U = hv \cdot T = 2.567 \times 10^{-9} (ML^2T^{-1}) = \text{angular momentum}.$$

The Beta factor $= v/c = 0.99$. We calculate numerically, leaving the period as before, $T = 3.14 \times 10^{-3}$ sec.

$$G_o = c^2 \left(\frac{P}{U}\right)^2 \beta = 1.893 \times 10^{-8} \text{ gm}^{-1} \text{ cm}^3 \text{ sec}^{-2}$$

This shows a modest decrease in the value of G_o when the orbital velocity of the oxygen electron reaches 99% of the velocity of c. Under high electric field intensities the atom becomes a miniature cyclotron.

12

Summary of the Theory of Psi-Plasma Control

We can now present a simplified version of our concept of the relationship between the physical fields of particles and the psi-plasma field. We have pictured the electron as a spinning sphere of quanta in the positive energy state. It is surrounded by its characteristic electric and magnetic fields. In phase with the particle and its fields is a psi plasma whose relationship is that of a die to a coin; in other words, it is an envelope isomorphic to the physical field, but has the form of a pseudosphere. As the value of the gravitational constant drops at the center of the spinning mass, the attraction on its physical field is weakened. This weakening of the force of attraction upon the physical field decreases the force of attraction upon the psi-plasma field and the latter undergoes expansion. However, the more accurate picture would be that derived from the concepts of four-dimensional geometry, which more correctly describes the translation from a three-dimensional sphere to a four-dimensional pseudosphere.

In general we expect that the increased frequency of rhythms due to adrenergia of short duration, that is shock, fright, and tension, would cause a local increase for the human body value of the gravitational constant. This would correspond to the state of the telepathic sender described earlier. Under these conditions the psi-plasma field would be attracted more tightly to the physical field.

In the state of cholinergia with its decreased frequency of rhythms we expect a body decrease in the value of the gravitational constant resulting in an expansion of the psi-plasma field. If we relate the field of an individual in adrenergia to one in cholinergia, we find that there will be a difference in gravitational potential between the two points. Since the value of the gravitational constant is greater in the sender, the more weakly bound psi-plasma field of the receiver will be attracted toward the sender. Such an attraction will create a singularity in what we have called the pseudospherical psi-plasma field (for the electron) and result in an axial extension at one end which can be thought of as the tubular end (the mouthpiece end) of a long trumpet.

Diagram A shows the relationship of the physical field and the psi-plasma field in the state of normal cholinergia. Drawing B shows the condition for normal adrenergia. In drawing C we show the relationship of the psi-plasma fields during a telepathic transfer.

This drawing shows that the increased gravitational force in the sender will create a center of attraction for the psi plasma of the receiver. The axial extension of the psi plasma follows the pilot wave as well as the lines of gravitational force universally present between bodies. In essence we see that the expansion of the psi-plasma field of the receiver has brought the mental field of both the sender and the receiver into a common field, a standing wave.

From this simplified picture we would expect that any decrease in the local gravitational field potential would lead to an expansion of the psi-plasma field of an individual who has telepathic sensitivity. From this we would predict that telepathy should be increased during such periods of decreased local gravitational field potential. About the only natural condition where this would obtain is during the full moon. An experiment performed for a

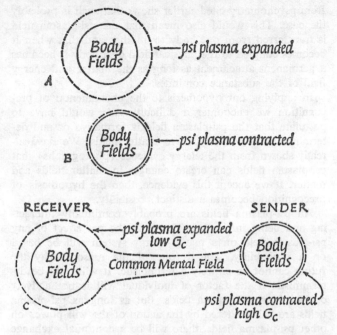

full lunar month showed, all other conditions being equal, an increase in telepathy during the full moon phase when the gravitational force is lowered. (See Appendix G.) This gives us an idea how small changes in the gravitational potential can produce large effects on telepathy. Unfortunately, no means has yet been found to artificially create changes in gravitational potential in regions of space large enough and long enough for experimental work in parapsychology.

The diagram shown earlier for the interaction of the psi-plasma fields during telepathy can also be applied to clairvoyance and psychometry. In this case the diagram shown for the sender would correspond to the psi-plasma field surrounding an object. This of course assumes that all material bodies have a psi-plasma field, and the evidence from psychometry cited earlier shows that such is probably the case. This would also mean that the psi-plasma field is transferred from one body to another and that when it becomes coupled to the physical field of a body it becomes a permanent attachment as long as the matter and energy field of the substance continues.

In applying our hypothesis to the phenomenon of precognition we encounter a difficulty. We would have to postulate that the psi-plasma field is formative of and determines what will happen to matter fields. We have already shown from the telergy evidence (photographs) that psi-plasma fields can create changes in matter fields and matter. If we accept this evidence, then the hypothesis of precognition becomes a distinct possibility.

All psi-plasma fields are probably continually interacting and being influenced. Therefore the net effect of any psi-plasma field on a matter-energy system will be based on a probability. This is one of the reasons why the future cannot be entirely deterministic. It will only be deterministic if the factor of individual will is not actively operative on psi-plasma fields. But as long as psi-plasma fields are being altered by the action of the will power on other psi-plasma fields, there will be a continual exchange between the various fields.

Some people have the notion that events are predetermined, and others believe that a large element of freewill exists in man. If we take a culture which is principally a passive one, where the exertion of will power is not a prominent feature of the way of life, these people will find more evidence for determinism in their lives. This is because they are passive to the psi-plasma field around them and do not by personal intervention upset the equilibrium.

On the other hand, if we take a culture where will power is a predominant feature of individual action, as for example in the long succession of Aryan cultures, we see that the psi-plasma fields are continually being influenced and changed by personal will. Such a culture will find less evidence for determinism in their affairs than will the passive culture.

It is implicit to our concept that since the psi-plasma field is a governing factor in the nature of energy and matter fields, and since the psi-plasma field is the a priori field, there must be a basic element of determinism behind the operation of our personal psi-plasma field. The net effect will be that there is an over-all determinism, but each individual has a small vote that can exert its small quantum of mental action on the over-all psi-plasma field. If the majority of individuals will, think, and exert telergic effects on their psi-plasma field, it would appear that they can determine the over-all probability of the outcome of any given event.

The reason I have earlier gone into the process of pair production and the annihilation of pairs is that a concept of empty holes in the plasma is necessary if we are going to follow through on the observation that a nuclear psi entity can exist outside of the physical body. In the physical body the particles making up that state must of course thoroughly fill the spaces between the vortices of the psi plasma. At first glance we cannot conceive of the psi plasma existing without its spherical cells being filled with particles. However, we see in the phenomenon of pair production that such holes do exist in plasma, however briefly in time. Therefore we can proceed from this knowledge to the hypothesis that the nuclear psi plasma can exist for certain periods outside of the physical body, that is, without containing any particles in it.

Assuming that the nuclear psi entity is some such vortical cellular structure and that its properties are those of mind, then we must face the next question and ask how long can a nuclear psi entity continue before particles fill its vortices? The only reasonable analogy we have from physics comes from the phenomenon of radioactive decay, or half-life of the elements. Just as individual elements disappear by radioactive disintegration to the extent of one-half of their mass within a given period for each element, so must we consider the opposite possibility, namely that empty holes in the psi plasma have a positive half-life of their own with respect to being filled.

This would mean that a nuclear psi entity minus a physical body could exist for a finite period of time in this empty state and then have its vortical cells filled by physical particles. This brings us to the question of the time of union of the nuclear psi-entity vacuosities and physical particles; namely the process of conception. As far as biology knows, in order to have conception we must have a germ-plasm cell from the male, the spermatozoa, and a germ-plasm cell from the female, the ovum. If the complex molecules of the germ plasm are simply the coin struck from the die of the nuclear psi plasma, then we can expect the nuclear psi plasma to have a form comparable to some part of the fertilized ovum or of the entire fertilized ovum. The question is whether the nuclear psi entity is always present in the never-dying germ plasm, or whether it enters *de novo* at the time of conception. There is no easy answer to this question

An equally difficult question is the one of biological death. If we are to accept the evidence of apparitions, we must assume that the nuclear psi entity does indeed part with the physical body at the moment called death. If we accept this hypothesis as holding for death, it would be just as easy to accept the hypothesis that at some moment in the process of conception the holes in the nuclear psi entity can be filled by the fertilized germ plasm.

This would mean that if life begins before the time of conception, and by that I invoke not only physical life, but I mean the life of a mind and soul, then we must assign a much more complex structure to the nuclear psi entity than the simple little double-trumpet surface we have pictured for elementary particles. Whatever the true case may be, it is safest for us to anticipate that the form or forms assumed by the nuclear psi entity are much more complex than that which we have envisioned for the elementary particles. The forms may be as complex as those which we encounter in the physical world of crystals, the network of cells present in the brains of the higher organisms, or even the totality of our most complex ideas in art, religion, and science.

Epilogue
A Test of the Theory

In order to test the validity of the theory there are certain experiments which could be carried out. We are testing the hypothesis that the expansion or the contraction of the psi-plasma field is a function of the value of the gravitational field potential.

Many preparatory experiments will have to be carried out before a definitive experiment is conducted. These will begin by gathering in a laboratory a number of individuals who will dedicate themselves to a long-term project. They will be individuals who have shown various degrees of psychic talent, that is, telepathy, clairvoyance, psychometry, telergy, and the ability to bring on the state of a mobile center of consciousness.

Each of these individuals would be subjected to various biological procedures whose purpose is to induce the proper type of stress-conditioning leading to an increase in the power of their psychic talent. We have indicated, particularly in the case of the Shaman and the Yogin, the general form which these techniques should take.

The individual whose general acuity has been increased by reaching a stage of general resistance would then be subjected to short-term physical, chemical, and psychological techniques whose purpose it is to slow down biological rhythms in conjunction with control over such slowing down. Such experiments should be able to duplicate, on a short-term basis, what the Yogin attempts to achieve over a long-term period of training.

An auxiliary group of experiments would have to be conducted to create the optimal environmental conditions around the subject. The purpose of these experiments is to cut down body-noise levels, atmosphere-noise levels, and if possible to decrease local gravitational field potentials.

The effectiveness of these multiplex techniques would always have to be measured against something. It is proposed that the simplest measuring technique would involve the use of a standard instrument which would consist of photographic emulsions carefully prepared for the purposes of the study. The photographic emulsion can be used as an index of telepathic and psychometric ability and telergic power. The choice of the measuring instrument for psychic powers is extremely important. In my opinion the photographic emulsion is an ideal instrument because its quantum mechanical properties can be accurately measured for changes resulting from the dynamics of psi plasma. The critical element in the photographic emulsion is, of course, the silver-halide crystal. There are a number of highly refined techniques in modern physics which would make the measurement of small quantum changes possible.

The five steps outlined above represent an enormous array of complex biological, physical, and psychological instruments and techniques. These could all be properly grouped under the heading of biophysics, if this term includes parapsychology as well. The entire purpose of collecting such subjects, techniques, and sciences would be to create controlled conditions both for the human beings involved and for the measuring instruments. Assuming that all these could be assembled and that successful solutions could be found for each phase, we would then be in a position to set up some critical experiments.

We would first want to test the proposition that psi plasma is attracted toward areas of increased gravitational field potential. This could best be done by placing our measuring instrument, the photographic emulsion for telergy experiments, in regions of high gravitational force. This could be done by placing the film in a centrifuge. Assuming that the telergist has reached a stage of maximum psi-plasma expansion, one would predict that the telergic effect on the film would increase as the gravational force was increased upon the emulsion.

Another experiment that shows promise would be an elevator experiment. We place the receiver and the sender, in the telepathy experiment, in two separate elevators in a tall building. The receiver, in the elevator which is going down, would be in the free-fall state, and, with respect to the elevator, floating. The sender on the other hand would be going up in a rapidly accelerating elevator and the gravitational force would increase on his body. If the accelerations of the two elevators are high enough, and the differential velocity is large enough, we would expect to find a marked increase in telepathic test scores under these conditions. Conversely, if we reverse the positions of the sender and the receiver with regard to the direction of their velocity, we would expect to get a decrease in telepathy scores.

This experiment can be further refined if we placed telepathic senders in the field of high "*G*" forces such as are found in a centrifuge. We place the sender in a large centrifuge, and it would be so arranged that, as he rotated, the visual field around him would rotate synchronously; so that it would appear to him, as far as his visual frame of reference is concerned, that he was not rotating. Once a constant velocity had been reached it would minimize the effect of vestibular disturbance (dizziness) upon him.

The same experiment could be carried out in the case of the telepathic receiver, by a technique proposed by H. J. Muller.[1] The receiver would be placed in a system

horizontally rotating very much like an object rotating on
a spit. If he was whirled around fast enough and the velocity was constant and his visual environment rotated
synchronously with him, a certain approximation to
a gravity-free condition could be obtained. In this case
the decrease in gravitational field potential would presumably increase expansion in the psi-plasma field and
once he got accustomed to this unusual environment we
expect that his powers of telepathy would increase.

There is another gravity-free condition of relatively short
duration which could be used in this experiment. It is well
known that in the ascending parabolic path of an aircraft
moving with respect to the earth there is an arc in the top
of the curve, lasting about thirty to sixty seconds, which
is gravity-free. Many experiments have been conducted by
the U. S. Air Force under such zero-gravity conditions.
The zero-gravity state occurs when the gravitational pull
of the earth is balanced by the forces caused by the parabolic path of the plane. In this condition one experiences
a sense of weightlessness, and the individual floats in the
air with respect to the plane enclosure around him. The
limiting factor with this technique is the short duration
allowed for the performance of any experiment. Since
we must deal with the probability outcome of events in
ESP experiments requiring much repetition, this would
not be long enough.

Perhaps the most critical experiment could be performed when man is capable of sending manned vehicles
into outer space. In outer space we would find conditions
where gravity-free conditions could be maintained for
prolonged periods. For example, in the region of space
between the earth and the moon we would find a null
gravitational point where the respective attractions of the
moon and the earth would be approximately equal. An
outer space laboratory would be an ideal platform from
which to conduct telepathy experiments toward earth.
In this case the receiver would be in the space platform,
and the sender on earth would be subjected to high

gravitational-force conditions. Under these circumstances we would expect to find the most remarkable increase in telepathic interaction.

It is a long-standing legend that Yogins in the state of samadhi are capable of physically floating off the ground. If this is true, it would mean that the psi-plasma envelope of the Yogin contains a shielded region of marked decrease in the value of the gravitational constant. Hence the pull of the earth would be shielded and the individual would float. This possibility should be included in the list of critical experiments. One would have to search the world for a few individuals who claim to be able to do levitation. We could then conduct experiments comparable to those done by Sir William Crookes on D. D. Home. Here the levitating individual is placed on a platform scale which under the constant gravitational pull of the earth would register a given amount of mass. The individual would then attempt to decrease this mass by undergoing the necessary mental operations to achieve levitation. This would be reflected in a loss of mass on the scale. There are a number of experiments from the last hundred years which state that weight losses up to 10% have been registered. If one could find such individuals one would have the simplest of all possible tests of the psi-plasma hypothesis.

NOTES Epilogue

1. Muller, H. J., "Approximation to a Gravity-Free Situation for the Human Organism Achieved at Moderate Expense," *Science,* Vol. 128, Oct. 3, 1958, p. 772.

Appendix A

Experiments with Faraday-cage method and apparatus for inducing various states of consciousness in an individual with particular application to Telepathy.

That telepathy exists has been repeatedly shown both in personal experience and in the laboratory. This does not mean that the controversy as to its existence has ceased, but quite the contrary. The controversy remains alive as ever because no rational explanation has been formulated as to the *modus operandi* of this unique means of gaining intelligence. This vacuum exists because of the inherent difficulties in studying telepathy, principally due to the absence of controlled repeatability in the laboratory.

Therefore, one of the principal goals of modern parapsychological research is to conquer the problem of repeatability. The principal method now used to achieve this goal is to work with human subjects of great talent in telepathy. A secondary method is to painstakingly uncover the hereditary, psychological, and environmental conditions that favor the appearance of demonstrable telepathy. The research work reported in this Appendix deals only with subjects of exceptional talent who were tested against controlled environmental factors.

The experiment was designed to test the hypothesis that telepathy is based on the transmission of electromagnetic waves between humans. Therefore, the null hypothesis states: *Telepathy can be blocked by appropriate shielding.*

In order to carry out such an experiment certain components had to be assembled. The first were subjects who could produce demonstrable telepathy under laboratory conditions. This condition was initially satisfied when Mrs. Eileen J. Garrett of New York volunteered to be the subject. She had proven her telepathic ability in a number of other laboratories both in Europe and in the United States. The second component concerned the choice of instrument to be used to test the null hypothesis, and it was decided to use the Faraday-cage principle as a controlled environment in which the subject would attempt telepathy. The third component had to do with the controls used to eliminate all sensory perception on the part of the subject, and the standards by which one determined the presence or absence of telepathy. These factors were embodied in the design of the test material used for the transmission of intelligence by telepathy and its interpretation by well-established statistical standards. Each of the three components will be described in greater detail as the experimental results are sequentially summarized.

The exploratory experiment, Project I, made use of a copper-screen Faraday cage of dimensions $7 \times 7 \times 7$ feet, the entire cubical enclosure being placed on insulating supports. The plan was to place the sensitive, Mrs. Garrett, in the cage, and a telepathic sender outside of the cage. The control test consisted of the following:

1 Mrs. Garrett as receiver in the cage.
2 A person in another room acting as the sender.
3 The cage door open, and the cage "floating," i.e., not grounded.
4 The test material, a pack of Zener Cards, with the sender looking at each symbol, and trying to "send" to the receiver.

Mrs. Garrett had chance-expectation results for telepathy in this control test. This was not a very encouraging beginning since the purpose of the experiment was to attempt to block telepathic transmission.

The test experiment in Project I was the same as the control with the exception that the cage door was closed. This also showed chance-expectation results.

The next step in Project I was to place an electrical field across the cage, testing discrete frequencies from 60 c.p.s. to 21.3 megacycles. This field was applied with the positive center conductor on the cage, and the ground shield on a plate above the cage with an air space between these two plates. Mrs. Garrett while in the cage was unable to detect when such a field was on or off, when it was placed across the plate and the cage. However, a curious finding was made during these experiments which eventually led in a fruitful direction. It was found that when an *interrupted* A.C. field was placed on the cage across the plates, Mrs. Garrett showed an involuntary gasp a second or so after the charge was placed on the cage in which she sat. There was no known precedent for this effect, and it was decided to explore it further.

It was found that Mrs. Garrett showed the most pronounced gasping reaction to a frequency of 640 c.p.s., interrupted five times per second. The voltage was 105 (rms) at 2 ma. and it was applied to the cage for a duration of ten seconds. With the appearance of the interrupted A.C. field on the cage Mrs. Garrett would show an inspiratory gasp of 2–4 seconds duration followed by an 8–10 second respiratory depression. This was monitored by a sensitive microphone that picked up her breath sounds, and the output of the microphone was integrated and recorded on a Sanborn Industrial Recorder. The time and duration of the cage charge was recorded on the same paper graph. The puzzling aspect of these observations was that Mrs. Garrett was the only person who showed the gasping reaction. Other subjects who made no claim to being telepathists did not show this reaction. Therefore, Project II was designed to test Mrs. Garrett under more rigorous conditions.

In Project II the 10-second interrupted A.C. charge was placed on the outside walls of the screen cage by means of an automatic random-switching multivibrator. The times of the charge, Mrs. Garrett's breathing, and her calls were automatically recorded on moving graph paper. Mrs. Garrett was supposed to guess when the charge was present on the cage in which she sat. The charges, which were the target she was to call, appeared over a range as close as 30 seconds apart to as long as 12 minutes apart. During Project II, 91 targets appeared, and in relation to these, Mrs. Garrett showed the gasping reaction 86 times. Besides the gasping reaction, it was observed that Mrs. Garrett was also able to accurately detect other electrostatic effects in the vicinity of the cage, such as refrigerator motors starting, cars approaching the building that were as yet out of range of hearing, etc. Thus we had two unknown effects to account for when the subject was inside of a screen cage.

It was reasoned that the gasping effect was due to a disturbance of the charged ions within the cage, and this disturbance in turn excited a physiological gasping reflex. It was known

that an excess of positive ions in the atmosphere has an irritating effect on the nasal and pulmonary mucosa. But the de-
tection of remote electrostatic disturbances could not be explained so easily. Therefore, it was decided to first rule out the
role of acute ion deficiency (or excess) by shielding the subject
from such effects.

This shielding was accomplished in the design of Project III
by placing a sheet-metal copper cage *B* inside of the afore-
described screen cage *A*. Cage *B* had double-rolled soldered
joints, and the entire structure was made airtight. The electrical
target was the same as in Project II with the change that the
negative-ground side of the circuit was connected to the sheet-
metal cage *B*, and the positive side to cage *A*. The subject, of
course, was placed inside the airtight cage *B*. Mrs. Garrett was
asked to guess the arrival time of the random electrical charge.
The first finding was that Mrs. Garrett no longer showed the
gasping reaction. Thus the inference that the gasping reflex was
due to an ionic effect proved to be plausible, although the
mechanism was far from clear. Thirty targets appeared during
the course of Project III, ranging in arrival time from 36 seconds to 11 minutes 10 seconds apart. It was found after the
experiment that the electrical targets were distributed in the
Poisson series with a mean of 1.11, and Mrs. Garrett's calls
with a mean of 1.08. Since the assumption is made that both
the electrical targets and the calls of the subject are random
events and independent series, such homogeneity of the two
series argues for an interaction between the electrical targets and
the cognition of Mrs. Garrett. We allowed Mrs. Garrett 15 seconds after the end of a target to make a call that could be considered as a hit. Using this standard she made 30 hits with respect to the 30 targets. This was six hits in excess of the
chance-expected score, and with a standard deviation of 1.04
hits, this gave a critical ratio of 4.3. This represents odds
against chance occurrence of such a score of 117,000 to 1.

Our problem had now become quite complex. We had eliminated the gasping reflex by shielding the subject from ionic effects, but had discovered an interaction between an electrical
field, from which the subject was shielded by the Faraday cage,
and her cognition processes. A long series of experiments was
carried out to clarify this problem. These led to the hypothesis
that certain Faraday-cage arrangements and electrical charging

of cages produced a state of mental tension (adrenergia) in humans. Other arrangements of cages and charging produced a state of relaxation (cholinergia) in humans. These experiments, which are much too laborious to go into here, led to the suspicion that the gasping reflex and mental tension were caused by a charged-ion deficiency in the respiratory gases. Therefore, an experiment was designed to test this hypothesis.

Ion-density measurements were made with a simple ion collector made up of parallel plates arranged in a rectangular duct with air drawn past the plates with a small blower. Recording of the ion density was made with a Beckman Model V vibrating reed unit in combination with a 50 mv potentiometer-type recorder. It was found that the air in cage *B* initially contained about 250 ion pairs per c.c., and that after an hour of occupancy by two people the count was reduced to about 40 ion pairs per c.c. with an excess of positive ions averaging about 20 ions. The purpose of the experiment was to reduce the total charged-ion count to as close to zero as possible. It was found that this could be achieved by introducing the collector electrode of an electrostatic dust sampler (Mines Safety Appliances) through an aperture cut into the wall of cage *B*. The sampler carried a 10 Kv D.C. negative potential on the center electrode, and the outer concentric two-inch electrode was at ground potential; the outer electrode was connected to the copper wall of cage *B*, thus placing the cage in which the subject sat at ground potential. Air was drawn out of the cage at the rate of three cubic feet per minute by the sampler. The like amount of air was replaced inside the cage from a compressed-air tank. By placing a copper screen over the negative center electrode the positive ions could be bound to the screen while the negative ions were repelled through the grating. This technique effectively reduced the charged-ion density down to 0–5 ion pairs per c.c. in about twenty minutes.

The effects from this method were quite remarkable, and may be classed under three headings:

1 Physiological Effects: After 20 minutes of exposure to this ion-deficient atmosphere the subjects showed an uncontrollable spasm and flexor rigidity of the hands and forearms. This was severe and painful. They also showed spasm of the facial musculature which gave

them the appearance of being subjected to high gravity force. There was present a continuous dry hacking cough, a sense of pressure on the top of the skull, and a headache.

2 Psychological Effects: All subjects reported a sense of inebriation as though they had been drugged. Some reported auditory hallucinations described as church bells, sleigh bells, or music.

3 Parapsychological Effects: Although this is ahead of our sequence, subjects who had previously shown extra-chance scoring rates in ESP tests were never able to exceed chance scoring under ion-deficient conditions, regardless of the type of test used, i.e., cards, electrical, or MAT.

Our next problem was to evaluate the effect of charging the Faraday cages in relation to the suspected interaction between the electrical field and the process of cognition. Because the electrical field appeared to be the critical factor influencing cognition, it was decided to make the control experiment one in which the subject sat in an uncharged cage, and the test experiment one in which the subject sat in a charged cage. This was carried out in Project IV with Mrs. Garrett as the subject.

It was first necessary to test the integrity of the Faraday cage as a shield against electromagnetic radiation. The low-frequency shielding was tested by making a coil that was sharply tuned to 640 c.p.s., the charging frequency of the cage. The output of the coil was fed into an amplifier. When the field was placed on the outside of cage *A* at 150 volts A.C. and the coil was placed inside of cage *B*, there was no detectable output from the coil. The high frequencies were tested by placing a Zenith All-wave receiver (with the automatic volume control eliminated) inside cage *B*, and spraying the outside of cage *A* and cage *B* with the output from a 10,000 volt A.C. transformer such as is used for neon lights. By testing all the frequencies present in the receiver it was determined that the cage was impermeable to this test charge.

Since the cage proved to be an effective shield against the frequencies tested, it was necessary to find out if the human body was acting as a detector for these frequencies. Silver-chloride electrodes immersed in saline were placed in contact with the skin of the human subject placed inside of cage *B*. These leads were fed into a D.C. amplifier of high impedance sensitive to, and stable for, one microvolt. The D.C. potential of the skin was found to be unaltered by applying the test frequencies mentioned above to the outside of the cage. The same negative results were found for electroencephalograph measurements made on the scalp. It must be pointed out that the four pieces of test equipment used inside the cage were battery-powered. No electrical lead crossed the barrier of cage *B* during these tests.

Since we were primarily concerned with the possible interaction of an electrical field across a Faraday-cage shield with the process of human cognition, it was decided to use an electrical target as a test of the alleged telepathic ability of the subject. The electrical target was a random generator pulsed by big cosmic-ray showers, and a moving paper graph recorded the ON switching period (of ten seconds). This provided an electrical target appearing in a random sequence which followed a Poisson distribution. The subject was separated from the electrical target by a distance of 0.3 miles. The subject was further shielded from the electrical target by being placed inside the double Faraday cage. This consisted of the airtight Faraday cage *B* wherein the subject sat, nested inside of cage *A* as previously described. Cage *B* was at ground potential, and cage *A* was continuously charged with an (5 per second) interrupted 640-cycle field only in the test experiment and not in the control experiment. The order in which the cage was to be charged (test), or uncharged (control), was determined by a table of random numbers unknown to the subject. This procedure ruled out psychological bias on the part of the subject for either the test or control condition.

Mrs. Garrett was asked to call the arrival time of the cosmic-ray pulse that activated the pen, and was allowed 15 seconds after the target in which to qualify for a hit. In Group 5 of the test experiment of Project IV there appeared a total of 59 targets, and these were distributed in the Poisson series with a mean of 0.475. In relation to these targets Mrs. Garrett made 61 calls distributed in the Poisson series with a mean of 0.491. Statistical analysis of Group 5 yielded a critical ratio of 4.87 with probability of 0.000001, or odds against chance of a million to one. The uncharged cage, control experiment, yielded a critical ratio of 1.08 or chance-expectation. The critical ratio of difference between these two experiments is 4.43 ($P =$ 0.000005). This result was considered statistically significant and argued for extrasensory cognition on the part of Mrs. Garrett. However, because of the possibility that large cosmic-ray showers could simultaneously strike the target area and the call area, it was felt that the evidence for "no electrical interaction" was incomplete. The main finding of Project IV was that the special physical arrangement and electrical charging of the Treated Faraday Cage was associated with statistically significant scoring. In order to ascertain whether or not the Treated Faraday Cage did indeed positively influence the outcome of ESP-test scores independently of cosmic-ray showers, it was decided to repeat the experiment, testing for the presence of extrasensory cognition by using playing cards as the test material inside and outside of the Treated Faraday Cage, instead of an electrical target. Due to other commitments, Mrs. Garrett was unable to participate in this experiment.

Mr. Frederick Marion was used as the subject in Project VII. His reputed telepathic skill was tested when performing outside and inside of the Treated Faraday Cage. As an additional control there was introduced into the experiment the same physical arrangement as the Treated Faraday Cage, but electrically uncharged. This is called the Ground Faraday Cage and has cage *B* grounded to earth, the same as the control in Project IV. It was found that Mr. Marion showed statistically significant scores in calling out whether a playing card was red or black under ordinary room conditions. It was found that blindfolded or unblindfolded he could attain significant scores only when the investigator held the cards in his hands, face down over a black-velvet surface, and offered each card separately for calling —the so-called "broken" technique. He did not show significant scores when no one held the cards, i.e., called down through the deck, or the so-called "down-through" technique. Mr. Marion argued that he was dependent for his knowledge of the card-order on psychometry, i.e., some human hand had to contact each card. This was our first clue as to the role of touch in such ESP-tests. This was to be explored later in the design of an ESP-test called the Matching Abacus Test. In all the tests with Mr. Marion the broken technique with playing cards was used. Mr. Robert Baker acted as the agent who handled the cards.

Using the broken technique, never allowing Mr. Marion to touch or see the cards, he achieved a critical ratio of 10.5 as a control under normal room conditions. Inside the Treated Faraday Cage he achieved a critical ratio of 14.8, and this represented a statistically significant increase over his control score under room conditions. In addition, it was found that his critical ratio in the Ground Faraday Cage was 13.7 and this was a statistically significant increase over the room control score.

Hence, it was concluded that both the Treated Faraday Cage and the Ground Faraday Cage were associated with significant increases in ESP-test scores over scores associated with normal room conditions in the case of Mr. Marion. According to our null hypothesis the scoring rates inside of the Faraday cages should have been lower than those under normal room conditions. Therefore, the null hypothesis was falsified in the experiments with Mrs. Garrett, where the subject was shielded from the target by the barrier of the Faraday cages.

This raises the question as to whether these experiments have really ruled out the role of electromagnetic radiation as the transmission system in telepathic communication. While the experiments are highly suggestive that electromagnetic radiation is not the means of transmission in telepathy, they are by no means conclusive. It would take a great deal of highly refined research with Faraday cages specifically impermeable for narrow bands to finally settle this vexing question. We did not pursue this specific problem since we had other more pressing problems to clarify. Having found that charged-ion deficiency within a cage is associated with chance ESP-test scores, it was desirable to observe the effects of an ion-enriched atmosphere. Before this experiment could be carried out it was necessary to standardize our experimental procedure so that any experiment in one series could be compared to any experiment in every other series.

The first standardization had to do with the cages. The screen cage *A* was used to carry the electrical charge. This was standardized by using a D.C. negative charge of 10–20 Kv at 4 milliamperes. Cage *B* was always used at ground potential. Inside cage *B* was placed a floating screen cage *C* just large enough for one person to sit in, leaving room for another person to occupy the remainder of cage *B*.

The ion generator, when used, was placed inside cage *B*. The ion source was a burning candle surrounded by a copper-screen cylinder. The copper-screen cylinder was charged to 10 Kv negative or positive, depending on which unipolar ion was to be produced. Such an ion generator was capable of maintaining a level of up to 500,000 ions per c.c. These conditions were combined into the technology of Project XV to be described later. The 10 Kv D.C. ion source in Project XV was a battery-powered Van de Graaf generator.

In order to standardize telepathic testing a procedure was devised that fitted our experimental requirements. This is the Matching Abacus Test (MAT), a fundamental probability set of 10. The problem is to attempt to match two sets, each of 10 distinct symbols. The chance-expected score is 5.4 for five such tests (a series of $5 \times 10 = 50$ trials). Eleven correct matches in 50 trials is significant at the 1% level. Each of the symbols was sealed in a plastic box so that all surfaces were uniform.

Each experiment was conducted as a block of 50 trials. Each experiment is expressed as the number of correct matches in 50 trials. Thus, 15 correct matches is given as 15/50. This score can also be expressed in terms of a probability, or 15/50 equals $P = 1.572 \times 10^{-4}$, or $P = 0.0001572$.

In order to clarify why the Faraday-cage technique apparently influenced ESP-test scores it was first used without an electrical field. Thus, only the physical arrangement of the Faraday cages in the form of the Ground Faraday Cage was used. This means that cage B was connected from one point to earth by a single copper wire.

Scores significant for ESP-cognition were obtained when the sender and the receiver were allowed full telepathic interaction.

I would define full telepathic interaction as follows:

1 Both the sender and the receiver must be consciously aware that the focus of their attention is on each other's mind, and not on the test material.
2 A physical focal point of interaction between the two minds is present. This can be furnished by allowing the receiver's hands to scan over the possible choices he has to make from a set of symbolic test material. The receiver is, of course, blindfolded and the test is hidden further by a screen. The sender must have full visual control of the test material and the receiver's hands.

As the receiver's hands move toward the correct target symbol there is built up in the sender the proper sense of tension and anticipation (adrenergia) which is the necessary prelude to sending the appropriate telepathic signal. By telepathic interaction the receiver feels the build-up, climax, and disappearance of emotion which serves as a feedback guide as to whether he is nearing the target symbol or moving away from it.

3 The receiver's mind should be as devoid as possible of verbal, symbolic, or image material, either conscious or unconscious. The presence of conscious cortical functions does not appear to favor telepathic interaction. Any self-consciousness tends to suppress telepathic reception. Alcohol, with its suppression of the cortical inhibitory function, has a most salubrious effect on the telepathic receiver. Conversely, fear, anxiety, or the tension generated by the pressure of spectators is an unfavorable condition for full telepathic interaction.

For two telepathic teams working under normal room conditions the MAT score average was 12/50 ($P = 0.003$) and 11/15 ($P = 0.008$) respectively. The scores for a comparable series of tests inside the Ground Faraday Cage averaged 27/50 ($P = 4.59 \times 10^{-11}$) and 28/50 ($P = 8.17 \times 10^{-13}$). This was a significant increase in scores over those for ordinary room conditions. A total of five telepathic teams achieved a comparable level of scoring inside the Ground Faraday Cage, averaging 5 hits per MAT run (approximately 25/50 or better). For each of these teams the critical ratio was 9.0 or better. These scores were obtained when the blindfolded receiver was allowed to manually arrange the matching pictures. This is termed the "arranging" technique of MAT utilization. When the receivers were not allowed to manually arrange the pictures, but were only allowed to call the name of the picture the scores were at a chance level. This is termed the "calling" technique of MAT utilization. As in the case of Mr. Marion, it was found that the sense of touch was important in the extrasensory cognition process. Hence, the term *extrasensory* is a misnomer if the process is indeed fortified by the sensory modality of touch. However, in order to avoid confusion the use of the term *extrasensory perception* (ESP) is retained keeping in mind the qualification cited for the MAT.

This problem was further clarified in subsequent studies. The experience of most parapsychologists with the Zener Card test is that the scoring rate declines with successive runs. For example, the first-run score may be 18/25, second 16/25, third 14/25, and fourth 10/25, etc. This illustrates a declining scoring rate and is associated with the "calling" technique.

Our experience with the arranging technique of MAT utilization with both subjects in the same charged Faraday cage shows an opposite curve of performance. For example, the first-run score may be 4/10, second 6/10, third 8/10, fourth 10/10, and fifth 10/10. In other words, ESP-test scores go up with prolonged confinement in the electrically charged cage, and with manual arranging.

A new finding was made in Project XV. In addition to making highly significant scores by the "arranging" technique, it was found that one telepathic team, for the first time, was able to achieve significant ESP-test scores by the "calling" technique. This means that transmission of symbols was possible by telepathy. Harry Stone was the sender, and Peter Hurkos the receiver. Both were inside of the Faraday cage *B* with the MAT between them. The position of each picture in the target row of the MAT was designated by the numbers 1 to 10. Before each trial the sender was to attempt to telepathically communicate the number of the position at which could be found the correct matching target picture. The receiver then called out the number which he thought he had received, and this was recorded. The receiver then completed the trial by attempting to find manually (by the arranging technique) the correct target picture (and disregarding the number that he had already selected). Thus a contemporaneous score was kept for each trial of success by *calling,* and success by *arranging.*

With this team the score for calling was 18/50 ($P = 4.014 \times 10^{-6}$), and the score for arranging was 50/50 ($P = 1.589 \times 10^{-33}$). But more striking than this difference in ESP-test scores was the fact that the calling scores showed a declining curve of performance. The first-run score for calling was 8/10, the second 2/10, the third 6/10, the fourth 2/10, and the fifth 0/10 making a total of 18/50. Conversely, the arranging technique scores started high and stayed high, or 10/10 for each run, making a total of 50/50.

Hence, the sensitivity of the arranging technique as a more

delicate meter of environmental factors was illustrated by this experiment. The difference in scoring between the two techniques has been confirmed in other experiments. It appeared that the curve of increasing performance found heretofore in the Treated Faraday Cage was due to the use of the relatively nonsymbolic technique of arranging, as against the symbolic technique of calling.

It was now possible to put to a crucial experiment the question of whether we were indeed dealing with true telepathic interaction. Mr. Hurkos was placed inside cage *C,* and given only the randomized *target* row of the MAT. Cage *B* was at ground and cage *A* was charged to 18 kilovolt negative D.C. with respect to ground with the ion generator on in cage *B*. Mr. Carl Betz was in cage *B* as the agent-investigator observing Hurkos. Mr. Stone was taken in an automobile to a distance approximately one mile away from the cage where Hurkos sat. When the car stopped, Mr. Stone was handed only the randomized *match* row of the MAT by Miss Marianna Rockwell, the other agent-investigator. At a prearranged time signal both Hurkos and Stone started the matching. Hurkos as receiver was to try to duplicate the order of the ten pictures set up by Stone as the sender. The ESP-test score was 36/50 *ON* hits ($P = 2.248 \times 10^{-19}$). This is the best evidence obtained in this laboratory for telepathic interaction between two humans. The evidence was now strong enough to falsify the null hypothesis.

Curiously enough, when the same test was repeated, but modified so that the sender and receiver were synchronized by the agent for the start and end of each trial, the scores fell to a chance-expectation level. Repetition of this type of experiment showed that when the sender and receiver had a free choice as to the timing of each trial within a run, the ESP-test scores were siginificant for telepathy. When the timing of each trial was controlled by the investigator, the scores were chance-expectation. This fact is illustrated by the following two experiments done for an investigating committee of the psychic research society of an Eastern university on September 30, 1956.

The subjects were in two separate rooms, the receiver being in the Treated Faraday Cage. Each had only one row of the MAT. When imposed synchronization was used for each trial the score was 6/50 *ON* hits—which is chance-expectation. When each subject started the run at his own discretion, and did each trial under his own sense of synchronization, the score was 18/50 *ON* hits ($P = 4.014 \times 10^{-6}$), or significance for telepathic interaction. In this experiment both Stone and Hurkos were blindfolded for the five runs, thus eliminating full telepathic interaction as defined earlier.

The team of Stone/Hurkos could not achieve extra-chance scores in this type of distance split-MAT test unless one of them was inside of the Treated Faraday Cage as described for Project XV. It is believed that the environmental conditions of the Treated Faraday Cage are essential for repeatable demonstration of telepathic interaction between two sensitives under acceptable scientific standards.

The following table summarizes all the effects on human consciousness observed with various Faraday-cage arrangements and charging. It is to be noted that most of the effects observed are due to the presence or absence of charged ions of the respiratory gases. The one exception is where ESP-test scores increase when cages *A* and *B* are grounded.

SUMMARY OF STATES OF CONSCIOUSNESS WITH DIFFERENT FARADAY CAGE ARRANGEMENTS AND CHARGING

Positive Effects on Consciousness	Negative Effects on Consciousness
SINGLE SCREEN CAGE—with Steady A.C. Field. Effect on Sensitive: No untoward effect. Ionization stable.	SINGLE SCREEN CAGE—with interrupted A.C. Field. Effect on Sensitive: Gasping, psychomotor depression, and tension. Ionization reversing. Deficiency of ions in cage.
SINGLE SCREEN CAGE—with subject grounded. Effect on Sensitive: Relaxation of tension. Ionization stable.	SINGLE SCREEN CAGE—with grounding, or interrupted A.C. Field. Effect on Sensitive: Neuromuscular reflex facilitation or spasm. Ionization reversing and deficiency of ions.
CAGES A & B STANDARD Effect on Sensitive: Exhilaration and well-being. No gasping, psychomotor depression, reflex facilitation, or tension. Ionization stable. Physical tension disappears, and a form of "psychic" tension appears as a residue. ESP-test scores significant.	
CAGES A & B GROUND No notable effects on sensitive, except significant ESP-test score increase. Ionization stable.	
CAGES A & B GROUND, AND ATMOSPHERE INSIDE AT 10 KV D.C. NEGATIVE WITH EXCESS NEGATIVE IONS. Effect on Sensitive: Disappearance of all untoward effects in opposite column. Chance-expectation ESP-test scores, or high ESP-test scores depending on who the subject is.	CAGES A & B. CAGE B GROUND, AND ATMOSPHERE INSIDE AT 10 KV D.C. NEGATIVE WITH ION DEFICIENCY. Effect on Sensitive: Activation of cough reflex, neuromuscular spasm, headache, auditory hallucinations. Chance-expectation ESP-test scores.
CAGE B GROUND; AND CAGE A AT 20 KV NEGATIVE POTENTIAL. RECEIVER IN CAGE C. NEGATIVE ION EXCESS. Effect on Sensitive: No untoward effects; exhilaration. Usually high ESP-test scores with telepathic teams in which sender is outside of cages and may be many miles away from the receiver in cage C.	

Appendix B

*Analysis of the Experimental Fragments of the
Environmental Conditions for Telepathy*

There is an ancient tradition that certain types of atmospheric disturbances have a negative effect, and that other atmospheric conditions have a positive or enhancing effect on the outcome of operations which we now term parapsychological. The earliest recorded reference that I can find on this subject is alleged to be the authorship of Solomon the King. *The Key of Solomon* is a classic on the techniques to be used in psychic operations, or Magic, as it was called. One of the admonishments given in this work is that before the operation is undertaken "It is necessary to make the following Experiments and Arts in the appropriate Days and Hours. . . . Note that the last three days [before the experiment] should be calm weather, without wind, and without clouds rushing hither and thither over the face of the sky."[1]

Repeated allusions of the same character, too numerous to mention, have been made throughout the history of such rituals, the ritual of the irrational. These are of such a consistent nature that they bear analysis. Almost three thousand years later we find a modern author coming to the same conclusion as King Solomon. J. Cecil Maby, an authority on the alleged *"extrasensory"* faculty of water dowsing,[2] makes the following statement (A.D. 1950):

"Probably no other single factor upsets dowsing so much as the weather, when it is stormy and unsettled; isolated, electrically-charged cloud masses, with their associated rising columns of damp air and subjacent electrostatic and ionisation effects, being capable of causing violent local fluctuations of intensity and also polarity of the serialized reaction bands of a radionic or dowsing field, as well as general perturbation of delicate instruments and animal physiology. And this is often the case on stormy afternoons, in, say, April and mid-summer. Wet gales, likewise, are most disturbing.

"In my opinion, therefore, and pending any final solution of this problem (which may prove insuperable) it is best simply to avoid such interference or perturbation by careful choice of time and place."[3]

Let us compare the weather facts[4] with the reported effects of fine weather and stormy weather on the ritual of the irrational in tabular form:

Type of Weather	ATMOSPHERIC ELECTRICITY	RITUAL OF THE IRRATIONAL
FINE	Ionosphere—Positive Earth—Negative (with positive Field)	Favorable
	Electrical Conditions—Stable. On a clear day, small ion concentration is high, Field P.D. is low.	Doubtful or Unknown
	Max. Field P.D. at 19 Hrs. G.M.T. falling to Min. at 6 Hrs. G.M.T.	Favorable
STORMY	Earth Field unstable with fluctuation from positive to negative. Fields tend to be high. Clouds—high conc. charges.	Unfavorable

We find three suggestive correlations here: a) Fine weather with a low P.D. (potential difference) positive field and high concentration of small ions coincides with a possibly favorable time for the ritual of the irrational. b) The fine weather high P.D. positive field of nighttime (falling from 1900 to 0600 hrs.) is also allegedly favorable for the ritual of the irrational. c) The traditional use of the ritual fire (burning of fats, vegetable matter, incense, terpenes, etc.) produces a high concentration of small ions (charges of both signs) and can augment the effects of (a) and (b).

Because of such a possible correlation it was decided in 1950 at the Round Table Laboratory to set up an experiment in which an approximation of the stormy-weather electrical effects could be duplicated in a laboratory procedure in order to test its effect on an individual who was in self-induced trance. In Projects I and II an interrupted electrical charge was placed on the outside of a single-screen Faraday cage, leaving the subject exposed primarily to the effects of the ion deficiency produced presumably by a diffusion outward through the screen. This condition was perfected under the better-controlled experiments of Project XI and produced marked physiological and psychological effects in other subjects.

The screen cage, as described in Projects I and II (Appendix A), can produce both positive and negative ions when using interrupted alternating current; and these can be made unipolar by a D.C.-grid negative charge that separates the negative ions. An opposite charge on the copper-screen grid will separate out the positive ions. Such devices are in commercial use; here the ion source is a hot electrode or a radioactive electrode (Polonium salts).[5] Biological experiments with such separated ions have shown that: 1) A sudden reversal in polarity of ionization momentarily disturbs the normal development and growth of animals,[6] 2) increases the carbon dioxide capacity of the plasma in hamsters kept in negatively ionized air,[7] 3) in rats it has been found that exposure to an excess of positive ions produces histological changes in the adrenal glands indicative of elaboration of both salt and carbohydrate regulating corticoids.[8] According to Ferrannini,[9] "given equal ionic concentrations, negative charges slow down respiration, whereas positive charges have an opposite effect" in humans. Gorriti and Medina[10] report that significant lowering of the blood pressure occurred in hypertensive patients given negative-ion therapy over long periods.

The studies with the use of unipolarized airborne electric charges, both in this country and abroad,[11] seem to indicate as a rule that with certain sensitive individuals negative ions produce a feeling of physical and mental well-being, mental alertness, and optimism. On the other hand, treatment with positive ions are frequently reported to be the apparent cause of headaches, fatigue, dizziness, ill-temper, and fear. In our experimental work the provisional assumption was made, on the basis of such reports, that the presence of an excess of small negative ions might be a favorable condition in tests of extrasensory cognition. Therefore, the following fair-weather criteria were used for the design of an environmental situation in which to carry out the studies: 1) Stable Electrical Conditions in which r (conductivity of small ions) is relatively constant. Any change in r would have to be in the direction of a slow decrease in resistance (comparable to that found in the nighttime falling potential difference from 1900 hrs. to 0600 hrs. G.M.T.). 2) Small ion concentration high in immediate environment of the subject, preferably with an excess of negative ions. 3) The external walls of the room in which the subject worked were to have a negative charge sign. This was achieved by connecting the external metal wall of the room to ground, which may be considered as a vast reservoir of negative electricity. Thus, with respect to the positive charge of the ionosphere, the subject would be in the center of a field in which the lines of force would run from the room to the ionosphere, and the direction of current flow would be from the ionosphere to the room.

Criterion 1 is satisfied by the use of the sheet-copper cage B described in Appendix A. Criterion 3 is satisfied by placing the sheet-copper cage B inside, and insulated from, the screen cage A, and connecting cage B to ground. This arrangement was reversed in Project XI in regard to charge sign. Criterion 2 was tested in Project XII D, and found to be associated with increased ESP-test scores.

Yaglou and his associates at the Harvard School of Public Health[12] found that the number of small ions in an unoccupied room was substantially the same as outdoors. When the room was occupied by a human being, however, the number of small ions decreased rapidly. The initial ion concentration in his tests was approximately 250 ion pairs per c.c. In one hour and twenty-five minutes, the count was reduced to 50 per c.c. Work at the Wesix Foundation[13] has shown that an unoccupied room tends to have a higher number of negative ions (about 100 ion pairs) than positive ions. In general, an occupied room will have a higher number of positive ions than negative ions, depending on the heat source, number of people present, humidity, etc. Thus one could assume initially that with a subject and one observer in a tightly closed room of 216 cubic feet capacity, there would not be a natural excess of negative ions. We have carried out a crucial experiment to decide whether Criterion 2 represents a favorable or an unfavorable condition. The results of Project

XII D argue for the favorable effect of an excess of negative ions.

Let us discuss separately the events going on *outside* of the metal skin of cage *B,* and events going on *inside* of the metal skin of cage *B.* As a model of the "stormy-weather" condition let us analyze the Single Screen Cage—Ground, without an A.C. charge. Here the outside wall of the screen cage *A* is negatively charged because of the connection to earth. The plate has a positive charge. The capacitor field between the plate and the cage will slowly accumulate a positive charge from the atmosphere. The negatively charged cage *A* will tend to bind positive charges, and any disturbance of the field, either by earth/atmosphere oscillation, capacitance change due to a moving object, etc., will allow negatively charged ions to drift into, or out of, the cage. This effect is increased when an interrupted A.C. field is placed across the existing D.C. field, by causing an attraction and repulsion of ions at the surface of the screen cage *A,* resulting in a gate-type of action propelling negative ions into the cage initially, and thereafter out of the cage. In the normal subject this action of negative ions causes tension symptoms; and in sensitives gives, for a period of a second or two, a psychomotor stimulation, followed by a marked psychomotor depression; and in certain conditioned sensitives produces an exaggerated facilitation of neuromuscular reflexes. A steady sine field neutralizes the ionic migration, and has no stimulating or depressing effect on a sensitive subject.

As a model of the "fine-weather" condition, let us analyze the Double Faraday Cage (cage *B*—Ground; cage *A*—not charged) with the Ground circuit. Here we have a double-cube capacitor, the inner cube sheet-copper cage *B* with a negative charge from the earth, and the outer cube screen cage *A* with a positive charge from the atmosphere. This is a large capacitor with a capacitance of 0.0014 microfarads. Nikola Tesla has shown[14] that such an arrangement acts as an accumulator of positive electricity from the atmosphere, and that such charging of the capacitor will continue indefinitely (provided insulation is adequate), even to the point of rupturing a high-order dielectric (if such is used). Thus the positively charged cage *A* will bind the negative particles and build up a field of positive ions (since cage *A* is a "permeable" copper screen) between cage *A* and cage *B.* Since in our experiments the cage *B* was elevated ten feet above ground level, there would be a normal D.C. potential of about 300 volts between cages A and B (assuming under ideal conditions a P.D. of 100 volts per meter above ground level). Any natural fluctuation of this field by normal earth/atmosphere oscillation, capacitance change induced by moving objects, or moving motor vehicles (electrostatic field), etc., would cause a fluctuation in the positive field between cages A and B. Such fluctuation of positive field is associated in *sensitive* subjects with psychic tension, which is experienced primarily as a sense of "lift" or well-being, and reflected by increased ESP-test scores. It is to be noted that in this case the subject is protected from any direct effect of ionic changes.

When this positive field in the capacitor is altered by the effect of pulse-modulated waves of five per second (640 c.p.s. interrupted five times per second) the sense of well-being of the sensitive subject is increased, and this is reflected in increased ESP-test scores, as compared to the Ground condition. What change is induced in the positive electrostatic field between cages A and B by the pulse-modulated waves? Such modulation would obviously increase the positive ion content and positive field strength of the air dielectric between the cages. The application of continuous pulse modulation would not only serve to increase the positive ion concentration, but would act to conserve it from dissipation. Loss of strength of field could occur primarily by dielectric leakage and since the system was not built with high-order dielectric strength this leakage would tend to diminish the field conservation established by the pulse modulation. It seems theoretically possible, however, that there was an energy transfer between the cages, on the assumption of an electrostatic charge moving at the velocity of sound[15] to ground through the cage-B surface. A movement of the electrostatic envelope of cage B could be pulsed by the five per second modulation. If this assumption is correct, a pulsating electrostatic envelope would have a definite effect on the ionic contents of the air (20.9% oxygen, 79.0% nitrogen, and 0.1% constituents such as the rare gases, hydrogen, and air impurities).

What happens to the above gases placed between electrodes (such as cage A and cage B) at the potentials used? The formation of ozone in an electrical discharge has been known since Van Marum's discovery of this effect in 1785.[16]

Siemens in 1857 showed that ozone could be produced by passing air through a silent discharge between two electrodes at high potential.[17] In commercial usage this potential is five to ten thousand volts in order to get high yields. The reaction of oxygen to ozone can also occur at very low energies as a photochemical polymerization and depolymerization reaction, according to the reaction $3 O_2 \rightleftharpoons 2 O_3$. Here the active radiation is 1970–1765 Å.U. and the absorbing molecule is the O_2.[18]

Oxygen, O_2, is an electronegative gas which attaches electrons directly to form negative ions, O_2^-. In O_2 the energy of formation of the O_2^- ion is between 0.1 and 0.3 volts. It involves the incorporation of the electron with its 0.2-volt energy of attachment plus its energy of heat motion into the molecule of O_2, the energy being taken up in the vibrational states of the O_2 molecule. This energy must be dissipated in collisions with other O_2 or N_2 molecules if the O_2^- ion is to remain stable. Unless it collides in a short time the electron will dissociate. When a positive ion, O_2^+, strikes a metal surface at about 180 volts potential, it bounces off as an O_2^- ion, picking up an electron after neutralizing itself.

Thus it may be that in the electrostatic field of cage B it is possible to have an excess of O_2^- ions by the nature of the double capacitor as defined. Since it can be shown by calculation[19] that the electric field intensity between the cages is greater at the surface of the cage-B metal wall than at the surface of cage A, this would increase the probability of collision of the O_2^+ with the copper metal wall, resulting in the production of a small amount of O_2^- ions as well. The presence of such ionic forms of oxygen would in turn favor the production of ozone at the low potentials involved. Ozone is believed to exist in the following resonance between structures:[20]

Ozone can also be formed by the collision between a photochemically activated oxygen molecule and a normal oxygen molecule:[21] $O_2^* + O_2 \rightarrow O_3 + O$. ($O_2^*$ = activated oxygen.) Thus there are a number of processes that could contribute to the production of ozone in small quantities. That this is so in our experiments is borne out by the fact that the smell of ozone is often detectable in the vicinity of the charged cages. However, since the field energy levels involved are rather low, one should expect to find a continuous transition of the oxygen to the ozone state, and the reverse, with each pulse of the field, with little or no conservation of stable ozone. This polymerization and depolymerization of oxygen and ozone would to some degree excite weak bands of the absorption and emission spectra of the molecules.[22] The subject is sealed off from any physiological activity of the oxygen in the electrostatic field, but may have some interaction based on the phenomenon of extrasensory cognition, and this presumably would be exerted via the psi-plasma field.

Let us leave this outer-cage surface activity for the moment and consider those events going on inside of the metal skin of cage *B*. Here again there are two phenomena to consider, the radiation and the chemical. We can consider the subject, sitting inside of cage *B*, as a radiator of electrical oscillation (albeit a feeble one) from the evidence of electroencephalography. That such an electrical oscillation is not entirely confined to the box of the cranium is evident from the fact that electroencephalographic recordings from the surface of the scalp are identical to those made from the surface of the exposed brain.[23] It is well known that waves, sonic or electrical, in an enclosure or box will result in standing waves. This problem has been analyzed for low-frequency sound in a room by Morse.[24] But let us first analyze the ideal case of an electron in a box.

"These considerations are well illustrated by the concept of 'the particle in the box.' If a particle moves to and fro in a box with parallel walls, its behavior may be treated by 'classical' dynamics, and the particle may have *any energy*, provided that the box is large. The equations of wave-mechanics require us to take account of the wave theory interpretation of the motion. The governing equations are:

$$mv = h\lambda^{-1}, \quad \text{and} \quad n\lambda = 2(a)$$

where mv is the momentum of the particle, lambda the wavelength, n an integer, and (a) the width of the box. These expressions embody the Uncertainty Principle and the assumption that if the motion has a wave character it must necessarily be a stationary wave, i.e., have nodes at the walls of the box, or otherwise the motion could not persist unchanged in time. Figure 10 shows the wave-forms of the first three quantum levels of a vibrating particle. It is possible to attach a physical meaning to the *amplitude,* Psi (ψ) of the above wave motion, or rather to its square (ψ^2). The square represents the *probability* that the particle will occupy any region of space. Experiment cannot establish simultaneously the exact momentum and position of the particle, if it determines the momentum within fixed limits, the *position* of the fixed particle can be expressed only as a probability curve in space. Such probability distributions are called the 'partial density' curves. In Fig. 10 it can be seen that ψ^2 for $n = 1$ has a maximum (electron density) in the center of the box. This is the opposite of the result given by classical theory for a particle vibrating in a box, which is there expected to be found with equal probability anywhere across the box. For $n = 2$ there are two maxima, for $n = 3$, three, and so on. It will be observed from the shapes of the curves, however, that at high values of n the forms of ψ^2 must tend to uniform probability of position across the box, i.e., to approximate to classical dynamics, which applies when n is large.

"These considerations lead us to the conclusion that when particles are relatively *unconfined* by walls of force fields they may be treated as particles in ordinary dynamical theory; when on the other hand they are restricted in space, they must be treated by wave-theory."[25]

The Rev. Father A. K. Glazewski[26] has analyzed this problem for the case of a human placed in a "box," and his analysis is here presented in synoptic form: "Let a human body, *m,* situated not far from other objects, e.g., in a room, be suddenly charged electrostatically with, say, a negative charge. At that precise moment the lines of the electric field will move with a certain velocity, *x* (at app. the velocity of light), towards the walls, and will end on a positive charge. On reaching the walls they will induce an additional charge of positive sign, which in its turn will reverse the process. Owing to slow discharge, the process will be maintained for a certain time, and a damping phenomenon will take place. But in addition it must be taken into account that the body, *m,* vibrates with its molecular, thermal, and electric

agitation; and statistically at a certain moment, 50% of the molecules of the body, m, will retreat from the direction of the wall
and at a moment, t, will again approach the wall. A resultant
wave will be produced, and an extremely faint mutual exchange
of induction and radiation between these two bodies, the wall
and the body, m, will take place. This change will be extremely
small relative to the size of the human body, but by no means
small relative to the size of the molecules in the surrounding air.
This mutual process between the body, m, and the walls, will
naturally produce a standing wave." (See Q. 5 Appendix C.)

Now, between the mass of the human body, m, and the walls
of the room there is a gaseous medium, the air. It is composed of
the same constituents as those cited for the air outside the cage,
with the addition that there is present the expired carbon dioxide
and other organic constituents of respiration, perspiration, and
sebaceous secretion. What happens to these molecules? We know
that they vibrate with thermal agitation in all directions. Suppose
that to a great extent they are electrically neutral. The moment
we charge the body electrically, all the neutral molecules of the
air, now in an electrical field, will become electrical dipoles, and
their thermal agitation will be polarized to a certain degree (plus-
minus an angle ϕ) in the direction of the field lines. This polarization will be a function of the intensity of the electrical field of
the body, m.

Owing to this polarization of the vibration of the molecules, a
sonic wave will necessarily result as a pulse-modulation effect.
However, the intensity of the field is too small to produce an
audible noise. Prof. T. J. J. See rightly compares a charged
capacitor to a singing bell,[27] and has given the mathematical
analysis for the relation between sound and electrostatics.

Thus we paint a theoretical picture of an ionized state around
the subject (which one can imagine to appear very much like the
traditional aureole) that may have nodal characteristics due to
a standing-wave phenomenon. The nodal points represent probability areas where the energy density is increased. Such an
energy density can be expected to result in transitions of the vibrational energy of the molecules. This would result in certain
observable changes in the absorption (or emission) spectra of
the molecules, depending on the level of energy in question, for
which we can look.

Let us turn for a moment to the results of direct observation
of a medium or a person in some advanced stage of the ritual of

the irrational. It has been repeatedly reported[28] that a field can actually be visually observed around such an individual that has the following characteristics: 1) It is of a gaseous type of appearance, and has been called the aura, or OD. 2) It, at times, has luminous qualities with different colors reported for different states. 3) It has an odor which is usually of a fragrant perfume quality often described as musk, heliotropin, jasmine, etc. The author can confirm these latter observations of odoriferous characteristics on the basis of personal experience. The appearance or production of such a gaseous field is traditionally associated with the degree of power exhibited by the sensitive, i.e., the greater the production of this odic substance, the greater the capacity to produce "physical phenomena." Assuming that these traditional observations are correct, and not illusions, what mechanism could produce such a substance?

The most apparent particle sources are the secretions of the sweat and sebaceous glands of the skin. The sebaceous glands secrete cholesterol, oxycholesterol, lanolin, simpler fatty acids including unsaturated fatty acids, and fatty-acid esters of octodecyl and cetyl alcohols, as well as albumins.[29] The sweat glands secrete urea, uric acid, creatinine, lactic acid, ethereal sulfates of phenol and skatol, amino acids, sugar, albumine, as well as water and sodium chloride.[30] Some of these substances, particularly the unsaturated fatty acids, can by such a simple operation as exposure to activated oxygen or ozone result in a "perfume" odor. Marchand[31] concluded that perfumes are compounds which contain oxygen in the form of a bridge linkage and contain oxygen in the form of a bridge atom. Esters, lactones, and ethers contain an oxygen linkage, but not ketones, aldehydes, or ionones. We can assume that such chemicals occur endogenously in sensitive individuals who are exhibiting parapsychological phenomena as a result of cholinergia.

What functional purpose would the production of such perfume-like substances serve? Zwaardemaker and Hogewind[32] found that the spray formed by extruding water from a fine jet is not electrically charged, but if the water contains an "odorant" in solution, even in very small quantities, then the spray carries a strong positive charge. The quantity of the electric charge per c.c. of saturated solution has been worked out for various substances by Zwaardemaker, Backman, and Huyer separately. The following are taken from a list compiled by Zwaardemaker in *International Critical Tables,* 1: 359, 1926.

ODORANT	SPRAY ELECTRICITY per c.c. of saturated solution 10^{-10} Coulombs
Aniline	0.4
Skatol	1.0
Trinitroisobutyl (Artificial Musk)	1.0
Toluene	5.1
Nitrobenzene	9.6
Phenol	15.2
Camphor	20.3
Heliotropin	52.0
Citral	360.0

We can now see the possibility of the fine apertures of the sweat glands increasing the ionic charge in the atmosphere around a sensitive. In addition to the phenol and skatol produced by the skin of the sensitive, other perfume-like substances would have the effect of increasing the positive charge in his vicinity. This effect would be increased by water vapor from induced sweating.

We have already theorized that the psi-plasma field of a sensitive will expand under the influence of cholinergia. Cholinergia increases secretions from the skin. The water and odoriferous substances would exist as particles in a *physical plasma* formed by the psi-plasma field. Such a physical plasma can be compared to the ectoplasm so frequently reported (and photographed) in the vicinity of mediums.[33] Being a physical plasma it would necessarily be a short-range effect; and this is how it has been observed to act. The curious fact is that such a physical plasma is capable of assuming many forms and exerting local action and force. Such physical plasma is usually observed to come out of a medium principally through the gross apertures, i.e., mouth, ears, etc.

Since we observed the greatest increase in ESP-test scores with increased concentrations of negatively charged ions in the cage, it would appear that these have a greater effect on building up the density of the physical psi plasma than the positive charges described for spray electricity. Building up the negative charge in the immediate environment of the subject would then presumably further build up the condensation of the physical plasma.

Let us further consider the ionized field around the subject in the cage. Activated molecules emit radiation in three wavelength regions: 1) the far infrared, 2) the near infrared, and 3) the visible or ultraviolet. The radiation in the first group is ascribed, in the simple theory, to changes in the rotational energy of a dipole molecule. The second group is ascribed to simultaneous changes of rotational and vibrational energy, and the third, to simultaneous changes in the rotational, vibrational, and electronic energy of the molecule. We can expect that the carbon dioxide in the atmosphere of the cage would be subject to rotational-vibrational stress and result in near infrared emission or absorption bands. It is known that CO_2 has two unusually strong absorption bands in the infrared, one at 15.0 microns, and the other at 4.3 microns. We have already shown the presence of activated oxygen and ozone in the electrostatic field outside of cage B (between it and cage A). It is a curious coincidence that ozone also has a strong absorption band in the infrared, one at 4.8 microns, and one at approximately 15 microns. Such emission and absorption bands may well account for the luminosity observed in the odic, or aura, field.

The intimate dependency of consciousness on oxygen is too well-known to describe here in detail. It became an intriguing question as to whether the observed increase in ESP-test scores with increased negative-ion concentration was in any way related to oxygen physiology as it affects consciousness.

Since all previous experiments had been conducted with both nostrils and the mouth open, and therefore available as airways, and since I had observed that all sensitives when doing ESP-tests seem to breathe not through the mouth but nasally, it was decided to selectively seal both nostrils, and then each one separately during ESP-tests. Project XIII used the conditions of Project XII D with the telepathic sender at a high electrostatic potential induced by a 10 Kv D.C. negative foot electrode, and an atmospheric negative-ion excess. The subject was in cage C.

Peter Hurkos—sender ⎱	Telepathy experiment with subjects facing each other.
Harry Stone—receiver ⎰	Receiver blindfolded.

Protocol: Project XIII.

Experiment No. 1
   Control Cage—floating, no charge, nostrils open.
      ON hits   9/50 $P = 0.036265$

Experiment No. 2
   Test Cage, charged, both nostrils plugged (papier-mâché mask).
      ON hits   9/50 $P = 0.036265$

Experiment No. 4*
   Test Cage, charged, both nostrils plugged tightly (collodion seal).
      ON hits   14/50 $P = 0.000471$

Experiment No. 5
   Test Cage, charged, left nostril open; right closed (collodion seal).
      ON hits   43/50 $P = 5.52 \times 10^{-26}$

Experiment No. 6
   Test Cage, charged, right nostril open; left closed (collodion seal).
      ON hits   24/50 $P = 6.47 \times 10^{-10}$

Experiment No. 11
   Test Cage, charged, both nostrils open.
      ON hits   44/50 $P = 5.50 \times 10^{-27}$

Summary:

Right Nostril Only Open	Both Nostrils Sealed	Left Nostril Only Open
Hits 24/50	Hits 14/50	Hits 43/50
$P = 6.47 \times 10^{-10}$	$P = 4.71 \times 10^{-4}$	$P = 5.52 \times 10^{-26}$

Both Nostrils Open
Hits 44/50
$P = 5.50 \times 10^{-27}$

* Experiments 3, 7, 8, 9 and 10 are not pertinent to this series.

The significant difference in scoring when both nostrils are sealed and only mouth-breathing is used and when the nostrils are open is dramatic. Of curious interest is the fact that the highest scores were associated with respiration through the left nostril. Since an adequate amount of oxygen is delivered by mouth-breathing through the pulmonary alveoli to the brain, one cannot look to the known functions of such oxygen absorption as being vitally related to telepathy under the conditions cited. Since the scores were the same with nostrils open in an uncharged cage and with nostrils plugged in a charged cage, it must be assumed that the nostril-plugging blocked some effect due to the electrical charging. This effect could only be the excess of negative ions. One can only make a guess when one suggests that the charged ions, O_2^-, collect in the roof of the nasal passage, and there exert some effect (paramagnetic?) on the brain or on the expansion of psi plasma. This, of course, is only a conjecture, but one which is subject to test.

NOTES Appendix B

1. *The Key of Solomon,* Translated from various thirteenth-century and fourteenth-century MSS in the British Museum by S. Lidell MacGregor Mathers, George Redway, London, 1889, p. 14.

2. J. Cecil Maby, *Internat'l Congress of Radionics,* London, 1950, p. 82. See also the *J. of the British Soc. of Dowsers,* 11: 80, p. 55 *et seq.,* 11: 81, p. 117 *et seq.,* 12: 85, pp. 7–26, 1954.

3. J. Cecil Maby, *op. cit.,* pp. 80, 82.

4. J. Alan Chalmers, *Atmospheric Electricity,* Oxford, 1949, pp. 17, 18, 22, 69, 72, and 74.

5. H. H. Skilling and John C. Beckett, "Control of Air Ion Density in Rooms," *J. of the Franklin Institute,* 256: 423–34, 1953. W. W. Hicks, U.S. Patents No. 2,594,777; 2,640,158.

6. J. C. Beckett, "Air Ionization as an Environment Factor," *Applications and Industry,* September 1954.

7. John L. Worden, "The effect of air ion concentration and polarity on the carbon dioxide capacity of mammalian blood plasma," Lecture before the American Physiological Society, April 12, 1954, at Atlantic City, N.J.

8. Christian B. Nielson and Harold A. Harper, "Effect of air

ions on succinoxidase activity of the rat adrenal gland," *Proc. Soc. Exp. Biol. & Med.*, 86: 753–56, 1954.

9. Ferrannini, L., *Revista de Meterologia e Scienza Affine*, Roma, julio-agosta, 1939.

10. Augusto M. Tobles Gorriti and Antonio Medina, "The application of Ion Therapy in Hypertension," *Nat. Ministry of Public Health*, April 12, 1954, Buenos Aires.

11. Manfred Curry, *Bioklimatik*, 2 Vols., American Bioclimatic Research Institute, 1946.

12. C. P. Yaglou, L. C. Benjamin, and A. D. Brandt, "The influence of respiration and transpiration on ionic content of air of occupied rooms," *Ind. Hygiene*, 15: 8, 1933.

13. Howard C. Murphy, "How ion density affects comfort," *Heating, Piping & Air Conditioning*, October 1954.

14. Nikola Tesla, "Apparatus for the Utilization of Radiant Energy." U.S. Patents No. 685,957; 685,958, November 5, 1901.

15. *International Congress of Radionics*, London, 1950, p. 60.

16. *Thorpe's Dictionary of Applied Chemistry*, Longmans, London, Fourth Ed., 1949, p. 192 *et seq.*

17. *Thorpe's Dictionary of Applied Chemistry*, Longmans, London, Fourth Ed., 1949, p. 193.

18. *Encyclopaedia Britannica*, 1953 Ed., Vol. 17, p. 786.

19. *Encyclopaedia Britannica*, 1953 Ed., Vol. 8, p. 241.

20. *Thorpe's Dictionary of Applied Chemistry*, Longmans, London, Fourth Ed., 1949, p. 194. Warren B. Boast, *Principles of Electric and Magnetic Fields*, Harper & Bros., New York, 1948, p. 60 *et seq.*

21. *Thorpe's Dictionary of Applied Chemistry*, Longmans, London, Fourth Ed., 1949, p. 193.

22. *Encyclopaedia Britannica*, 1953 Ed., Vol. 23, p. 639.

23. Identical means for the practical purpose of clinical diagnostic procedures. Some absorption of the energy is obviously incurred in the passage through the bony and soft tissues.

24. Philip M. Morse, *Vibration and Sound*, "International Series in Pure and Applied Physics," McGraw-Hill, New York, 1948, p. 381.

25. E. J. Bowen, *The Chemical Aspects of Light*, Oxford, 1946, p. 60–63.

26. *International Congress of Radionics*, London, 1950, p. 138 *et seq.*

27. T. J. J. See, *Wave Theory*, 12 Vols., Wheldon and Wes-

ley, Nichols Press, Lynn, Mass., 1938–52. See Vol. 5, pp. 94–102.

28. Gerda Walter, "The Human Aura," *Tomorrow,* 2: 81–87, 1954. Hans Driesch, *Psychical Research,* G. Bell, London, 1933.

29. *Howell's Physiology.*

30. *Howell's Physiology.*

31. R. W. Moncrieff, *The Chemical Senses,* John Wiley & Sons, New York, 1944, p. 230.

32. Zwaardemaker and Hogewind, *Proceedings of the Academy of Sciences,* Amsterdam, 22: 429–37, 1920.

33. See the photographs in "The Margery Mediumship," *Proceedings of the American Society for Psychical Research,* 3 Vols., 1928.

Appendix C

Some Questions and Speculations about the Physical Plasma

There is reason to believe that the type of telepathic interaction observed in Project XIII (Appendix B) is somehow dependent on the gaseous constituents in the atmosphere which are related to respiration. Although one may invoke a physical plasma, it is best to consider this effect under some generic title, and I propose to use the word *OD* (coined by Reichenbach) until the gaseous elements can be identified chemically and their role established. OD is conceived as a gaseous plasma in which atoms and organic molecules are molded into some form by the psi-plasma field.

The following line of speculation, in the form of questions and provisional answers, is put forth with reserve:

Q. 1. What is the origin of OD?

    A. OD probably is constituted of atmospheric gases and biological vapors, and formed by the psi-plasma field.

Q. 2. Which is the important constituent of the gaseous atmosphere?

    A. It may be one that is absorbed in respiration.

    Possibilities:

      1. O_2, O_2^-, O_2^*. At. no. = 8. At. wt. = 16. Mol. wt. = 32

      2. O_3. Ozone = 48. O_4 oxozonide = 64

      3. H. At. no. = 1

      4. CO_2 produced by the organism

Q. 3. What is unique about the respiratory system of a sensitive that would give a clue as to active atmospheric-gas constituent?

    A. An analysis of mediumistic trance-breathing phenomena shows that:

      1. Left-sided nasal intake is traditionally alleged to be

the receiving function in telepathy. (See Yoga literature.)

2. Mediums usually develop left-sided upper respiratory pathology, with symptoms based on cholinergia. Sensitives tend to hypercapnea and increased pCO_2 rather than hyperventilation.

—Paramagnetic property of O_2 and N_2O and its relation to nasal chambers?

—When charge flashes on single-screen cage, medium's breathing is momentarily cut off. (Gasping reaction or reflex.)[1] (Charged ions pulled out of cage.)

B. Breathing block of medium:

1. A 2-second electric charge on screen cage is sufficient to produce this effect—momentary (for 1–2 seconds).

2. Primary blocking occurs in 2–4 seconds after end of charge.

3. *Full* secondary blocking occurs approximately 7 seconds after end of charge. This secondary blocking lasts for approximately 8 seconds. The telepathic "sensitive" is refractory to "receiving" for approximately 15 seconds after showing response. This suggests an adrenergic effect and a contraction of the psiplasma field.

4. Tertiary partial blocking effects last for at least 2 minutes.

Q. 4. What does the blocking effect mean?

A. 1. It means as electrical energy (ionic) is pulled out of the screen cage, initiated by an electrical charge outside the cage, that this has the effect of initial stimulation (adrenergia) on sensitive subject (psychomotor) followed by profound respiratory effect (which starts on expiratory phase of breathing) and psychomotor depression, possibly due to inhibitory phase of adrenergia.

2. This primary effect (mostly depressive) is eliminated by the use of a double Faraday cage which, however, does not remove the ESP-stimulating effect. This is well-proven in our experiments.

3. This may point to an ionic effect that has a double component:

a. Initially there may be an ionization of gas due to sudden energy change in the ions in the cage atmosphere.

b. When deficiency of ions occurs, adrenergic depression results. When direct deficiency ionic effect is blocked out there remains an important *secondary effect* of the electrical charge which is able to act through a solid-copper air-tight Faraday cage.

Q. 5. What is the nature of the secondary effect?

A. The electrical charge may induce a potential electromagnetic signal inside cage B. Calculating from the values 640 c.p.s. and 2 ma., this would produce a field of 2×10^{-5} volts per meter in the cage. The subject would then absorb a power of approximately 4×10^{-10} watts. The thermal noise of the body is approximately $1.6 \times 10^{-20} \times \Delta f$ watts, where $\Delta f =$ band width of filter. Allowing the subject 15 seconds for a response corresponds to a filter of band width 0.1 c.p.s. The atmospheric noise is approximately 10^{-8} watts $\times \Delta f$ (unpolarized through 4π radius); and 3×10^{-9} watts $\times \Delta f$ polarized in one dimension. Comparing the absorbed power $= 4 \times 10^{-10}$ watts, with atmospheric noise 3×10^{-9} watts $\times$ 0.1 c.p.s. $= 3 \times 10^{-10}$ watts, we see that the atmospheric noise is reduced to a signal-to-noise-ratio of unity. The secondary effect could then be due to the charged cage serving as a filter which rejects noise. (Analysis by Jack J. Grossmann.)

Q. 6. Does the electrical charging of the cage create any ionic effects which act as a filter to atmospheric noise?

A. 1. The interrupted pulses may create an oscillatory movement of ions such as O_2^-, O_2^*, etc. Since these are all polarized by the field they may tend to polarize the "atmospheric noise" which in turn favors psi-plasma expansion.

2. However, it may be due to a *property* of these ions which is not blocked by the barrier of the Faraday cage.

   This property could be:

   a. Magnetic fields.
   b. Paramagnetic resonance.

        c. Gravitational effect, allowing psi-plasma expansion.

Q. 7. It is a fact that thus far only mediums, or sensitives, can experience the increased ESP-test scoring effect of the cage. What distinguishes the medium or sensitive from the ordinary human?

A. It may be the ability to maintain a concentration of OD, or to properly control it, or to respond by cholinergia to cage environment.

Q. 8. Do we have observational clues as to what OD is?

A. OD is alleged to be seen by sensitives and it has been photographed by scientists as ectoplasm.

Q. 9. From these sources what do we know about the aura?

A. 1. It envelops the human body.

2. It probably has a gaseous composition, O_2, N_2, and H.

3. It is luminous—has form and color to the eye of the sensitive.

4. It has the properties of an odorant. This may mean that it may activate either the central or peripheral centers for olfaction.

5. It has been described by sensitives as contracting or condensing about a human inside of the charged cage B.

6. The appearance of the aura to the sensitive is alleged to be indicative of past or present disease as well as the present state of health. Therefore, it has the properties already ascribed to the psi plasma in psychometry.

Q. 10. What conclusion can we come to from these observations as to the nature of OD?

A. 1. Mediums are able to utilize it to gain intelligence about humans; and to concentrate it for use in bringing about physical phenomena.

Q. 11. What time factors are associated with OD?

A. 1. I have observed that it takes good mediums about 2 minutes to go into trance and establish contact for "control." This is the same time period as the duration of tertiary depression induced by an electrically charged screen cage. This may mean that OD is dispersed by a single screen cage and that it takes about 2 minutes to condense a new supply in the absence of further cage charging. Likewise, 2 minutes may represent the time for a medium to bring about an expansion of his psi-plasma field. This would correspond to the time period of elastance calculated for the psi plasma in Note 12, Chapter 11.

2. After this 2-minute tertiary period it takes 8–10 more minutes for the sensitive to recover and *demonstrate* ESP-cognition. This may mean that 2 minutes is required for the medium to gain control of the psi-plasma process initially, but that it takes 10 or more minutes to fully recover from the effects of an inhibitory adrenergia, achieve cholinergia, and concentrate enough OD to utilize it precisely.

3. Thus one may say that it takes a medium about 12 minutes in which to concentrate enough OD to demonstrate ESP-cognition, after the biological, psychological, and psychical shock of acute ion deficiency.

4. Stone, in ESP-tests in the cage, always does poorly on the first MAT run which normally takes him from 12–20 minutes. His best score appears in the last two runs of a series of five. Therefore, he may be much slower than other sensitives in controlling psi-plasma expansion and OD.

5. Hurkos takes only 3 minutes to warm up to ESP-tests, and his best scores occur in the first few runs (approximately 30 minutes) of testing.

Q. 12. Since the entire air supply for the medium is confined to the cage volume (216 cu. feet), what is it that the medium does to "process" the respired air?

A. 1. Before going into trance most mediums go through a breathing exercise which is the first step in processing the air.

2. First processing may occur in nasal chambers as a selective filtration and absorption of certain ions or molecules, or even a concentration of OD.

3. It is conceivable that the medium processes OD in the left side of the respiratory passage, as stated in the Yoga doctrine.

4. Oxygen is absorbed in greatest quantity through the

pulmonary alveolar wall. Trace amounts of N_2 and H are also absorbed.

5. Special breathing techniques may act to ionize the gas molecules, as per the observation cited by Floyd that respiration creates an electrical potential on membrane surfaces.

6. As stated earlier, CO_2 is concentrated in the blood, and pCO_2 may also be increased. This may influence OD concentration, and needs to be studied.

7. The OD component of air may not necessarily be transferred into the body via the pulmonary blood stream, but nevertheless it appears that it probably undergoes chemical linkage there. Since OD has an odor, there must occur some linkage by a molecule of gas (O_3, O_2) and an atom or molecule of an organic substance which gives off the scented odor. This is then excreted through skin pores and apertures as OD, or seen as the aura.

What could this linkage be?

a. Sex steroid?
b. Adrenal ketosteroid?
c. Choline compounds?

d. Unsaturated fatty-acid compound: Lecithin-glutathione-O_2 Glycer-ides-linolenic acid?
e. Glutathione system?
f. Indole compounds?

What clues do we have?

a. The medium loses a few ounces weight during an hour trance, but over a number of such sittings gains weight. Weight increase is mostly due to edema fluid. Overactivity of the adrenal cortex is implied.

Q. 13. What substance could be lost during a trance that accounts for weight loss, and then leads to compensatory edema?
A. Water would be the only substance that could be lost so rapidly. Water would most likely be lost by a diuretic effect, combined with a sudorific or perspiratory reaction. The release of some compound from the adrenal

cortex can be suspected (electrocortin?). Such a fluid loss would entail a loss of electrolyte, and probably an excess production of cortisone compound which would lead to a compensatory edema.

Q. 14. It would appear that there could be a sequence of events in the realm of gas phenomena, respiratory physiology, and stress-reaction physiology that may furnish clues to the mode of OD production, and to the identification of OD. If this be so, then what experiments should be conducted to test the above hypothesis?

A. A minute gas analysis in the cage—before, during, and after the medium worked—compared to a control study. A continuous spectrographic analysis would be the most satisfactory. Excretion studies of the urine, specific gravity, electrolytes, ketosteroids, etc.

Q. 15. Is there any possible relation between the 15-micron absorption band of CO_2 and brain-cell function?

A. It has been observed in the case of Mr. Hurkos that there is present on EEG recording a form of self-excited synchronous discharge in the right temporal cortex at times contemporaneous with an act of ESP-cognition. Let us assume that such cortical cells are behaving as a cavity resonator. The formula for the wave length of a cavity resonator is $\lambda = 2.28$ radius. Substituting in the place of lambda the value of a wave length of 15 microns, we can calculate that the radius of the nucleus, or cytoplasm, of such cells would be approximately 6.5 microns, or 13 microns in diameter. This conforms to the size of the cell body of the ordinary small cell in the temporal cortex. The assumption that the cortical cell body could behave like a cavity resonator must be based on some structural characteristic compatible with such a function. The following structural characteristics are present that are compatible with such an assumption: 1) The geometry is correct. 2) It can be argued quite plausibly that the plasma membrane of the cell body has properties that fit closely the properties of a piezoelectric crystal of the Rochelle-salt type. 3) The elements of resistance (R), capacitance (C), and inductance (L) in a nerve are postulated by Curtis and Cole[2] to exist in the form of a series-resonant circuit.

In a piezocrystal these same elements are arranged in a parallel-resonant circuit. A parallel-resonant circuit would satisfy the electrical requirements of the "after-discharge" phenomenon observed in humans showing self-excited synchronous discharge. Hence, it is suggested that the series connection of L and C of the "series-resonant" circuit in a nerve in the normal state, is shifted in a sensitive to a parallel connection between L and C which is in series with the rest of the circuit, thus resulting in a parallel-resonant circuit. Such a change could be effected by a reorientation of molecular elements as the result of chemical shifts. 4) The energy and power requirements are satisfied. 5) It is suggested that sonic activation (8–14 c.p.s.?) is the simplest method of activating a cell body of the temporal cortex to shift its function toward being a parallel resonant circuit and act as a cavity resonator of wave length 15 microns, and that this is related in some unknown way to the 15-micron absorption band of CO_2. The hypothetical 15-micron resonance of the activated temporal-cortex cell body is put forward to show that it is desirable to perform the following experiment: If intermittent 15-micron radiation from the brain and absorption of the same by carbon dioxide, ozone, or other like molecules in the atmosphere can increase the "power factor" of the subject, it should be possible to test this by introducing such monochromatic radiation and then to test its effect on the ESP-test performance of the subject. We must not forget that 15-micron radiation induces heat, and we may be talking of the "inner heat," or *tumo* that Yogins generate.

Q. 16. Why is the ground connection of cage B important in the phenomenon described, and why is pulse modulation of such an arrangement contributory?

A. The following line of speculation might be helpful in finding an answer. Consider the surface of the earth as the inner shell of a capacitor, and the atmosphere or ionosphere as the outer shell of a capacitor. What are the requirements to produce a standing electromagnetic wave in a shell of such dimensions? Using the circumference of the earth as one physical dimension (approximately 40,000 kilometers), and the circumference of the ionosphere 200 kilometers above the earth as another dimension, simple calculation reveals that it would require a frequency of about 8 cycles per second to form a standing electromagnetic wave whose node would be at the opposite pole of the earth from the point of origin. One could pulse (with suitable power) a double Faraday cage at this frequency and maintain such a standing wave. It would be interesting to activate by photic stimulation, or auditory stimulation, the brain electrical oscillation at a frequency of 8 c.p.s., and since the earth-atmosphere oscillation is resonant at approximately 8 c.p.s., it might be possible to get these factors in synchrony. In order to achieve this certain requirements would have to be met. The first is that the geometry of the inner cage *B* should be such that it resonates (sonically) at a fundamental of 8 c.p.s. This could easily be done with the use of a 64-foot-long organ pipe which has a fundamental of 8 c.p.s. This tube can be made of a good dielectric, and a Faraday sphere placed on top of this column.

Q. 17. In regard to Project XV what electrical conditions exist on cage-*B* wall?

A. Charged copper in the wall of a Faraday cage tends to have all free electrons pulled to the outer surface of the cage. This leaves an excess of positive charge on the inside of the copper wall which attracts electrons from the outer surface of the dielectric (wood) lining. Since the charges are bound in the dielectric, the inside surface of the dielectric will tend to become positively charged with respect to the outer surface. This will induce a certain stress in the dielectric whose direction will be outward. A human being inside the cage will then be subject to the stress of a high potential of positive electricity in respect to his own electrostatic field. This will tend to pull negatively charged ions away from his body. This effect is neutralized by the addition of negative ions to the cage atmosphere. With a steady D.C. charge on the cage, equilibrium conditions are obtained.

The following points may be enumerated as to what

may be the function of the Faraday cage in increasing ESP-test scores and cognition:

1. It shields out all electrical disturbance which would make the gaseous components of the odic field unstable.
2. It provides a closed volume of space which can concentrate gaseous energy around the sensitive.
3. The Ground arrangement of the Faraday cages may act as an atmospheric noise filter, and as a signal filter for ESP. This effect is increased by adding charged negative ions into the cage.
4. The maintenance of electric-charge potential on the cage aids telepathic cognition to gain intelligence from outside of the walls of the cage. Hence, some filter function must exist for the copper metal boundary of the cage.

Q. 18. Is there any function of the copper as a psi-plasma filter?

A. A basic function of the copper may be polarization. The face-centered cubic crystal structure of copper (tough pitch copper with 0.03% O_2) may be the polarizing structure. As far as ESP-cognition is concerned it would be the O_2 and O_3 in the copper that may polarize the consciousness system involved.

Q. 19. What properties of copper[3] support this hypothesis?

A. Gold, silver, and copper are diamagnetic. A diamagnetic metal offers a favorable lattice work for paramagnetic domains. Dispersed throughout copper is oxygen. Thus high electric fields on the copper would produce high electric-field intensities in the interionic volume of oxygen.

Q. 20. What property of oxygen[4] would form domains in the diamagnetism of copper resulting in polarization?

A. O_2 is strong in paramagnetism. Under the impress of a high potential difference across the cage certain changes would occur in the oxygen. We recall that the gravitational constant $= c^2(P/U)^2\beta$. We can decrease the local gravitational constant in oxygen by influencing its angular moment, U, by: 1) Increasing v, the orbital frequency of the ionic electron. 2) Increasing the period of the ionic electron, T, by pulsing the charge on the cage at approximately 8 c.p.s. Thus $U = hv \cdot T$, and as we have shown earlier such a change in v and T results in a marked local decrease in the value of the gravitational constant, and this will occur in each atom of oxygen contained in a spherical shell of copper around a sensitive. The net result will be a polarized shell of lowered gravitational field potential around the subject. This will allow expansion of his psi plasma. Each atom of oxygen will be a center of lowered G_o polarizing psi plasma. Oxygen will have this effect because it is the one chemical in nature most closely linked to consciousness.

The faster the ionic electron orbits around the atom, the closer will the atom approach the ground state—the atomic state of least energy. In this state the atom cannot radiate at all. If this atom is oxygen in the brain, we can see that such cessation of radiation means quietude for the mind. The mind will become the calm mirror surface of the void sought in the state of samadhi by the Yogin.

There are several ways to increase the oxygen orbital-electron velocity. Each presupposes that the subject is in a hollow spherical shell of metal, the type depending on the technique. We consider the case of a magnetic shell first. The P. Langevin equation for magnetic moment of an orbital electron is:

$$M = \frac{ve/c}{2\pi r} \pi r^2$$

where v = orbital velocity
e = e.s.u. charge of electron
c = light velocity
r = radius of the orbit

The velocity of the oxygen electron, where $r = 1.12 \times 10^{-8}$ cm:

$$v = \frac{cM}{e\pi r^2} 2\pi r$$

$$= 1.033 \times 10^8 \text{ cm/sec.}$$

We can solve for v^2 in this equation by using the e.m.u. value instead of the e.s.u. value of electron:

$$v^2 = \frac{cM}{e\pi r^2} 2\pi r$$

$$= 3.128 \times 10^{18} \text{ cm}^2 \text{ sec}^{-2}$$

Increasing the orbital velocity of the electron (by means of a magnetic field) will create an orbital "current" and this increases the magnetic moment, M.

Let us assume that $v^2 = c^2$, and we solve in e.m.u.

$$M = \frac{v^2 e/c}{2\pi r} \pi r^2$$

$$= 2.69 \times 10^{-18} \text{ erg/gauss,}$$

i.e., if the magnetic field is applied to the atom, without loss. This increased velocity can be achieved with an applied field to a single atom of approximately 300 gauss. To get the same order of effect on the scale of a human would require a corresponding increase in field strength. This might prove to be a considerable engineering problem. I believe the simpler technology lies with a charged hollow copper sphere.

We want to establish a potential difference (calculated in e.m.u.) between a proton in the nucleus of oxygen and an orbital electron such that the orbital electron is accelerated to about 99% of light velocity, or $v^2 \cong c^2$.

The electron at this velocity will have its mass increased by a factor $1 / \left(1 - \dfrac{v^2}{c^2} \right)^{\frac{1}{2}} = (e)^2 = 7.39$, where e is the number e. (See Appendix F.) All calculations are based on this mass.

The radius, as before, is 1.12×10^{-8}.

The gravitational constant $= 6.67 \times 10^{-8}$.

The proton mass is unaffected, being at the center.

$$E = (c^2 G)^{\frac{1}{2}} = \text{Potential Difference (volts)}$$

$$= 2.068 \times 10^{-6} \text{ e.m.u.}$$

$$\text{Abvolts} = \frac{2.068 \times 10^{-6} \text{ e.m.u.}}{1.602 \times 10^{-20} \text{ e.m.u.}} = 1.29 \times 10^{14}$$

$$\text{Volts} = \frac{1.29 \times 10^{14}}{10^8} = 1.29 \times 10^6 \text{ volts}$$

This is the order of potential difference that we would seek to maintain between the center of a hollow sphere (with our subject therein) and the outer surface of the copper sphere.

We can apply this principle in a general way to the technology of the Faraday cage.

We place a human in a hollow copper sphere. His weight is approximately 63 Kgm. The amount of charge placed on the sphere will be calculated from his mass. We make the sphere large enough for human comfort, say 100 cm. radius. The mass of the copper in the sphere should equal the mass of the human as a minimum. The human is assumed to have his mass concentrated at the center of the sphere. The equivalent mass of the copper sphere will also have its mass concentrated at the center of gravity. We take the product of these masses:

$$M^2 = M_h \times M_{ou} = 3.96 \times 10^9 \text{ gm}^2$$

We derive the amount of charge to be placed on the sphere as follows: One coulomb charge is equal to 6.226×10^{20} electrons per second $= N$.

Divide N by $M^2 = 1.57 \times 10^{11}$ electrons/sec. Multiply the mass of a proton and electron, respectively, by this number:

$$P = (1.672 \times 10^{-24} \text{ gm})(1.57 \times 10^{11}) = 2.62 \times 10^{-13} \text{ gm.}$$

$$e = (9.108 \times 10^{-28} \text{ gm})(1.57 \times 10^{11}) = 14.28 \times 10^{-17} \text{ gm.}$$

The product of these masses represents the mass of electrons added to the copper sphere as charge; and the mass of the protons affected by this charge. As the voltage goes up we have to add a correction factor for the mass increase of the electrons, but we ignore this now.

$$E = c^2 G_o \frac{(mpN)(meN)}{4\pi r^2}$$

$$E = .83 \times 10^6 \text{ volts}$$

If we increase this value by the proper mass correction factor, we will have achieved the voltage given for the single proton and the electron. This type of experiment is, I believe, a simple test of the general hypothesis. It would require a polished sphere (of copper) charged by a Van de Graaf generator capable of generating about 3 million volts at less than one ampere.

ESP-communication facts and theory have shown that all things are within the grasp of our observation dependent on the bits of information available. We need only to establish the proper steps of perceptive transformation between the seer and the object. The example of the telescope, microscope, radio, and television come readily to mind. In addition, some element of redundancy is necessary.

In the case of telepathic ESP-cognition, what are the necessary theoretical transforming steps that we must establish in order to realize such communication?

I would suggest:

1. A proper focus of consciousness in the percipient on the point in space-time of which we desire intelligence.

2. Proper amplification of the correct focus of consciousness.

3. Elimination of noise interfering with the line of communication between the point of consciousness and the object point of perception (inanimate or animate).

We can assume that the proper focus of consciousness can be achieved by training and experience by the same methods necessary for a comparable power of concentration in any other pursuits of life such as art, logic, and science. In the study of humans exhibiting ESP-cognition it has been found that better orientation can be achieved if the sensitive comes into tactile contact with some object belonging to or related to the target area in question.

Having achieved the proper focus of consciousness the sensitive needs the aid of a power factor in order to carry out the proper transformation of ESP intelligence into rational expression. This is where the concept of a physical ODIC field appears to be helpful. It appears that the transformation can best be carried out if the sensitive is inside of a dense shell of OD.

Amplification of consciousness by our theory would appear to be due to the expansion of the psi-plasma field, and this seems to be a function of gravitational field potential.

Elimination of noise is, I believe, a problem of internal body noise. This can best be eliminated by bringing the energy level of body atoms to the ground state. This is a function of the orbital velocity of electrons. We have indicated the probable biological, psychological, and physical techniques available to achieve this ground state.

For practical purposes, this line of proposed research will have reached maturity when normal "nonsensitives" can yield extra-chance scores in ESP-tests by the aid of the techniques cited.

NOTES   Appendix C

1. Bell, Davidson, and Scarborough, *Textbook of Physiology and Biochemistry,* Williams & Wilkins, 2nd Ed., 1953, p. 512, for physiology of gasping center at posterior end of 4th ventricle.

2. Curtis and Cole, *J. Cell. & Comp. Physiology,* 19: 135, 1943.

3. *Isotopes — Copper. At. No. = 29*

Protons	Mass No.	Neutrons	% Abund.	½ Life	Trans to
	58	29	0	7.9 min.	Ni 58
29	60	31	0	81 sec.	Ni 60
	61	32	0	3.4 hrs.	Ni 61
	62	33	0	10.5 min.	Ni 62
29	63	34	70.13	*stable*	—
	64	35	0	12.8 hrs.	Zn 6
	65	36	29.87	*stable*	—
	66	37	0	5 min.	Zn 66

4. *Oxygen. At. No. = 8*

Protons	Mass No.	Neutrons	% Abund.	½ Life	Trans to
8	15	7	0	126 sec.	N 15
8	16	8	99.757	—	—
8	17	9	0.039	—	—
8	18	10	0.204	—	—
8	19	11	0	31 sec.	F 19

Appendix D

An algebraic notation is used: A significant decrease of a chemical concentration or a function is indicated by minus one (−1). A significant increase of a chemical concentration or a function is indicated by plus one (+1). A normal concentration or function, or where the direction of the shift is unknown, is indicated by a blank space. An algebraic summation is then made for each biochemical or functional component. Brief reference is made to the major authorities whose work has been extrapolated in order to compile the table.

It is permissible to deduce from Table I that the *possible* biochemical shifts and their summation may result in the following physiological states during the ritual of the irrational at that point in the performance where excitatory effects are reaching a peak.

I. Metabolic Acidosis

Metabolic acidosis (primary alkali deficit) may result from excess production of organic acids (ketone bodies and lactic acid), excess loss of base, retention of acid (phosphate and sulfate), administration of acid salts, etc. This condition is found in the *adrenal cortical hyperfunction, starvation, violent exercise,* etc.

II. Normal or increased Basal Metabolic Rate with increased Calorigenic output

The basal metabolic rate is usually expressed as the amount of energy produced per unit of surface area of the body per hour when the subject is in the basal state (12 hours after the last meal and after a night's sleep). This value is calculated from the amount of oxygen consumed during a fixed period. An increased calorigenic output usually refers to an increase in the heat production of the body without an accompanying increase in the B.M.R., although the term calorigenic refers to an increased heat production without reference to the accompanying change in B.M.R. In the Shaman the B.M.R. would tend to be increased by the increased thyroid function induced by cold and athletics. The increased calorigenic output can be attributed to

TABLE I: STRESSORS

SERUM	Normal Mgm/100 ml	Cold-Acute-24 hrs.	Cold-Adaptation	Fasting	Exercise	Algebraic Summation	Effect on Neurone
Cations (base)							
Sodium	326.0	−1	1		−1	−1	Inc. in membrane potential
Potassium	20.0	1	−1		−1	−1	
Calcium	10.0	1				1	Inc. membrane rectifier and therefore inc. in capacitance & resistance
Magnesium	2.4						
Anions (Acid)							
Bicarbonate	60.5 (mlCO_2)				1	1	Acid
Chloride	365.7	−1			−1	−2	Inc. in membrane potential
Phosphate	3.4	1			1	2	Acid
Sulfate	1.6						
Lactic Acid	15.0	1			1	2	Acid
Proteinate	6500.0	1				1	
Organic Acids				1	1	2	Acid
Pyruvic Acid					1	1	
Whole Blood							
Cholesterol	140-215	−1				−1	
Creatinine	0.1-1.2				1	1	
Glucose	68-96				1	1	Inc. fuel for brain
Non-Prot. Nit.	29-43			1	1	2	
Urea	16-35			1		1	
Uric Acid	1.6-3.9	1				1	
pH	7.35-7.45	−1		−1	−1	−3	Acid
Thyroxin			1			1	Increased heat production
CO_2					1	1	pH-acid Inc. wave amplitude

TABLE I: STRESSORS (*continued*)

SERUM	*Normal* Mgm/100 ml	Cold-Acute-24 hrs.	Cold-Adaptation	Fasting	Exercise	Algebraic Summation	*Effect on Neurone*
BLOOD							
Protein Bound Iodine	6.4µgm/100 ml	-1	+1				
Ascorbic Acid	75 mgm daily	-1	1	-1		-1	This should be compensated by a therapeutic daily dose.
Ser. Ac. Phosphatase	0-1 Bodansky Units						
Ser. Alk. Phosphatase	1-4 Bodansky Units						
ACTH			1			1	Adrenergia
Gluco-Corticoids		1	1		1	3	Adrenergia
Mineral Corticoids		1			1	2	Adrenergia
Adrenaline		1	1		1	3	Adrenergia
B. M. R.	+10 to -10		1	-1	1	1	
Calorigenic Output			1		1	2	Inc. heat production
Mu Value							
Internal Temp.		-1	1		1	1	
C. M. R.	1		1			1	Inc. fuel for brain cells
A/V O$_2$ Diff.	6.4-6.9 vol. %				1	1	Inc. fuel for brain cells
Cere. Blood Flow	250-400 c.c./Min				1	1	Inc. fuel for brain cells
Urinary 17-ketosteroid Excretion		1	1			2	
Hydration		-1	-1	-1	-1	-4	Inc. in membrane capacitance
Nitrogen Balance		-1		-1	-1	-3	
Cholinergics			1		-1		

the hyperfunction of the adrenal cortex and adrenal medulla, as well as the heat production of exercise.

III. Normal or elevated Internal Body Temperature

The body temperature would tend to rise as a result of cold adaptation, exercise, and dehydration.

IV. Normal or elevated Blood Sugar

There is no evidence to show that the blood sugar is depressed by cold adaptation or fasting, and the sympathetico-adrenal stimulation of the dancing, breathing, and excitement of the performance would tend to raise the blood sugar.

V. Normal Oxygen Supply to the Brain

There is no evidence to show that the Shaman is in danger of suffering from hypoxia and its resultant changes in consciousness. Increased supply in Yogin due to breathing exercises.

VI. Hypercapnea and pCO_2

This term refers to an excess of carbon dioxide in the blood. The sources of such an excess in the Shaman are: increased carbon-dioxide production as a result of exercise, and retention of alveolar carbon dioxide as a result of singing; breathing plant smoke. In the Yogin the retention of breath between inhalation and exhalation would increase the pCO_2.

VII. Dehydration

This refers to the loss of body water particularly from the extracellular space. In the Shaman this is brought on as a result of fasting, and the sweating of the dancing and exercise. This is accompanied by the loss of large amounts of sodium chloride. In the Yogin this occurs as a result of fasting and hygienic measures.

VIII. Negative Nitrogen Balance

The difference between the nitrogen taken in the food and that excreted in the feces and the urine is spoken of as the nitrogen balance. If the output (excretion) exceeds the intake, the balance is said to be negative, i.e., the body is losing nitrogen. On a low protein intake, starvation, or severe exertion, the individual excretes nitrogen derived from the dissolution of his own protoplasm and so goes into negative nitrogen balance.

IX. Activation of the Sympathetico-Adrenal System

Since this is a vast subject, it is sufficient to say that in the opinion of the author there is a preponderance of sympathetic autonomic activity with its multiplex effects that gird the organism for "fight or flight" and increased central-nervous-system excitability. Higher thresholds require high-potential electrical discharges, which in turn require a state of cholinergia to balance the adrenergia.

The material in the table was extrapolated from the following sources:

Selye, Hans, "Stress," *Annual Reviews,* Montreal, 1951, p. 9.

It is interesting to recall at this point the condition which is called "arctic hysteria." This form of hysteria is to be seen after acute exposure to cold, or after prolonged exposure to cold (the long Arctic winter). Arctic hysteria has been invoked as the explanation of the hysterical manifestations of some Shamans. The alarm reaction, or the stage of exhaustion, should be considered as mechanisms involved in this reaction.

Cold and Metabolic Rate, *The Bulletin,* U.S.A. Med. Dept., Vol. VIII, No. 11, 1948, p. 849.

Cold and Heat Production, Best & Taylor, p. 724.

Cold and Metabolic Rate, *Cold Injury* (abbrev. *C. I.*), 1951, Transactions of the First Conference, Ed. M. Irene Ferrer, Josiah Macy, Jr., Foundation, New York, 1952, Robert Kark, p. 184.

Cold and Acclimatization, *C. I.,* 1951, Robert Kark, p. 185.

Cold and Basal Metabolism, *C. I.,* 1951, Robert Kark, p. 189.

Cold and Cortisone, *C. I.,* 1951, Joseph Blair, p. 230.

Cold and Histological Changes in the Adrenals and Thyroid, *The Bulletin,* U.S.A. Med. Dept., *op. cit.,* p. 849.

Cold and Protein-Bound Iodine, *C. I.,* 1951, Robert Kark, p. 193.

Cold and Calorigenic Activity, *C. I.,* 1951, J. W. Conn, p. 199.

Cold and Thyroid, *C. I.,* 1951, C. W. Gottschalk, p. 200.

Cold Adaptation and Thyroid, *C. I.,* 1951, Gottschalk, p. 201.

Size of the Adrenal Cortex and Cold Adaptation, *C. I.,* 1951, Robert Kark, p. 193.

Gellhorn, E., "Adrenocortical Hormones and E.E.G.," *Physiological Foundations of Neurology & Psychiatry,* University of Minnesota Press, 1953, p. 53.

Liver Oxygen Consumption and Cold, *C. I.,* 1952, p. 124.

Cold and Increase of Metabolic Rate, L. Chevillard and A. Mayer, *Ann. De Physiol.,* 15: 411, 1939.

Cold and Liver Hypertrophy, Chevillard, *ibid.*

Best & Taylor, *Physiological Basis of Medical Practice,* Williams & Wilkins, 4th Ed., "Physiology and Fasting," p. 698 *et seq.* (abbrev. B. & T.).

Fasting and Nitrogen Excretion, B. & T., p. 633.

Muscular Activity, Physiology of, A. V. Bock, C. Vancaulaert,

D. B. Dill, A. Folling, and L. M. Hurxthal, *J. Physiol.*, 66: 153, 1928.

Bell, Davidson, and Scarborough, *Textbook of Physiology & Biochemistry,* Livingstone, 2nd Ed., "Physiology of Severe Exercise," p. 737 *et seq.* (abbrev. B. D. & S.).

Weisberg, Harry F., "Water, Electrolyte and Acid Base Balance," Williams & Wilkins, 1953, "Acid-Base Balance & Exercise," p. 58.

"Acid-Base Balance & Brain," I. Page, *Chemistry of the Brain,* Williams & Wilkins, Baltimore, 1935, p. 230 *et seq.*

"Sweating," Weisberg, *op. cit.,* p. 71.

"Fasting and Metabolic Acidosis," Weisberg, *op. cit.,* p. 120.

"Excess production of organic acids in fasting and exercise," Weisberg, *op. cit.,* p. 112.

"Alkali reserve and exercise," Weisberg, *op. cit.,* p. 113.

Weisberg, *op. cit.,* Table 23, p. 114 *et seq.*

B. & T., p. 620 *et seq.* B. D. & S., p. 136.

C. I., 1951–52. B. D. & S., p. 731 *et seq.* B. & T., p. 727.

B. & T., pp. 721 *et seq.,* 728.

B. & T., p. 630. Himwich, H., *Brain Metabolism and Cerebral Disorders,* Williams & Wilkins, Baltimore, 1951.

Himwich, *op. cit.,* Chap. 2.

Hypoxia is a decreased supply of oxygen to the brain due to a decrease in the concentration of oxygen in the air supply, such as is usually found at high altitudes.

Weisberg, *op. cit.,* p. 135.

The total body water is divided into compartments: the intracellular fluid (fluid inside of the cells) comprises 50% of the body weight; the extracellular fluid comprises 20% of the body weight. The extracellular compartment is subdivided into the interstitial fluid (fluid between the cells) and the intravascular fluid, which are 15% and 5% of the body weight respectively. The remaining 30% of the body weight is made up of solids.

Weisberg, *op. cit.,* p. 13.

B. & T., *op. cit.,* p. 639.

Gellhorn, *op. cit.,* Part V, p. 291 *et seq.*

Appendix E

Table II is constructed according to the same scheme as Table I. Plus one (+1) stands for either an augmentation or an excitation of a function. Minus one (−1) stands for either a depression or an inhibition of a function. Where no notation is used it means that the effect is either unknown or remains normal or unchanged. An algebraic summation is used to denote the state when ecstasy is reached. However, since the transition from ecstasy to exhaustion is marked by a sudden and dramatic reversal of previously existing states the use of a "conversion" factor is introduced. This means that if it is known, for example, that adrenaline suddenly passes over from an excitatory effect to one of inhibition, the plus value is changed to an equal minus value. While this is an artificial device, the usage conforms to known or expected physiological shifts.

Shifts are indicated only where some experimental basis can be cited for the expected shift. In spite of the paucity of evidence bearing on this problem, the main shifts appear to be quite clear. Briefly stated these are (For the End Point):

1 Depression and inhibition of the frontal cortex. Adrenergia.

2 Activation of Cell bodies (soma) of Temporal Cortex and Occipital Cortex with synaptic blockade.

3 Self-excitatory repetitive electrical discharge of the Temporal Cortical Cells. Cholinergia.

4 Probable decrease in frequency and increase in amplitude of the alpha wave.

5 Depression and inhibition of the posterior hypothalamic nuclei and the ascending reticular activating system. Adrenergia.

6 Anterior and midline nuclei of hypothalamus—normal sleep activity. Depression of sympatho-adrenal system with preponderance of the parasympathetic system. Cholinergia.

7 Possible increased acetylcholine content of the cerebrospinal fluid.

TABLE II

	I. Metabolic Acidosis	II. Inc. Calorigenic Output	III. El. Int. Body Temperature	IV. Norm. or El. Bl. Sugar	V. Norm. Oxygen—Brain	VI. Hypercapnea—CO₂	VII. Dehydration	VIII. Neg. Nitrogen Bal.	IX. Sym-Adrenal Sys.	X. Cholinergia	Darkness—Night	Interrupted Auditory Stim.	Carbon Dioxide	Camphor	Alcohol (EtOH)	Tobacco Smoke—Nicotine	Summation—Ecstasy
CORTEX																	
Frontal–Soma													−1		−1		−2
Frontal–Synaptic													−1		−1	−1	−3
Temporal–Soma							1					1	1	1			4
Temporal–Synaptic												1	1	1			3
Temporal–EEG												1	1	1			3
Occipital–Soma											−1		−1				−2
Occipital–Synaptic											−1		−1				−2
Occipital–EEG											−1						1
EEG–Alpha		1	1								1				1		4
SUBCORTEX																	
Afferent Long Tract System																	
ARAS–Soma												1	1	1			1
ARAS–Synaptic												1	1	1			3
ARAS–EEG												1	1	1			3
HYPOTHALAMUS																	
Anterior Nuc.																	3
Midline Area																	
Parasympathetic																	
Lateral Area									1								1

TABLE II (continued)

	I. Metabolic Acidosis	II. Inc. Calorigenic Output	III. El., Int. Body Temperature	IV. Norm. or El. Bl. Sugar	V. Norm. Oxygen—Brain	VI. Hypercapnea—CO_2	VII. Dehydration	VIII. Neg. Nitrogen Bal.	IX. Sym-Adrenal Sys.	X. Cholinergia	Darkness—Night	Interrupted Auditory Stim.	Carbon Dioxide	Camphor	Alcohol (EtOH)	Tobacco Smoke—Nicotine	Summation—Ecstasy
HYPOTHALAMUS																	
Posterior Nuc.						1			1				1	1			4
Sympathetic		1							1			1	1				4
Pituitary-Ant.									1								1
Pituitary-Post.																1	1
Pineal Gland									-1								
Medulla									1					1			
CEREBROSPINAL																	
Fluid-AcCh																	1
CEREBRAL																	
A/V O_2 Diff.						-1							-1		1		-2
Blood Flow	1					1							1		1		4
Metabolic Rate								1					1				3
Adrenaline	1		1				1					1		1		1	3
Acetylcholine			1		1					1		1		1		1	1
Histamine																	
pH													-1				-1
Electric Constants	1	1					1			1							4
Convulsant Effect		1										1		1		1	5
Anti-Convulsant	1				1	1					1		1				6

TABLE II (continued)

CORTEX	Conversion to, Exhaustion	Light Sleep	Hypothetical End Point	
Frontal–Soma			-2	Depression
Frontal–Synaptic			-3	Inhibition
Temporal–Soma		1	5	Excitation
Temporal–Synaptic	-3	-2	-2	Inhibition
Temporal–EEG		1	4	Freq. & Amp.–Inc.
Occipital–Soma	2	2	+2	Excitation?
Occipital–Synaptic			-2	Depression
Occipital–EEG			-1	Awareness Response?
EEG–Alpha		1	5	Freq. Dec. & Amp.–Inc.
SUBCORTEX				
Afferent Long Tract System	-1	-1	-1	Depression
ARAS–Soma	-3	-3	-3	} Inhibition
ARAS–Synaptic	-3	-3	-3	} &
ARAS–EEG	-3	-3	-3	} Depression
HYPOTHALAMUS				
Anterior Nuc.		1	1	} Normal Sleep
Midline Area		1	1	} Activity
Parasympathetic		1	1	

TABLE II (continued)

HYPOTHALAMUS	Exhaustion, Conversion to,	Light Sleep	Hypothetical End Point	
Lateral Area	−1	−1	−2	Depression & Inhibition
Posterior Nuc.	−4	−1	−5	
Sympathetic	−4	−1	−5	
Pituitary-Ant.	−1		−1	Depression
Pituitary-Post.			1	Normal, or Inc.
Pineal Gland				Unknown
Medulla		−1	−1	Depression
CEREBROSPINAL				
Fluid-AcCh			1	Inc. Content
CEREBRAL				
A/V O₂ Diff.			−2	Decreased
Blood Flow	−4	1	1	Increased
Metabolic Rate	−3			Decreased
Adrenaline	−3		−3	Inhibitory Effect
Acetylcholine	−1	+2	+1	Inhibitory Effect on Synapse?
Histamine			1?	Unknown
pH	−1	−1	−4	Lowered
Electric Constants			+4	Increased
Convulsant Effect		1	6	Balanced
Anti-Convulsant			6	

Appendix F

X, Y, Z, co-ordinates of 3-space are laid out as spherical co-ordinates. To each co-ordinate is assigned a physical dimension based on mass, M, length, L, and time, T. To each co-ordinate is assigned a number value derived from powers, x, of the transcendental number e, and of 10.

The number e is based on the integer 1 arranged in the series:

$$e = 1 + \cfrac{1}{1} + \cfrac{1}{\cfrac{(1+1)}{\cfrac{(1+1)+(1+1)}{(1+1+1)+(1+1+1)}}} \quad \text{etc.,}$$

or this can be expressed as:

$$e = 2 + \cfrac{1}{1 + \cfrac{1}{2 + \cfrac{2}{3 + \cfrac{3}{4 + \cfrac{4}{5+5}}}}} \quad \text{etc.,}$$

or

$$e = 1 + \frac{1}{1!} + \frac{1}{2!} + \frac{1}{3!} + \frac{1}{4!} + \frac{1}{5!} \cdots = 2.71828182 \cdots$$

The number e itself appears to represent a quantum manifestation of energy in nature when increased by powers (x) of the number ten.

To the x-axis is assigned the physical dimension of mass, as $M^{\frac{1}{2}}$ for OX, with unit number value $[(e)(10)^{-24}] = 2.7182 \times 10^{-24} \text{ gm}^{\frac{1}{2}}$. This is illustrated in Fig. 1.

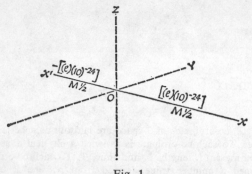

Fig. 1.

To the Y-axis is assigned the physical dimension of length as L for OY with unit number value

$$[(e)^7(10)^{-24}]^{-1/2} = 3.01 \times 10^{10} \text{ cm.} = \Lambda$$

This is illustrated in Fig. 2.

To the Z-axis is assigned the physical dimension of time as T for OZ with unit number value $(e)^{2\pi i} = 1$ sec. This is illustrated in Fig. 3. $i = \sqrt{-1}$.

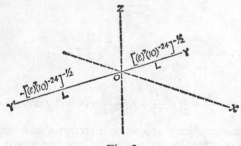

Fig. 2.

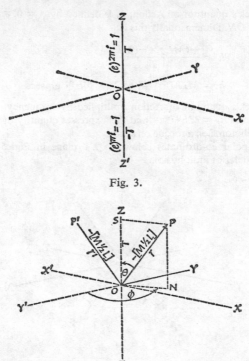

Fig. 3.

Fig. 4.

Figure 4 shows the two polar co-ordinates r and r' whose product quantizes waves and particles of physics in time, T. The points P and P' are defined by r, θ, ϕ. The locus of P is a hyperbolic spiral.

The position of P is expressed by radians of revolution denoted by β, dimensionally this is $T^{-\frac{1}{2}}$, and β^2 is T^{-1}. The frequency of any photon is given by $e\beta^2$.

Planck's quantum of Action, h, is defined by $\phi = 0$, $\theta = 90°$, and $r = ON$. Dimensionally this is:

$$h = \frac{-(ML) \times -(ML)}{T}$$

$$h = ML^2T^{-1} = 6.626 \times 10^{-27} \text{ ergsecs}$$

Planck's quantum of Action multiplied by frequency, $(e\beta^2)$, v, becomes $hv = ML^2T^{-2}$, and this expresses quantity of energy of the photon, i.e., a torque on space.

The polar co-ordinates below the XY plane in Fig. 5 define the particles of antiphysics.

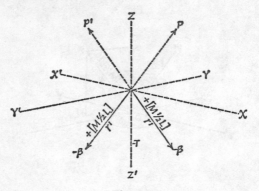

Fig. 5.

The antiquantum must also exist in the negative energy state of antiphysics.

$$\bar{h} = \frac{(M^{1/2}L)(M^{1/2}L)}{-T}$$

$$\bar{h} = -(ML^2T^{-1})$$

$$\bar{h}v = -(ML^2T^{-2})$$

or negative quantum energy, or antitorque.

Figure 6 shows the locus of the point P, and the general form of the hyperbolic spiral. P' has a locus spiral opposite in direction to P.

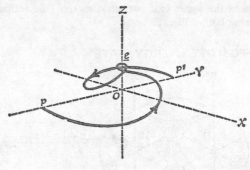

Fig. 6.

Figure 7 is a cross-sectional model of the relation postulated between the pseudospherical psi-plasma vortex, and the elementary particles and radiation. Only four spheres are shown, but eight properly belong in the figure, four in the upper half and four in the lower half. Each of the spheres occupies one octant. Figure 6 represents only one of these cells.

The pseudosphere is under angular rotation, an absolute motion. This imparts a spin to each of the spherical cells which latter must be regarded as being stationary with respect to the framework of the pseudosphere. It may be possible that the entire assembly has a precession, but I have not calculated this. The sphere El. (the electron) is in the quadrant opposite to the sphere Pr. (the proton). Their spin axes are in the X-axis. This spin axis will always be parallel to a tangent to the surface of the pseudosphere. As can be seen in the figure the direction of rotation of these two spheres is opposite to each other. The other two spheres in the upper half of Fig. 7 (not shown) are in the quadrants between El. and Pr., spin on the Y-axis, and their direction of rotation is opposite to each other. These are, respectively, the neutron and the neutrino.

The electron in the upper half has below it another spherical cell Pos. (the positron). Both of these spin on the X-axis, but with respect to each other the spins are in opposite directions. Thus all of the spin axes and rotations are quantized with respect to the pseudosphere surface and axis. Each of the four particles in the upper half has an isomorph (the antiparticle) in the lower half of Fig. 7.

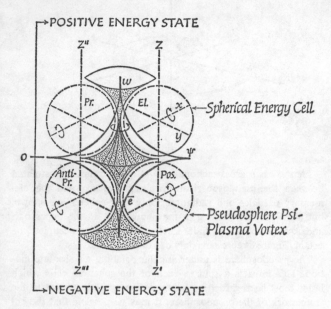

Fig. 7. The relation between the psi-plasma vortex (pseudo-sphere) and the elementary particles (spheres).

The curve, ψ, is the probability curve of the potential energy for each spherical cell. Any point on this curve is found from $e^{-\beta^2}$, and the energy at this point is given by $E = he^{\beta^2}$, where h is Planck's Constant. The α tail of the ψ curve represents the lowest frequency of radiation, and the ω head of the curve represents the region of cosmic radiation. In the sphere El., the intercept of ψ and the surface of the pseudosphere (where $\beta = 6.283$ radians) marks the region of the conversion of linear radiation into mass, i.e., the formation of the electron. The region beyond this point toward ω is the domain of atomic structure. The upper half of Fig. 7 may be used to represent the hydrogen isotope Deuterium, mass number two.

The extension of the loci of the spirals P and P' below the X, Y, plane shows a torque opposite to that of the spirals above this plane. This torque direction defines the energy state of the particles. For example, the point $\underline{e}$ is equal to 2π radians on the hyperbolic spiral where the polar co-ordinates r and r' (points P and P') approach a parallel to each other. The line SP achieves the critical length of 2.84×10^{-13} cm. The points P, P' on reaching this critical length at 2π radians enter a torque vector of the psi-plasma vortex to create the electron, e, probably in the form of a torus. Likewise, the opposite torque below the X, Y, plane at 2π radians creates the positron, $\bar{e}$.

Up to 6.28 radians the energy of torsion of the psi plasma appears in photonic radiation form expressed by hv. At 6.283 radians energy appears in particle form and is expressed by the following equation, where $\lambda = SP$ (Fig. 4).

$$e^2 = \lambda hv = ML^3T^{-2}$$

$e = (\lambda hv)^{\frac{1}{2}} = M^{\frac{1}{2}}L^{\frac{3}{2}}T^{-1} = $ e.s.u., specific electronic charge. Classical Electron Radius $= \lambda = e^2/mc^2 = 2.84 \times 10^{-13}$ cm.

Having derived the electrostatic unit of charge, we can show that the difference of electrical potential between two particles, i.e., two electrons, is a property of the mass.

$$E = (c^2G)^{\frac{1}{2}}$$

where E = potential difference in electromagnetic units.

c^2 = velocity of light squared.

G = gravitational force.

$$G = \frac{mM}{\pi r^2} G_c$$

where m, and M = rest mass of electrons increased by a beta factor of $(e)^2 = 7.389 = 6.73 \times 10^{-27}$ gm.

This means they have a velocity approximately 99% of that of light. r = unit distance = 1 cm.

$$E = 1.649 \times 10^{-20} \text{ e.m.u., or one abvolt.}$$

This shows that the potential difference (electrical) between two electron masses is a product of c^2 and G. G is a property of mass, and c^2 appears to be a property of the psi-plasma vortex imparted to the electron as spin.

$$c^2 = \frac{E}{G} = 8.98 \times 10^{20} \text{ cm.}^2 \text{ sec.}^{-2}$$

$$c = \left(\frac{E}{G}\right)^{\frac{1}{2}} = 2.99 \times 10^{10} \text{ cm. sec.}^{-1}$$

Appendix G

The Expansion and Contraction of Psi Plasma by Gravitational Influence

One problem of great interest is the possible effect of lunar phases on telepathic reception. It took five years of preparation before I could complete a satisfactory series of telepathy tests for a full lunar month. The principal obstacle was gaining control of all conditions for telepathy, except the test condition. Many problems had to be solved, as well as getting one subject into a harmonious state for a full month.

The subject was Harry Stone, and six months of laboratory work had thoroughly disciplined him to control conditions. I also had learned how to handle him. The Faraday cage was used for the constant environment, as the Ground Faraday Cage. A matching card test (the MAT) was used throughout the experiments to evaluate telepathic ability. (See Appendix A.) Three senders were used who rotated through the series of five runs done each afternoon at 2:30 P.M. The senders were myself, Leo Narodny, and Henry Jackson.

The results of the tests run from September 16, 1955, to October 13, 1955, are shown in Note 1 as a graph. Two peaks of scoring are evident, one on the new moon phase, the second around the full moon phase. The latter shows the most pronounced increase in scoring rate. These two phases of the moon coincide with the periods in which the range of tides is increased. In the new moon phase the moon's attraction is added to that of the sun and the combined gravitational attraction on earth is at its greatest for the lunar cycle. In the full moon phase the moon's attraction on earth acts against that of the sun, and the gravitational attraction on the earth is at a minimum during this phase of the lunar cycle.

It would appear that our paradoxical results have an explanation. The increased gravitational attraction during the new moon phase acted principally on the sender. That is, the increased gravitational force contracted their psi-plasma fields and increased their efficiency as senders, but not the efficiency of the receiver. During the full moon phase the decreased gravitational force affected the receiver principally, by allowing greater psi-plasma expansion. The lesson to be learned is that the experiment should be repeated using only one subject—one who has clairvoyance, or psychometry. Then his powers can be measured alone against the effect of gravitational field forces.

However, this preliminary experiment is highly suggestive that decreased gravitational field potential favors the receiver in telepathy.

The question arose as to whether a charged Faraday cage had any effect with respect to gravitational force. An opportunity to test this idea presented itself in 1957 when William Cantor appeared at the laboratory claiming he could influence a spinning silver dollar to fall heads or tails as per wish. Cantor brought his own two coins, and it was soon found that his "lucky" coins were biased, one to fall heads, the other tails. He was not aware of this factor, but when it was pointed out to him he still agreed to go ahead with a series of tests. The following is a brief summary of a part of this series. The Faraday cage was arranged and charged as in Project XV. (See Appendix A.) This is an experiment in telergy with the spinning-coin test, using both an unbiased coin and a biased coin.

The subject, William Cantor, makes the claim that he can influence the fall of a spinning silver dollar.

1. Cantor using laboratory unbiased coin, in *room,* calling *Tails.*

               Score: Tails 29   Heads 21

                  The Standard Deviation is 3.5. Results: Chance.

2. Cantor using laboratory unbiased coin in *Charged Faraday Cage* calling *Tails.*

               Score: Tails 52   Heads 48

                  The Standard Deviation is 5.0. Results: Chance.

3. Cantor using laboratory unbiased coin in *Charged Faraday Cage* calling *Heads.*

               Score: Heads 28   Tails 22

                  The Standard Deviation is 3.5. Results: Chance.

4. Cantor believes that he can do better with his own coin. The Cantor coin is tested for bias by Puharich and Beveridge.

    a. Puharich using "tail" coin of Cantor in *room* calling *Heads.*

        Score: Heads 14   Tails 36

    b. Beveridge using same "tail" coin of Cantor in room—no calling.

        Score: Heads 9   Tails 41

    Control Totals: Heads 23 Tails 77

    The Standard Deviation is 5.0. C.R. is 5.2, showing that the coin is heavily biased for tails.

    c. Cantor using biased "tail" coin in *room* calling *Tails.*

        Score: Tails 41   Heads 9

    The Standard Deviation is 3.5. The C.R. is 4.5, which does not exceed the control level. The results are at a chance level for this biased coin.

5. Cantor using same biased "tail" coin in *Charged Faraday Cage* calling *Tails.*

    a. Control by Puharich under same conditions calling *Heads.*

        Score: Heads 9   Tails 41   Results: Chance.

    (See No. 4b Beveridge.)

    b. Test by Cantor.

        Score: Tails 47   Heads 3 (Run No. 1)

                 Tails 44   Heads 6 (Run No. 2)

    Totals: Tails 91 Heads 9

If we compare the Control Total of 77 *Tails* (for No. 4) with the Test Totals of 91 *Tails* for No. 5, we find a critical ratio of difference between the two experiments with a value of 3.33 ($P = 4.3 \times 10^{-4}$). This is significant at 0.0001% level. From this one can argue that the biased "tail" coin is influenced by the mind inside a charged Faraday cage. Another interpretation is that the biased coin simply becomes more biased in the cage, but the control run does not support this interpretation.

6. Control using Cantor's biased "head" coin in room.

a. Puharich calling *Tails.*	Tails 14	Heads 36
b. Tart calling *Tails.*	Tails 15	Heads 35
c. VanderHurk calling *Tails.*	Tails 16	Heads 34
d. Beveridge calling *Tails.*	Tails 12	Heads 38
Control Totals:	Tails 57	Heads 143

These figures represent the bias of the coin for 200 trials.

7. Cantor claims that he can exceed 36 heads per run with the biased "head" coin. Cantor using biased "head" coin in *room*, calling *Heads*.

> *Score:* Heads 42   Tails   8

The score of 42 heads is not a significant deviation from the mean of 35.7 heads in the control experiment per 50 trials.

8. Cantor claims that he can make the biased "head" coin come out 50% heads and 50% tails whether he spins it or someone else spins it.

> a. Cantor using biased "head" coin in *room*, spinning it himself, and willing 25 *Heads* and 25 *Tails*.
>
> > *Score:* Tails 22   Heads 28
>
> b. Cantor willing 25 *Heads* and 25 *Tails* with Beveridge spinning biased "head" coin.
>
> > *Score:* Tails 22   Heads 28
> > Totals: Tails 44   Heads 56

The score does not exceed 2.33 Standard Deviations (C.R. = 1.2). This gives a normal probability distribution, and Cantor makes good his claim to "unbias" the coin which was earlier proved to be biased.

9. Cantor now claims that he will take the biased "head" coin which he has just proven that he can "unbias," and whether he spins it or not, will try to influence it to fall *Heads* in the *charged cage*.

> a. Cantor using biased "head" coin in *charged cage*, spinning it himself, and calling *Heads*.
>
> > *Score:* Tails   0   Heads 50
>
> b. Cantor willing *Heads* with Beveridge spinning same biased "head" coin (still in charged cage).
>
> > *Score:* Tails   5   Heads 45
> > Totals: Tails   5   Heads 95

We take the mean of the Control Total in No. 6 (143/2 = 71.5) and subtract this from the actual score of 95 heads and get the actual deviation of 23.5 from the mean expected. The Standard Deviation is 4.5, and this gives us a critical ratio of 5.22. The $P = 8.9 \times 10^{-8}$, and odds against chance occurrence of such a score are better than a billion to one. Mr. Cantor has made good his claim under the charged-Faraday-cage condition.

We summarize the results of this telergy experiment:

Cantor cannot significantly influence the fall of an unbiased coin—in the room or in the charged Faraday cage.

The control totals for both biased coins, both in the room and in the cage, for 400 trials is 302 hits and 98 misses. Since we wish to compare these scores to the series of 200 test trials in the cage, we take the mean of 302 for 200 trials, which equals 151 hits. This is chance expected hits for 200 trials. The Standard Deviation is 6.14.

The Cantor test scores in the charged Faraday cage were: hits = 186, misses = 14. The actual deviation is $186 - 151 = +31$. The critical ratio is 5.04 and $P = 2.3 \times 10^{-7}$, or odds against chance of 4 billion to one.

Significantly enough, Cantor using the biased coins under room conditions cannot exceed chance expectations. However, in the room, using the biased coins, he was able to "unbias" them and obtain a normal distribution for heads and tails for each coin. The control score for the biased "head" coin in the room is 72 heads and 28 tails (mean for 100 trials from sec. 6). The S.D. = 4.44. His "unbiasing" test score was 56 heads and 44 tails. The actual deviation = -16. The critical ratio = -3.49. $P = 2.42 \times 10^{-4}$. This is a remarkable feat in that in 50 trials he did not spin his own coin, and the distribution of heads and tails was normal (the actual deviation for $P = 0.5$ is $+6$; C.R. = 1.2; a chance score).

He could not duplicate this latter feat in the charged cage. In other words, he proved he could *"unbias"* a coin under room conditions, and *increase the bias* of a coin under charged-Faraday-cage conditions. The effect was highly selective for the two conditions when biased coins were used.

A coin is biased because the rim has become beveled on an angle to the true 90° angle (to the face); or the rim is rounded and the peak of the rim is off center. Let us consider the case of the beveled coin, and say that the head face is on the side of the acute angle, and the tail face is on the side of the obtuse angle of the bevel. Such a coin cannot stand on end—it will fall, and tend to fall head face-up. The second fact about such a biased coin is that it cannot spin for long vertically, it soon precesses (wobbles) around its vertical axis. The more biased the coin the faster it will precess. It is a known fact that the faster the rate of precession, the more a coin will tend to rise against gravity. In the case of a biased coin this simply means that the force which holds the coin up (while spinning) against gravity, will for a longer time than an unbiased coin maintain the zero-gravity null point before it falls down. This gives the telergic mind slightly more time in which to influence the coin fall.

Now I have closely observed Cantor influencing the coin. As the spin and precession slow down, one can for a few moments see which face is going to land up. When Cantor did not want this face to land up, say tails—and I observed this especially in his run of 50 straight hits—one could see the coin suddenly flip from tails to heads, at that angle of precession when the upward force of the spin was about equal to the downward pull of gravity. I am convinced that this is the moment of telergic interaction of mind with coin. I am sure that high-speed motion pictures would reveal this effect dramatically.

Now let us analyze what happened telergically when Cantor unbiased the coin in the room. Here the natural tendency of the coin is to fall away from the acute angle of the bevel and land heads up. The rim of the acute angle is on the head face. This means that at the zero-gravity precession angle the coin is precessing on the axis of the obtuse angle of the rim. Cantor, in order to make this coin come up tails, can either apply a positive force under the coin, directed upward to flip it, or he can apply an attractive force from himself to the top of the coin and draw it toward him suddenly, in order to flip it. Of the two possibilities it is most likely that under the stress of the test he can exert a pulse of adrenergia. This will increase his local gravitational field, and the coin being at a zero-gravity state—for a long time —will be atracted to him and flip against the bias of the bevel. Conversely, any telergic push from above the coin downward would make it fall heads and so increase the bias score.

Now let us look at the situation in the cage. Here the problem is easier. One has only to push the biased coin down each time in order to get a perfect score. This is much easier than flipping the coin over against its bias. In order to make the biased "head" coin come heads each time Cantor can: (a) telergically increase gravitational field potential under the coin to make it fall heads, or (b) he can exert a telergic downward push on the head face of the coin. If he has adrenergia, he can only attract the coin up toward him, and this he could not do in the cage. (c) However, if we assume that he had the relaxation of cholinergia in the cage, and his psi plasma expanded toward the coin, then he would exert telergia by decreasing the gravitational field potential over the coin so that it would be pulled down more strongly by the earth. In order to flip the coin over when it was at a zero-gravity angle he would have to place the low gravitational potential under the coin, which would allow the precession to make a sudden rise and perhaps flip the coin. But this he could not do in the cage.

Since Cantor could not unbias the coin in the cage we must assume that he was neutralized as far as exerting an attractive upward force on the coin (force 2 in table).

ROOM CONDITION	CAGE CONDITION
Required Force: Must act upward in direction from table through coin to Cantor. Pulsed Force.	Must act downward in a direction from Cantor through coin to table. Steady Force.
1. Low G_o under coin (cholinergic state).	1a. Low G_o above coin (cholinergic state: decreased Cantor G attraction on coin).
2. High G_o above coin (adrenergic state: Cantor exerts G attraction on coin).	2a. High G_o under coin (adrenergic state).
3. Positive force pushing coin up from table. Odic Force? (See Appendix C.)	3a. Positive force pushing coin down on table. Odic Force? (See Appendix C.)

Since Cantor could not increase the bias of the coin under room conditions, it means he could not exert a downward push on the coin (force 2a), or could not create a lowered gravitational potential over the coin (force 1a).

We can summarize these possible effects in a table, and therefore reach a conclusion as to which mechanisms were operative.

(3) and (3a) cannot be considered because he should have been able to exert these effects on an unbiased coin, and (3) requires more force on Cantor's part than (3a), yet his (3a) scores were higher than (3).

(1) could not be operative in the room, because he should have been able to exert this effect to a greater degree in the

NOTE 1. Graph of MAT scores during a full lunar month.

HITS

LUNAR DAY	HIT SCORES/50	0	5	10	15	20	25	30	35	40	45	50
1	28											
2	17											
3	10											
4	8											
5	11											
6	10											
7	9											
8	9											
9	8											
10	9											
11	16											
12	28											
13	32											
FULL MOON	46											
15	Subject Could Not Complete Test—Due To Trance											
16	44											
17	22											
18	8											
19	10											
20	9											
21	10											
22	10											
23	9											
24	9											
25	11											
26	20											
27	31											
28	18											
TOTAL	454											

Hit Av.=16.8/50

cage, which he could not do, i.e., he could not unbias the coin in cage.

We are left with (2) as the operative mechanism in the room, and (1a) as the operative mechanism in the cage. (2) shows that he exerted an attractive force on the coin toward him in the room; and he did not show the reverse effect in the room, i.e., he was not able to "push" the coin down. Conversely, in the cage he was able to use (1a) to control a gentle steady downward pull of gravity on the coin. This means he lowered the G_c field potential above the coin.

We can conclude that the G_c effects were not directly from the cage to coin, because the control scores were the same in the cage as in the room. The G_c effect must have been from the cage to Cantor's psi plasma to coin. It is my opinion therefore that this experiment shows that the charged Faraday cage exerts an expansive stress on the psi plasma of the subject. Therefore, we must look for some influence of the cage on personal gravitational fields. (See Q. 20 of Appendix C for the theory.)

Appendix H

In the summer of 1960 I lived with the Chatinos of Oaxaca, Mexico, and participated in their sacred mushroom rite. I include this account of my experience in order to give the reader a more vivid idea of a series of hallucinations which had a high degree of ordering up to a certain point.

After due arrangements were made for the rite with the Brujo Blas Garcia, aged eighty and healthy and vigorous, we assembled in a small warehouse building belonging to Don Alfonso Zavaleta at nine o'clock on the evening of July 18, 1960, in the village of Juquila. Permission had already been granted to take motion pictures of the rite, and to tape record the ritual. This necessitated more light in the room than is usually used by the Brujo. Besides the two candles usually used, a Coleman gasoline lantern was used for additional illumination. Present in the room were the Brujo Blas, Puharich, and Sergio Zavaleta, who was serving as the cameraman.

At 9:10 P.M. Blas and Puharich sat down at a small table upon which were two candles, a small pail containing fresh mushrooms, and an incense burner containing copal. The mushrooms were of medium size and of chartreuse color (of a species not yet classified by Western science). Blas called them the Sacred Rabbit Mushroom, or in Chatino, KWI' YA HO' O KWITŠI. He prayed out loud over the mushrooms in the Chatino language for about two minutes, then lifted the pail and held them over the copal smoke for about thirty seconds. He prayed for another minute or so, and then placed two of the sacred rabbit mushrooms in my hand and asked me to eat them. At 9:21 P.M. I began to eat these two sacred mushrooms, and they tasted quite pleasant. After this the Brujo Blas demanded absolute silence and appeared to be quite annoyed by minor noises such as that of the motion-picture camera running. I was allowed, however, to get up occasionally to change the film in the camera, or to check

the lighting conditions for the filming. The Brujo also ate two
of the mushrooms after I had eaten mine. Occasionally Blas
would break the silence to make a short statement to me. He sat
quietly, tending the incense burner occasionally, or watching
my reactions from time to time. I myself felt perfectly normal,
and kept notes of my pulse, pupillary diameter, and other
physiological reactions. The room slowly filled with incense
smoke which was not unpleasant, and I realized that the terpene
compounds in the copal must also be having some effect on me.
In addition the copal smoke was saturating the atmosphere with
large amounts of carbon dioxide, which in itself has a profound
effect on the state of the central nervous system, as well as on
one's feelings and mental dynamics.

At 10:26 P.M. I began to feel the first effects of the mushroom
chemical, a feeling of a fullness rushing up into my head accompanied by a mild sense of inebriation, as though one had had a
cocktail in a hurry on an empty stomach. I would say that this
was a pleasant sensation. Occasionally I closed my eyes to observe for the presence of hallucinations. At 10:30 P.M. I observed my first hallucination. With my eyes closed I saw a single
wine-colored hexagonal cell (like a honeycomb cell) with sharp
yellow borders. The honeycomb cell multiplied into many such
in a flat plane. What impressed me immediately was that while
I was aware of the total pattern of the cells and their rich color,
I was also intensely aware of the existence of each unit cell in
the complex. After due expansion this flat plane abruptly converted into a long narrow trough looking very much like a long
narrow cobblestone street with high stone walls. I fancied that
this looked very much like a street from ancient Peru. The individual cells were now well-fitted dark-brown stones, and the
spacers were a yellowish mortar. Again each stone impressed itself individually upon my consciousness, and still the whole pattern retained its form for me. I appeared to be sort of a disem-
bodied consciousness observing this scene from a central vantage
point, and it all appeared quite impersonal to me. The individual
cells of this field now expanded to become a sort of link-chain
fence pattern that displaced the stone street and walls. The color
did not change with this transition in geometry. As I calmly observed this unfolding scene the cameras were started by Sergio,
and I suddenly realized that the clicks of the shutter had dis-
pelled my hallucination. Now I understood why it was necessary

to maintain silence. As I found out from this and subsequent experiences, sounds and noise definitely work to dispel or deteriorate visual hallucinations. Unlike the Shaman, the Yogin demands such silence.

At 10:35 P.M. the state of light-inebriation seemed to have passed and in its stead I found myself growing rather heavy and immobile. It seemed as though my mass had increased as the heavy feeling settled over me. However, I continued to make notes, and to keep an eye on the camera and lighting problems. With my eyes closed and the room silent again I found that the hallucinations resumed their evolution. The link-chain fence trough that I observed now became stonework again, this time a broad wide esplanade of stairs such as are found at the pyramids of Monte Alban. However, the stairs were covered on the sides and roofed with stonework, and I had the feeling that I was ascending this long endless stairway. All this time the stones and the mortar stood out brilliantly in their individual units and at the same time impressed upon me their total pattern. As I ascended the stairs the entire tunnel structure began to whirl around me while I stood upright and stable in the center of this whirlpool. With this experience I felt that a definite threshold had been passed, and I was no longer firmly rooted in the three-dimensional world of my surroundings. Yet when I opened my eyes the hallucinations vanished, and I found that I could bring them on or turn them off at will. I felt in complete control of myself and still in good contact with my companions and duties.

With the whirling I found myself projected into the interior of buildings. First I was in the interior of a vast and beautiful medieval Norman-type castle. I could feel exquisitely the shape, color, and texture of each individual stone, and at the same time be aware of and awed by the flying pattern of the interior architecture. One stone architectural triumph after another formed and transmuted before my mind's eye—European castles, Mayan temples, Peruvian buildings, etc. Blas and I quietly nodded to each other. We had a deep sense of mutual understanding and communion that needed no words for expression. I knew that he, too, was soaring with his mind's eye in a world that the physical eye had never seen.

At 10:48 P.M. I received Blas' unspoken permission to leave the room. I stepped out into the night sky which was brilliant with stars. I looked at them with a new-found sense of being a vital part of this external world of light beams, linked with it by the light and illumination within me. I felt not only the ubiquitous pervasion of light in the universe, but was overwhelmed by the geometrical structure of all light in and outside of the mind. With this mindward reach into the world of light I paradoxically enough became aware of a sense of pressure in the bladder. I wondered whether this was the pharmacologic action of the mushroom or whether I had to urinate. I soon found that it was a sense of bladder urgency without much issue.

When I closed my eyes to the starlit night, I found that my hallucinations were there ever-ready to display their panoply. Again, inky purply stonework, but now opening and closing in fan-shaped segments around me like the integrated parts of a diaphragm shutter. I returned to my companions in the room, and all looked quite normal to me. The copal was burning strongly. I realized that my hallucinations in the fresh night air were just as strong as in the smoke-filled room, and again wondered about the role of the carbon dioxide and the terpenes. I took some measurements upon myself and recorded them, checked the lighting and the cameras, and then returned to my seat by Blas.

At 10:53 P.M. I began to feel for the first time a mild nausea. I began to feel heavier and somewhat drowsy. Still I was able to assure myself that I was in good contact with my environment. But I was beginning to fear that this would not last long, and I became concerned as to how I would be able to run my recording instruments, take notes, and direct the filming. My hallucinations seemed more like living visions now, so intense were they becoming, but only with my eyes closed. I cannot adequately report now the complexity of the architectural scenes that unfolded before me. I seemed to be recapitulating all the architectural and geometrical heritage of mankind as one vast building after another was created before me. I remember especially one vast mosque that evolved before me. Its entire interior was decorated with square brilliantly colored tiles. The pattern and color of each of the millions of tiles burned into my consciousness, and yet I was always aware of the over-all architecture and the position of each tile in this vast complex.

At 11:03 P.M. I noticed that as the visions mounted in intensity of color, complexity of geometrical structure, and vividness of the unit cells of such architecture, I began to feel more inebriated. Actually, to outer appearance at this point, my companions told me later that I did not appear to be inebriated except for the huge dilatation of my pupils. But inwardly it was otherwise. I felt heavy and rooted to my chair. There was a heavy dragging pull on all the muscles of my shoulders and neck as though I were resisting a downward force. Curiously enough, I had no inward sense of vertigo, and the room itself appeared to be quite stable. The inebriation did not seem to affect my balance, or muscular co-ordination. But everything seemed to be slowed down enormously.

As I looked at my notebook, the white paper appeared to be yellow and luminescent. As I looked at my Mongoloid companion, the Brujo Blas, he no longer was familiar nor did I have any sense of rapport and intimacy with him. He now began to look more and more like a giant gorilla; in fact, I recalled that he looked akin to the ape Gargantua that I had seen in a circus many years ago. But he looked quite harmless and friendly, and this ape-like appearance transformed into the benign Ape of Tehuti, so well-known from Egypt; and even this ape-like appearance transformed into an Egyptian Priest of Tehuti. He now appeared to be my, for lack of a better word, mentor. He was there to see me through this experience of loosening of the bonds of flesh, and the flight into this world of brilliant color and elegant geometry. As all this went through my mind I wondered whether he was an hallucination on my part or an illusion that was projected far beyond the sensorium as a result of my inebriation. When I opened my eyes, the geometrical hallucinations were blanked out, but he sat there solidly in his ape-like role. When I closed my eyes, the hallucinations would actually resume—that is, begin where they had left off. I felt sure at this moment that by opening my eyes the hallucinations actually ceased, like a motion picture that is stopped, and resumed from the same end point when I again closed my eyes. Often, at this stage, as I closed my eyes, the geometrical complex that I viewed would begin to whirl around me as though framed on the walls of a giant centrifuge. And with such whirling there was an increase of nausea—and yet I did not feel that this was true vertigo. I felt that I was a stable observer of a fast-moving scene, and sometimes got caught up in it.

At 11:06 P.M. I noticed that my face was beginning to feel numb. The inebriation seemed to be settling more heavily upon me. I now began to feel a bit silly inside, and often smiled broadly for no good reason. I noticed in looking at the films of myself of this moment, later on when they were developed, that my grinning appeared quite idiotic when viewed with a sober mind. Yet the hallucinations mounted in speed, intensity and variety of color, and complexity of design. The architectural scenes were no longer held together by the massiveness of stone. They were now made up not of unit cells, as before, but of lines; lines of filigree, lines of basket weaves, lines of cord, all woven into geometrical patterns far beyond the power of words to describe or the pen to draw. It seemed as if the architectural evolution was moving toward finer lines, smaller units, and more complex patterns, all soaring up into the immensity of an unbounded space. And never, never was there a living thing to relieve the mathematical precision of the pattern. As this weaving went on and on, I noticed that more and more metallic strands of silvery color made up the grand design.

At 11:18 P.M. I noticed that the severe and awesome geometry of my visions began to deteriorate. The forms began to get more plastic, and at times rigid geometric structures slowly began to bend and fold very much like the rigidity of stone dissolving into putty distortion. This brought on more softly colored and monochrome scenes that were reminiscent of the landscapes made so familiar by the brush of Dali. I began to get more introspective, and felt I understood the necessity of silence in the mushroom rite: noise definitely disturbed the order of evolution of the light patterns and geometry of the mind. I felt that I had at last grasped the meaning of prayer. It served to place the mind in the best focus and most receptive state for visions of the far reaches of consciousness. The rain began to beat on the tin roof at this time and I definitely felt that this further disordered my experience. I resented it, although ordinarily I am quite pleased by the sound of rain on the roof. It was now 11:38 P.M. Blas broke the silence by asking in Spanish if it was midnight. He then said something in Chatino to me, which I could not understand but which he said with grave countenance. It all had the profound and inconsequential meaning of a trite phrase like "Bananas are cheaper," and I am sure that I smiled indulgently at him. I could no longer take him or his words seriously.

But with this lack of respect for Blas, my Brujo, he again began to transform before my eyes. His mongoloid Chatino appearance now made me feel that he was a mongoloid from Turkestan. I don't know now how much time passed, but when I looked at my watch again it was 11:55 P.M. and I realized that I had not been in contact with my immediate environment for some time. I seemed to be not in a hut in Juquila in 1960, but in far-off Turkestan (the word came to me as such), and it was hundreds of years ago. In this period of displaced time and scene I was sitting around a smoky camel's dung fire, and Blas was a Tibetan Monk who watched over me. The scene was not the room in Juquila, but an open plain that was cold and dusty, and we huddled in blankets around the fire. All this came to me in retrospect as I returned mentally to my immediate environment in Juquila. This was a weird feeling, not having any reference points with respect to my body, the room I was in, or even the time in which I lived. I still cannot explain this incident to myself. It was like a dream, but more tangible. However, even though I was now aware of this being 1960 and Juquila, the feeling persisted of having been in the heart of Asia.

The rain beat heavier on the roof. I began to feel chilly and put on a jacket. The smoke was rising heavily from the burner and the room was dense with copal. When I closed my eyes there were no hallucinations. At 12:10 A.M. I realized that I was coming back to the reality of this room, such as it was, and to the body-rooted consciousness of myself as I normally know myself. At 12:20 A.M. I was certain that the effect of the mushroom had left me, and that I was my usual dull self again. Outside of feeling quite dull (as my normal self) I felt fine. There was no hangover. I looked at Brujo Blas quite rationally now and felt no sympathy with him. He appeared to me to be a quite ridiculous senile old man. My primitive surroundings and companions had only the flavor of ashes and dregs.

I went to bed shortly and slept deeply for eight hours. I awoke feeling alert and fit. I realized I had had no dreams and that my night and awakening were completely uneventful. What impressed me the most in this morning hour was the quantal nature of my visions and the vast field effect that created the architecture and geometry. Such is the nature of the impressions from the mushroom vision that one can recapture on paper in retrospect.

Bibliography

BRAIN

von Bonin, Gerhard
  Essay on the Cerebral
    Cortex
  Charles C Thomas
  Springfield, Ill., 1950
Elliott, K. A. C.
Irvine, H.
Quastel, J. H.
  Neurochemistry
  Charles C Thomas
  Springfield, Ill., 1955
Himwich, Harold
  Brain Metabolism and
    Cerebral Disorders
  Williams & Wilkins
  Baltimore, Md., 1951
Page, I.
  Chemistry of the Brain
  Williams & Wilkins
  Baltimore, Md., 1935
Penfield, Wilder
  Epilepsy and the Func-
    tional Anatomy of the
    Human Brain
  Little, Brown
  Boston, Mass., 1954
Penfield, Wilder
Rasmussen, Theodore
  Cerebral Cortex of Man,
    The
  Macmillan
  New York, N.Y., 1950
Strauss, *et al.*

Diagnostic Electroen-
  cephalography
  Grune and Stratton
  New York, N.Y., 1952
Walter, W. Grey
  Living Brain, The
  W. W. Norton
  New York, N.Y., 1953

CHEMISTRY

Bowen, E. J.
  Chemical Aspects of
    Light, The
  Oxford, 2nd Edition
  New York, N.Y., 1946
Moncrieff, R. W.
  Chemical Senses, The
  John Wiley & Sons
  New York, N.Y., 1944
Thorpe's Dictionary of Ap-
  plied Chemistry
  Longmans, 4th Edition
  London, Eng., 1949

GENERAL

Blood, Benjamin Paul
  Anaesthetic Revelation
    and the Gist of Phi-
    losophy
  Amsterdam, N.Y., 1874
Blood, Benjamin Paul
  Pluriverse
  Marshall Jones Co.
  Boston, Mass., 1920

Bouquet, A. C.
  Comparative Religion
  Penguin Books
  Baltimore, Md., 1942
Bromage, Bernard
  Occult Arts of Ancient
    Egypt, The
  The Aquarian Press
  London, Eng., 1953
Budge, Wallis
  Mummy, The (A Hand-
    book of Egyptian Fu-
    nerary Archeology)
  Cambridge   University
    Press
  London, Eng., 1925
Christian, Paul
  History and Practice of
    Magic, The
  Forge Press
  London, Eng., 1952
Encyclopaedia   Britannica
  1953 Edition
Geldner, Karl Frederick
  Der Rig Veda (Aus dem
    Sanscrit ins Deutsche
    uebersetzt und mit
    einem laufenden Kom-
    mentar Versehen)
  Harvard Oriental Series,
    Vol. 35
  Cambridge, Mass., 1951
Hrozný, Bedřich
  Ancient History of West-
    ern Asia, India and
    Crete
  Philosophical Library
  New York, N.Y., 1953
Huxley, Aldous
  Perennial Philosophy
  Harper & Bros.
  New York, N.Y., 1945
James, William
  Varieties of Religious
    Experience, The
  Longmans

London, Eng., 1908
Maby, J. Cecil
  International Congress of
    Radionics
  London, Eng., 1950
Mathers, S. Lidell Mac-
    Gregor (translator)
  Key of Solomon, The
  George Redway
  London, Eng., 1889
Monardes
  Segunda Parte del Libro
    de la Cosas Que Se
    traen de Nuestras India
    Occidentales
  Seville, Spain, 1571
Underhill, Evelyn
  Mysticism
  E. P. Dutton
  New York, N.Y., 1931
Yule, Sir Henry (translator
    and editor)
  Travels of Marco Polo
  Cordier Edition, John
    Murray
  London, Eng., 1921

PARAPSYCHOLOGY

Bjorkhem, John
  Die Verborgene Kraft
  Walter Verlag
  Olten und Freiburg, Ger-
    many, 1954
Blondel, David
  Treatise of the Sibyls, A
  London, Eng., 1666
Boirac, Emile
  Our Hidden Forces
  deKerlor, W., translator
  F. A. Stokes & Co.
  New York, N.Y., 1917
Chadwick, Nora K.
  Poetry and Prophecy
  Cambridge   University
    Press
  London, Eng., 1942

Driesch, Hans
Psychical Research
G. Bell
London, Eng., 1933

Fukari, T.
Clairvoyance and
Thoughtography
Rider and Co.
London, Eng., 1931

Greber, Johannes
Communication with the
Spirit World
Macoy
New York, N.Y., 1932

Hettinger, J.
Exploring the Ultra Per-
ceptive Faculty
Rider and Co.
London, Eng., 1940

Johnson, Raynor C.
Imprisoned Splendor, The
Harper and Bros.
New York, N.Y., 1953

Kroll, W.
De Oraculis Chaldaicis
Breslauer   Philogische
Abhandlungen
VII, I, 1894

Lambert, Helen C.
General Survey of Psy-
chical Phenomena, A
The Knickerbocker Press
New York, N.Y., 1928

Maeterlinck, Maurice
Unknown Guest, The
Methuen and Co.
London, Eng., 1914

Margery Mediumship, The
American   Society   for
Psychical Research
3 Vols., 1928

Miller, Paul
Science in the Seance
Room
Psychic Press, Ltd.
London, Eng., 1945

Muldoon, Sylvan
Carrington, Hereward
Projection of the Astral
Body, The
Rider and Co.
London, Eng., 1951

Myers, F. W. H.
Human Personality
Longmans
London, Eng., 1907

Osborn, A. W.
Superphysical, The
Ivor Nicholson & Watson
London, Eng., 1937

Osterreich, T. K.
Possession, Demoniacal
and Other
Kegan   Paul,   Trench,
Trubner
London, Eng., 1930

Osty, Eugene (de Brath,
Stanley, translator)
Supernormal Faculties in
Man
Methuen and Co.
London, Eng., 1923

Parkes, A. S., Chairman
Ciba Foundation Sympo-
sium on Extrasensory
Perception
Little, Brown
Boston, Mass., 1956

Pratt, J. G.
Rhine, J. B.
Smith, B. M.
Stuart, C. E.
Greenwood, J. A.
Extrasensory Perception
after Sixty Years
Henry Holt
New York, N.Y., 1940

Rhine, J. B.
Reach of the Mind, The
Faber and Faber
London, Eng., 1948

Soal, S. G.
   Modern Experiments in
      Telepathy
   Yale University Press
   New Haven, Conn., 1954
Stromberg, Gustav
   Soul of the Universe, The
   McKay, 2nd Edition
   Philadelphia, Pa., 1943
Tenhaeff, W. H. C.
   Beschouwingen Over Het
      Gebruik Van Parag-
      nosten
   Erven J. Bijleveld
   Utrecht, 1957
Tyrrell, G. N. M.
   Apparitions
   Pantheon
   New York, N.Y., 1953
Tyrrell, G. N. M.
   Man the Maker
   E. P. Dutton
   New York, N.Y., 1952
Tyrrell, G. N. M.
   Personality of Man, The
   Pelican Books
   Baltimore, Md., 1948
von Urban, Rudolf
   Beyond Human Knowl-
      edge
   Pageant Press
   New York, N.Y., 1958

PHARMACOLOGY

Adriani, John
   Pharmacology of Anes-
      thetic Drugs, The
   Charles C Thomas, 3rd
      Edition
   Springfield, Ill., 1954
Gaddum, J. H.
   Pharmacology
   Oxford University Press,
      4th Edition
   London, Eng., 1953
Hess, Erich

   Narcotics and Narcotic
      Addiction
   Philosophical Library
   New York, N.Y., 1946
Meduna, L. J.
   Carbon Dioxide Therapy
   Charles C Thomas
   Springfield, Ill., 1950
Sollman, Torald
   Manual of Pharmacology
   Saunders
   New York, N.Y., 1948
Weisberg, Harry F.
   Water, Electrolyte and
      Acid-Base Balance
   Williams & Wilkins
   Baltimore, Md., 1953

PHYSICS

Boast, Warren B.
   Principles of Electric and
      Magnetic Fields
   Harper & Bros.
   New York, N.Y., 1948
Butler, J. A. V.
   Electrical Phenomena at
      Interfaces
   Methuen and Co.
   London, Eng., 1951
Chalmers, J. Allan
   Atmospheric Electricity
   Oxford University Press
   London, Eng., 1949
Glasser, Otto (Editor)
   Medical Physics, Vol. I
   Yearbook Publishers
   Chicago, Ill., 1944
Lodge, Sir Oliver
   Beyond Physics
   Greenberg
   New York, N.Y., 1931
Margenau, Henry
Margenau, Lindsay
Bruce, Robert
   Foundations of Physics
   Dover

New York, N.Y., 1957
Morse, Philip M.
  Vibration and Sound
  International Series in
    Pure & Applied Phys-
    ics
  McGraw-Hill
  New York, N.Y., 1948
Pender, Harold
McIlwain, Knox
  Electrical Engineers
    Handbook
  Wiley
  New York, N.Y., 1950
See, T. J. J.
  Wave Theory (12 Vols.)
  Weldon and Wesley,
    Nichols Press
  Lynn, Mass., 1938–52
Whittaker, Sir Edmund
  Aether and Electricity,
    History and Theories
    of
  Philosophical Library
  New York, N.Y., 1951
Wiener, Norbert
  Cybernetics
  Wiley
  New York, N.Y., 1948

PHYSIOLOGY

Bell, George H.
Davidson, J. Norman
Scarborough, Harold
  Textbook of Physiology
    and Biochemistry
  Williams & Wilkins, 2nd
    Edition
  Baltimore, Md., 1953
Best, Charles Herbert
Taylor, Norman Burke
  Physiological Basis of
    Medical Practice
  Williams & Wilkins, 5th
    Edition
  Baltimore, Md., 1950

Cannon, W. B.
  Bodily Changes in Pain,
    Hunger, Fear and Rage
  Appleton
  New York, N.Y., 1920
Cannon, W. B.
  Wisdom of the Body, The
  W. W. Norton
  New York, N.Y., 1932
Curry, Manfred
  Bioklimatik (2 Vols.)
  American Bioclimatic Re-
    search Inst., 1946
  Riederau/Ammersee
Dale, Sir Henry Hallet
  Adventures in Physiology
  Pergamon Press, Ltd.
  London, Eng., 1953
Ferrer, M. Irene, Editor
  Cold Injury
  Transactions of the First
    Conference, 1951
  Josiah Macy, Jr. Founda-
    tion, 1952
Gellhorn, E.
  Physiological Founda-
    tions of Neurology and
    Psychiatry
  University of Minnesota
    Press
  Minneapolis, Minn., 1953
Selye, Hans
  Stress
  (Annual Reviews)
  Montreal, Can., 1951, etc.

PLANTS AND DRUGS

Dickson, Sarah Augusta
  Panacea or Precious Bane
  N. Y. Public Library
  New York, N.Y., 1954
Heim, R.
Wasson, R. G.
  Les Champignons Hallu-
    cinogènes du Mexique
  Edition du Muséum Na-

tional d'Histoire Naturelle
Paris, France, 1958
Moldenke, Harold N.
Moldenke, Alma L.
  Plants of the Bible
  Chronica Botonica
  Waltham, Mass., 1952
Petrullo, Vincenzo
  Diabolic Root, The
  University of Pennsylvania Press
  Philadelphia, Pa., 1934
Puharich, Andrija
  Sacred Mushroom, The
  Doubleday and Co.
  New York, N.Y., 1959
Reko, Victor
  Magische Gifte
  F. Enke
  Stuttgart, Germany, 1949
Wasson, R. G.
  Hallucinogenic Mushrooms of Mexico
  Trans. of the N. Y. Academy of Sciences
  Vol. 21, No. 4, 1959
Wasson, V. P.
Wasson, R. G.
  Mushrooms, Russia and History
  Pantheon Books
  New York, N.Y., 1957

PSYCHOLOGY

Bender, Morris B.
  Disorders in Perception
  Charles C Thomas
  Springfield, Ill., 1952
Heron, Woodburn
Doane, B.
Scott, T. H.
  Readings in Perception
  Edited by Beardslee and Wertheimer
  Van Nostrand
  New York, N.Y., 1958
Monnier, E.
  Problems of Consciousness
  Josiah Macy, Jr. Foundation
  New York, N.Y., 1952
Morgan, Clifford T.
Stellar, Eliot
  Physiological Psychology
  McGraw-Hill, 2nd Edition
  New York, N.Y., 1950
Rawcliffe, D. H.
  Psychology of the Occult
  Derricke Ridgway
  London, Eng., 1952
Sheldon, W. H.
  Varieties of Temperament, The
  Harper & Bros.
  New York, N.Y., 1944
Sorokin, Pitrim A., Edited by
  Forms and Techniques of Altruistic and Spiritual Growth
  Beacon Press
  Boston, Mass., 1954

SHAMANISM

Bouteiller, Marcelle
  Chamanisme et Guérison Magique
  Press Universitaires de France
  Paris, France, 1950
David-Neel, Alexandra
  Magic and Mystery in Tibet
  Claude Kendall
  New York, N.Y., 1932
Eliade, Mircea
  Le Chamanisme et les Techniques Archaïques de l'Extase

Payot
Paris, France, 1951
Lévy-Bruhl, Lucien
Soul of the Primitive, The
Kegan Paul, Trench,
Trubner
London, Eng., 1930
Meuli, K.
Griechschen Opfer-
brauche
Phyllobodia für Peter van
der Muhl, 1946
de Nebesky-Wojkowitz,
René
Oracles and Demons of
Tibet
Mouton and Co.
The Hague, 1956
Shirokogoroff, S. M.
Psychomental Complex
of the Tungus
Kegan Paul, Trench,
Trubner
London, Eng., 1935 (Pe-
king Edition)
Walter, Ruben
Schamanismus im Alten
Indien
Acta Orientale Lugduni
Bata Vorum, 1940

YOGA

Bailey, Alice
Yoga Sutras of Patanjali,
The
Lucis Publishing Co.
New York, N.Y., 1949
Behanan, K. T.
Yoga: A Scientific Evalu-
ation
Macmillan
New York, N.Y., 1937
Bromage, Bernard

Tibetan Yoga
The Aquarian Press
London, Eng., 1952
Danielou, Alain
Yoga: The Method of Re-
Integration
Christopher Johnson
London, Eng., 1949
Eliade, Mircea
Yoga, Immortality and
Freedom
Bollingen Series LVI
Pantheon Books
New York, N.Y., 1958
Evans-Wentz, W. Y.
Tibetan Book of the
Great Liberation
Oxford University Press
London, Eng., 1954
Evans-Wentz, W. Y.
Tibet's Great Yoga Mil-
arepa
Oxford University Press
London, Eng., 1950
Evans-Wentz, W. Y.
Tibetan Yoga and Se-
cret Doctrines
Oxford University Press
London, Eng., 1946
Johnson, Charles
Yoga Sutras of Patanjali,
The
John M. Watkins
London, Eng., 1949
Prasad, Rama
Nature's Finer Forces
Theosophical Publishing
House
Madras, India, 1947
Prasad, Rama (Translated
by)
Yoga Sutras of Patanjali
Vasu, Sudhindramath Al-
lahabad, 1924

Author Index

General Index